THIS DAY IN MUSIC'S GUIDE TO
THE JAM

RICK BUCKLER & IAN SNOWBALL

This Day in Music's Guide To The Jam

This first edition published 2018 by
This Day in Music
www.thisdayinmusic.com

Email: editor@thisdayinmusic.com

Printed by CPI Group (UK) Ltd, Croydon CR0 4YY

A catalogue record for this book is available from the British Library

ISBN: 978 1 999592 77 6

www.thisdayinmusic.com

Thanks to: Simon Wells from *Mod Culture* for his account from The Jam's final concert. *Sound on Sound* magazine, *NME*, *Melody Maker*, *Record Mirror* and *Sounds*. Barry Caine for his assistance, Nicky Weller for her help with images and photographs. Thanks to Walt Davidson for additional photos. Phil Potter for the cover songs list, Andy Kennedy for compiling the books list and Brian Kirlew for his help with the live recordings list. Additional material by Neil Cossar and This Day in Music.

Front cover photo credit: Derek D'Souza
Page 189 photo credit: Mike Searle

Front and back cover concept by Liz Sanchez

Cover design by Oliver Keen

This Day In Music Books
2B Vantage Park
Dashingly Road
Huntingdon PE29 6SR

Exclusive Distributors:
Music Sales Limited
14/15 Berners St
London W1T 3JL

CONTENTS

PREFACE

"Time is short and life is cruel..."

Sad, bleak words from the pen of the ever-acerbic Paul Weller, written when he was young and uncertain but also capable of dressing up those feelings in melodic finery that The Supremes would've died for. That's genius. That's understanding teenage souls implicitly. That's communicating. That's saying I know what you feel because I feel it too – the uncertainty and the despair, the passion and the love. Let's face the music and fucking dance...

That's Paul Weller and that was The Jam, a rock 'n' roll band that dished out the passion and love to those uncertain and despairing wasteland teenagers more than any other band I've ever known. After a shaky start, they cornered the market in credibility and cool and no doubt would've carried on cornering for many years if Uri Weller hadn't broken the silver spoon and adopted a Style Council estate of mind.

Was he right? I used to think not. I used to think he was insane. I used to think The Jam would've gone on to achieve greatness but they managed to throw it all away.

Now? Now I think in the 35 years that have passed since the split, they've gone on to achieve greatness anyway. And Paul Weller has gone on to achieve greatness in his own right, in his own way, on his own terms. The Jam were, in effect, his teenage years, y'know, hanging out with your mates and railing against the world and constantly thinking of girls and booze and football. Bruce and Rick were in his gang, watching his back, making him, them, tick, creating a unit

of imperious measurement that delighted and provoked, the very essence of rock 'n' roll. 1977-1982. I followed them every step of the way. The Hope and Anchor, spring '77, was the first time I saw them live.

The Royal College of Art, the Rainbow, the opening show of their debut UK headlining tour at Barbarella's in Birmingham on the same night as the Pistols silver jubilee boat trip, Newcastle, Battersea, Stuttgart, Munich, and more, many more. First interview, a boutique in Carnaby Street, May '77, when they were swathed in Union Jack jackets and rancour – "I can't imagine how anyone can go on stage at the age of 32 and sing 'My Generation' and still be a force." Last interview, Paul and Rick in a West London pub autumn '82, days after after the end was announced (Bruce was a no show)
Paul: "When I first met Jill I totally cut myself off from Rick and Bruce which I now kinda regret because I think we could have been, well...we are still mates, still close, ain't we?'
Rick: "Yeah and we always will be."

I lived the dream with The Jam and when I saw them in Brighton for that last show I shed a tear. Our paths crossed rarely after that. Marriage, kids, lives in overdrive heading in different directions. From around 1984, I never saw any of them again for 25 years until I hugged Bruce and Rick at the funeral of Bruce's first wife, Pat.

Another five years went by before I bumped into Rick at a pub in the West End where a band he managed was performing. I asked him if he wanted to do a photo session and interview for a revamped online version of *Flexipop!*, a magazine I co-created in 1980 in which The Jam often appeared – even providing the exclusive flexi disc for issue two, 'Pop Art Poem' and a 'Boy About Town' remix. He agreed and a few weeks later, Rick asked me to read his book, *That's Entertainment*, before it came out and he kindly mentions me in the 'Thanks' section. Reminded me of 'Special Thanks To Mr. B. Cain' on the back of *This Is The Modern World*. Teenage blue anyone...?

A year later, the *About The Young Idea* documentary, coupled with The Jam exhibitions at Somerset House and the Cunard in Liverpool, threw me into their paths again. I ended up having a coffee and a fag with Paul at the café in Somerset House, our first meeting in over thirty years. A few months later, he agreed to appear in the republished '*77 Sulphate Strip* as the final interview in the book.

In common with many supremely successful bands, there seems to be none of the one for all, all for one attitude between these three musketeers. The last time Rick saw Paul, Mr. Weller was fatherless. now he's the proud dad of eight kids. Time flies when you're having fun. It's always sad when friends fall out, it borders on the tragic when those friends were once members of the biggest band in the land. Shit happens, especially in your own backyard.

But let's not dwell on the shit. This is a celebration of a new book about The Jam from someone who knew the story inside out, none other than Rick Buckler, alongside a man who knows Rick Buckler inside out, celebrated author Ian Snowball.

We should be concentrating on the legacy – the six glorious studio 33s, the stream of classic 45s, the hundreds of spectacular gigs, the style, the Mod osmosis or mosmosis as it never came to be called, the indefatigability, the joy. Above all, the joy.

As the musician said to his colleagues in the *Titanic* movie – and let's face it, we're all sinking ships – "Gentlemen, it's been a privilege."

The Jam, joybringers.

Sometimes, just sometimes, I don't envy my kids their ages...

Barry Cain

THE JAM

ABOUT THE AUTHORS

RICK BUCKLER:

Rick was the drummer for The Jam from its formation in the early Seventies through to its break up in the early Eighties, during which time it became a critically acclaimed and commercially successful band. The Jam's rhythm section of Buckler and Bruce Foxton (bass guitar) were integral to its sound. His 2015 book *That's Entertainment – My Life in The Jam* became an Amazon No 1 best seller.

Dedicated to Jam fans everywhere.

IAN SNOWBALL:

Ian who wrote his first novel *Long Hot Summer* in 2009 is the co-author of the 2015 book *That's Entertainment: My Life In The Jam* by Rick Buckler, and wrote *Paul Weller - Sounds From The Studio* (published in 2017), as well as *Thick As Thieves (Personal Situations With The Jam)*, *Supersonic (Personal Situations with Oasis)*, *Black Music White Britain*, *The Kid's Are All Square* and many more.

Dedicated to all those that have supported my books so far.

WOKING
1955–73

THE JAM

1

"Although the punk thing was vastly different from what we were doing, in some ways it was very similar – like fast rock & roll, really, energetic and youthful. So we took to that like a duck to water."

Rick Buckler

WOKING

1

The Jam story begins with four friends who met at Sheerwater Comprehensive in Woking a satellite town to the south west of London's urban sprawl. It's the same story that was happening all over the country as friends with shared musical tastes got together to play in bedrooms, school halls and youth clubs. A shared passion for Sixties bands ranging from The Beatles to The Kinks and The Who along with Motown and early rock 'n' rollers saw the first version of The Jam take shape.

John and Ann Weller's first child was born on 25 May 1958. At the time of the arrival of their brand new baby boy, they still hadn't decided upon a name, so for the first few days their son was named John William Weller, he became known as Paul later on. Two months after the birth the Wellers moved from Walton Road in Woking to nearby Stanley Road, where the rent was cheaper at only one pound and twenty-five pence a week. Stanley Road had three bedrooms, an outside loo, no bathroom and no running hot water.

It would be in his bedroom in Stanley Road that Paul's first indulgences into music would begin and go on to shape the man he became and forge the career that ultimately secured him a place as one of Britain's finest and most prolific songwriters.

John held down many jobs during Paul's childhood and before he became The Jam's manager. His jobs included being a taxi driver, a hod carrier and a bricklayer. Ann also worked and her jobs included being a cleaner around properties in Woking.

Paul never really took to school and this possibly began with the experiences of his first, which was the Maybury Primary. It was around the time of him being enrolled into

the school that Ann gave birth to Nicola, who in time would simply be known as Nicky. Like John and Ann, Nicky too would have her part to play in The Jam's story because she helped run The Jam Fan Club with her mum. By the time Paul was starting school The Beatles were gearing themselves up to take over the world and change the landscape of popular music. It was virtually impossible to have not been touched by the songs of John, Paul, George and Ringo in the Sixties and, like so many children and teenagers, Paul embraced The Beatles.

Paul became obsessed with The Beatles. Ann got him all of the issues of *The Beatles Monthly* magazine and he pored over the content. He added to his collection with anything Beatles-related that he could lay his hands on including the records. So precious was Paul's collection that he kept it safe in one of the drawers in his bedroom, where his clothes were meant to be kept. The clothes were stored on a pile on the floor.

By the time Paul had reached double figures in age, another thing he had developed an interest in was clothes. Woking was a town that like so many others had an army of teenagers who had their interests

THE JAM

rooted in music and fashion.

When Paul was just ten years old the Mod thing had given way to the skinheads, Spirit of 69 and the suedeheads. It was the merging of the Mod, skinhead and suedehead styles that Paul gravitated towards. Such was the importance to Paul that he would save up what money he had earned from his paper round (which Ann sometimes did for him because he wanted to go to a disco rather than trudge the streets carrying a bag of papers.) He would take trips to Petticoat Lane Market in London so he could buy a pair of Sta-Prest trousers or a button-down shirt. And it would be this look (and more strongly the Mod look) that Paul would embrace and carry forward throughout his Jam years and many years beyond whilst in The Style Council and his solo years.

Like his heroes, The Beatles, Paul was drawn to the idea of being in a band. To do this he accepted he'd need to be able to play an instrument. It would have to be a guitar, and one Christmas, when Paul was twelve, he was given a guitar. After the initial strumming and plucking Paul lost interest and he tucked it away under his bed, where it stayed for several months before being resurrected with a more optimistic and ambitious attitude. Paul talked about seeing The Beatles appear on one of the *Royal Variety* Performances and after that he "was hooked from there onwards".

Now armed with a more positive frame of mind Paul set about learning to play the guitar, which John encouraged, such was a

'There was this sense that your future's decided for you: that was the insulting thing. I remember going to see the careers officer, and when I said I wanted to be in a band he just laughed. It sounds arrogant, but I always knew I'd make it. I didn't have any other career options. It was either this or nothing.'

Paul Weller

feature in the Weller family make-up and certainly helped to steer the formative days of The Jam towards realising the potential which John felt.

John could play the piano (only the black keys) that was located under the stairs and there was a record player that got used on a regular basis and which would often play records including the likes of Chuck Berry, Elvis Presley and artists on the Tamla Motown label. It was this sort of music that served as the backdrop for Paul's upbringing and along with his own discovery of groups like The Beatles, The Kinks and The Who, the foundations for what The Jam would become were being laid. Indeed throughout The Jam's career they covered songs by The Beatles, The Kinks and The Who, along with songs on the Tamla Motown label.

Having now enrolled at the Sheerwater Comprehensive Paul met Steve Brookes. Steve had recently relocated to Woking. He had been living with his family in London. Steve also had an interest in learning to play the guitar and this helped to form the bonds of friendship that he and Paul enjoyed. They were also very close in age, Paul being just one day older. In time Steve came to live with the Wellers. They liked him and wanted to help him out. Steve considered John to be his 'surrogate' dad.

Steve shared Paul's bedroom. They did everything together, except probably their homework because neither held their school education in particularly high regard. What they did share was a passion for The Beatles and they spent hours learning Beatles songs from their precious copy of *The Beatles Song Book*.

They were allowed to strum their guitars until 9pm. After that they had to

John Weller bought his son his first proper guitar when he was 12. In 1972, the teenagers played at their school, Sheerwater Secondary, and a lunch-time gig at a local pub organised by John. Named The Jam, they won a talent contest in Woking in 1973.

THE JAM

1

stop because it was around that time that Stanley Road started to quieten down and Ann didn't want the guitar playing to annoy the neighbours.

The first songs Paul learnt to play were 'Elusive Butterfly' by Bob Lind and 'A Groovy Kind Of Love' by The Mindbenders. He now had these under his belt and he added to these with Beatles songs.

At Sheerwater School a gang called The Clan started to form in the music room at lunch times. The school's music teacher, Mr Avery, encouraged the boys that were interested in music and trying to learn instruments to use the music room. These included boys called Dave Waller, Richard Flitney, Nigel Constable, Neil 'Bomber' Harris and Howard Davies amongst others.

It was in the music room that Paul and Steve got to know another pupil. His name was Paul Buckler and he was one of the drummers around. Like Paul and Steve, who had their own thing going on and who were starting to venture out as a duo playing rock and roll classics (their first public performance was in 1972 in the Woking Working Men's Club, which was just a few steps from the Weller's home in Stanley Road), Paul Buckler was also in his first band. Along with Howard Davies and Paul's brother Pete they had a group called Impulse. They never ventured any further than rehearsals in Howard's bedroom, so Paul was lacking any actual live performance experience.

RICK BUCKLER

Paul Buckler was slightly older than Paul and Steve. He was born on 6 December 1955 and in time would be known as Rick Buckler. He received his education at

Sheerwater Secondary School, in Woking.

After taking piano lessons at an early age, a young Paul quit piano and took up drumming instead. In 1970 Paul Buckler formed his first band called Impulse, with his twin brother Pete on bass.

A friendship between Paul and Steve Brookes formed in the Sheerwater School music room and it was Rick who Paul and Steve turned to when they needed a drummer to replace Neil 'Bomber' Harris, the drummer they had been using.

Rick would find himself sitting behind the Sheerwater School's drum kit and because of this his interest grew in drumming. He also found himself making some drum shells in his woodwork lessons and from then on it would be the drums for Rick.

Learning the drums and improving his skills, Rick went to see Buddy Rich play at Royal Albert Hall. "It was phenomenal. The great thing about the gig was that I'm sure everyone in the audience was a drummer, because he was such an icon for drummers. I don't think anyone was there to listen to the other music, just to see him. We got great seats right near the front so we could see everything that he actually did. I probably learnt more in the hour or so watching him than anything else. He could do all sorts of things that most drummers can't even dream of."

Neil 'Bomber' Harris was a proficient drummer and had experience in playing live with other bands. Paul and Steve and Dave Waller, who also played guitar in the band, had a gig booked at the Sheerwater Youth Club but Neil couldn't make it.

Paul approached Rick asking him if he'd play the gig and Rick agreed. On 8 June 1973 Paul Buckler joined (John) Paul

THE JAM

1

Weller and The Jam were taking shape. Paul started being called Rick (his middle name) to avoid confusion with Paul who preferred not to be called John, his given name.

Paul quickly handed Rick a bunch of records to take away with him to learn and then a couple of rehearsals were arranged and held in Paul's bedroom and then the gig at the Sheerwater Youth Club went ahead. It was from this point on that Rick effectively joined Paul, Steve and Dave's band, which was the earliest version of The Jam.

Following the success of the Sheerwater Youth Club gig, further rehearsals were arranged and more songs were learnt. And it was around this time that Paul's father John Weller started to take a keen interest in what the band were trying to do.

The formation of what would become The Jam was rapidly taking shape. But the line-up in the band would change and adapt to the next needs. In time Steve Brookes and Dave Waller left the band, preferring to explore other interests. But by this time Bruce Foxton was a member of the band.

BRUCE FOXTON

Bruce Foxton was born on 1 September 1955, the youngest of three boys, to parents Henry and Helen. He grew up on Albert Drive, Sheerwater and attended Sheerwater Junior and Secondary Schools where he showed great skill in football and technical drawing. In 1972, he left school to work at a local printing firm, the Unwin Brothers, with his brother Derek. While there, he formed a band with his colleagues but he abandoned the project out of frustration due to lack of progress. Paul and Rick knew of Bruce and were aware that he was already playing in a band called Zita. Not being put off by this they still asked him to join The Jam and after a hesitant start Bruce did indeed join up.

Initially Bruce was brought into the band to play guitar. Paul was playing bass, a Hofner Violin bass, just like his Beatles hero Paul McCartney had played. However, after a gig one night Bruce accidently sat on Paul's bass and broke it. The instrument did get repaired but in time Paul would move to playing guitar and Bruce the bass.

Bruce Foxton recalls: "Paul said, 'Let's swap instruments,' so I took over the bass, and he showed me a couple of little bass lines, and I just developed my own style from there. I just stumbled around it until I had developed what I do now. Even though I came about it naturally and taught myself, I was obviously influenced by Paul McCartney and John Entwistle."

The Jam were also going to end up as a three-piece with Paul Weller, Rick Buckler and Bruce Foxton. "Punk," says Bruce, "gave Paul a direction that he really liked and gave the band encouragement to keep going. I don't think there has ever been anything like that since. Good bands have come out but there has been no explosion (like punk). It gave the industry a kick up the backside. It was very exciting to see the Pistols and The Clash and realise they had a similar direction and sentiment to us. The only difference was we didn't wear ripped t-shirts and safety pins but we had a lot in common with those bands. From getting the record deal with Polydor to 'Going Underground' becoming our first UK No 1 there are still a lot of fond memories. Daft things, like hearing 'In The City' being played on the jukebox in your local pub and just getting your first record in your hand. It was very exciting."

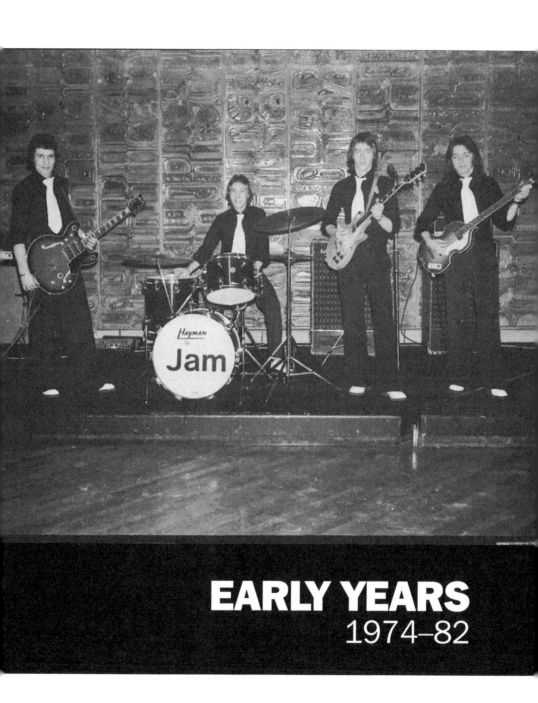

EARLY YEARS
1974–82

THE JAM

2

> *"The Jam were a very real manifestation of the kind of band I would have wanted to be in myself. They were like a cool, smart punk band. I only saw The Jam once. They were simply spectacular"*

Pete Townshend

EARLY YEARS

The intensity of Paul Weller's ambition shines through from the beginning with the young band playing in local venues from early on – assisted by Paul's Dad John hustling for gigs. Three years before breaking through on the national scene the band, like so many successful outfits before, were learning their stagecraft playing 70 gigs in 1974 alone.

The Jam worked hard playing most weekends in the working men's clubs and pubs around the Woking area. Such venues as the Woking Working Men's Club (where Paul and Steve had first played) and Michaels Club often saw The Jam racing through their set that consisted of cover songs by the likes of Elvis Presley, Chuck Berry, Little Richard and The Beatles.

They continued playing local gigs and building up a following. Paul discovered The Who's debut album, *My Generation*, and became fascinated with Mod music and lifestyle. As he said later, "I saw that through becoming a Mod it would give me a base and an angle to write from, and this we eventually did. We went out and bought suits and started playing Motown, Stax and Atlantic covers. I bought a Rickenbacker guitar and a Lambretta GP 150 and tried to style my hair like Steve Marriott's circa 1966."

Eventually Brookes left the band, and for a period was not replaced. Up to this point Paul had been playing bass and Bruce had been the band's second guitar player: Paul persuaded Bruce to take over bass duties and developed a combined lead/rhythm guitar style influenced by The Who's Pete Townshend as well as Dr. Feelgood guitarist Wilko Johnson.

During 1974, The Jam played over 70 gigs,

> *"John wasn't a professional manager: he was with The Jam purely on the fact that he was Paul Weller's dad. When we first signed to Polydor, they turned round to John and said, 'We don't want you managing the band.' This shocked all of us. Out of loyalty to John, we refused to sign to Polydor unless John Weller was The Jam's manager."*
>
> **Rick Buckler**

mainly in the Woking and Guildford area learning their stagecraft. 1974 also saw The Jam play a darts club party in Basingstoke and a gig at Coldingley Men's Prison in Woking, Surrey. The following year saw an equal amount of gigs

THE JAM

2

including gigs in London as well as an audition for the TV talent show *Opportunity Knocks* at Surbiton Town Hall. They failed the audition.

Along with John Weller's hustling for gigs and Paul, Rick and Bruce's desire to establish themselves in the London live music scene, by late 1976 they could be found playing on the modest stages of venues such as the Hope and Anchor, The Red Cow, The Nashville Rooms, The Marquee and the 100 Club. Dressed in their black suits with white shirts and black ties and clutching their Rickenbacker guitars, they were building an impressive fan base.

At this stage The Jam were starting to write some of their own songs. An early song was 'Takin' My Love' which was also one of the first songs that The Jam recorded when they signed to Polydor Records in 1977 (and which was later included as the B-side to their debut single 'In The City').

The Jam's concerts became better too. They supported The Clash and the Sex Pistols. For the Sex Pistols gig, The Jam even had a keyboard player. Bob Gray played keyboards with The Jam for just a handful of gigs before Paul, Bruce and Rick decided their sound didn't suit keyboards and they preferred The Jam as a three-piece outfit. It would be a few more years before a keyboard player next joined The Jam when Jim Telford and Mick Talbot (who would later go on to become a founding member of The Style Council) joined.

Throughout this time John Weller was also approaching record companies. John, Paul, Rick and Bruce were intent on getting a record deal. Their aim was to get signed and release records. Despite them getting the attention of some record companies, Chiswick offered a deal with a mere £600 advance and a loan of a PA system. Decca Records was another but they turned The Jam down and it was Polydor Records who

stepped up and offered The Jam a deal.

One of Polydor's A&R men, Chris Parry, had seen The Jam play live in The Nashville Rooms on Cromwell Road, London and after the gig approached them to express his interest. Parry would also sign Siouxsie and The Banshees to Polydor and later created his own label Fiction Records and signed The Cure, who he managed for some years.

Initially Paul, Bruce and Rick took this approach with a pinch of salt. But Parry did have a genuine interest in the band and he contacted them to say he'd arranged for them to come down to Anemone Studios on Poland Street, London and record some demos.

However, on the day there was an IRA bomb scare so the session was cancelled. Then on 9 February 1977 The Jam did enter the studio and laid down four songs: 'In The City', 'Time For Truth', 'Sounds From The Street' and 'I've Changed My Address'.

Parry was pleased with the results of the demos and invited The Jam to the Polydor Records offices to discuss a 'singles only' record deal. The Jam and John Weller attended the meeting and a deal was agreed. Polydor signed The Jam for £6,000, which wasn't a great sum of money - especially compared to what The Clash had from CBS Records (£100,000) and the Sex Pistols from A&M (£75,000). The money was handed over to John Weller in cash because at that time he still didn't have a bank account!

IN THE CITY

Recording sessions took place during March 1977 at Stratford Place, London, England, resulting in The Jam's debut single 'In the City' being released the following month. The track was influenced by The Who's early music (it borrowed its title from an obscure Who song of the same name), but with an energy and attitude updated for the punk era.

Weller recalled writing the song in an interview for Q magazine in April 2011: "It was the sound of young Woking, if not London, a song about trying to break out of suburbia. As far as we were concerned, the city was where it was all happening: the clubs, the gigs, the music, the music. I was probably 18, so it was a young man's song, a suburbanite dreaming of the delights of London and the excitement of the city. It was an exciting time to be alive. London was coming out of its post-hippy days and there was a new generation taking over. The song captured that wide-eyed innocence of coming out of a very small community and entering a wider world, seeing all the bands, meeting people, going to the clubs, and the freedom that it held."

On 29 April 1977 'In The City' was released where it reached No 40 on the UK charts - their first Top 40 single and the beginning of their streak of 18 consecutive Top 40 hits in the UK. The Jam had arrived. Following the successful recordings of the first tracks The Jam were booked into Basing Street Studios, London (where the boys found The Bee Gees also there, recording the classic 'Stayin' Alive').

This wasn't such a tough job for Paul, Rick

and Bruce because they had the material and they knew the songs inside out after playing most of them live for at least a couple of years. So armed with a collection of songs and having been bolstered by the record label, family, fans and friends, The Jam recorded their debut album, also to be called In The City. All the tracks were written by Paul Weller, plus the set featured two cover songs, 'Slow Down' and the theme to the Sixties television series, Batman, the latter of which had also been previously been covered by The Who, The Kinks and Link Wray.

Upon the album's release on 20 May 1977 In the City received all-round positive reviews. In the Record Mirror, Barry Cain wrote, "Armed and extremely dangerous The Jam stalk the decrepit grooves. If you don't like them, hard luck they're gonna be around for a long time. It's been a long time since albums actually reflected pre-20 delusions and this one does."

The NME said Weller's songwriting "captures that entire teen frustration vibe with the melodic grace and dynamic aplomb of early Kinks and Who". Melody Maker was equally impressed, proclaiming that "Weller-composed songs are anything but an embarrassment, he has a deft touch that places his material on a much higher plateau".

THE PRODUCER

Producer Vic Coppersmith-Heaven mixed The Jam's live gigs right up until they were playing the larger venues like the Rainbow in North London. Vic was on the road with The Jam for their college gigs, as well as at one of their most popular venues, The Red Cow in Hammersmith, and later took care of the many radio and TV mixes around Europe. Talking to Sound on Sound magazine he said: "I kind of grew up with the band and progressed along with them. We all developed - the musicians developed, the songwriting developed, the technology developed, and we kind of moved with that, introducing harmony guitars and harmony vocals. These things just happened naturally, embellishing the style of the progressive songwriting."

THE JAM

2

THIS IS THE MODERN WORLD

The Jam were known as one of the hardest working bands in the music business and they loved to play live. This was an attitude they carried with them throughout their career and with a successful debut single and album under their belts, in between touring Polydor Records booked them back into the studio to record a follow up album. Recording sessions took place at Basing Street Studios, London, England during late summer of 1977. Basing Street Studios (later known as SARM Studios), were the home of Island Records artists which saw the likes of Bob Marley, Steve Winwood, Free, Jimmy Cliff, Nick Drake, John Martyn and Mott the Hoople all recorded there.

It had only been a few months since In The City and The Jam hadn't really had the time to write a whole bunch of new songs. However, The Jam put their heads down and got on with the task and within a matter of weeks they had recorded an album's worth of material.

The Jam's second album This Is The Modern World was released in November 1977. Polydor had paid £20,000 for the album to be made and it took slightly longer than the eleven days that it had taken In The City to be recorded. There had been other single releases too in 'All Around The World' and 'The Modern World.' Plus The Jam had appeared on Top of the Pops and the Marc Bolan TV Show in the UK and were venturing into Europe to play gigs and festivals.

By the end of 1977, The Jam had played over 125 gigs and recorded two albums in 12 months. The fan base was growing after successful shows in major UK cities such as Leeds, Manchester and Edinburgh and an appearance at the Paris Punk Festival in France.

ALL MOD CONS

It was only a matter of time before The Jam found themselves touring America, albeit to mixed reviews and responses, but they did get to play two nights at CBGBs in New York City where they met punk heroes Joey Ramone and Patti Smith backstage at the world-famous club.

The Jam were now truly on their way backed by the support of fans rooted in the punk and New wave scenes. But going into 1978 a new scene was starting to spring up in London. This scene took its influences from the Mods that had ridden Vespas and Lambrettas, and that had worn parkas and sharp tailor-made suits with desert boots and stylish Italian shoes a decade earlier. This new 'revivalist' Mod blended the attitudes and styles of the Sixties Mods with the influences of their generation and punk.

It was only a matter of time before Mod bands started to emerge including The Chords, The Purple Hearts, The Lambrettas and Secret Affair (who scored the 1979 top 20 hit 'Time For Action'). An army of Mods started to build across the UK and while this was happening The Jam were the trailblazers.

In many ways The Jam's third album All Mod Cons reflected this rapidly-growing Mod trend. The album's title suggested an obvious link and this was reinforced even further when the inner sleeve, designed by Bill Smith (who would design most of The Jam's single and album record sleeves) included images of a Creation record, a Sounds Like Ska album and a diagram of a scooter. The Jam's tribal allegiances were clear.

The Mods did indeed make up a large part of The Jam's audience and fan club but the band also appealed to a wider range of people from the record-buying public. Sales and chart positions of The Jam's releases mirrored this. 'All Around The World' released in July 1977 peaked at No

13 on the UK singles chart, 'News Of The World' at No 27, 'David Watts' No 25 and 'Down in the Tube Station at Midnight' was a No 15 hit giving The Jam a total of six Top 40 hits from April 1977 to the end of 1978.

All Mod Cons did well, reaching No 6 in the charts. Recorded between 4 July and 17 August 1978 at RAK and Eden Studios in London the album featured the single 'Down in the Tube Station at Midnight', (which Weller had originally discarded because he was unhappy with the song's arrangement). The track was rescued from the studio bin by producer Vic Coppersmith-Heaven and became one of the band's most successful chart hits up to that point. Another highlight from the album was the cover of The Kinks' 'David Watts'.

Reviewing the album for *NME*, Charles Shaar Murray said that the album was "not only several light years ahead of anything they've done before but also the album that's going to catapult The Jam right into the front rank of international rock and roll: one of the handful of truly essential rock albums of the last few years." *NME* later ranked *All Mod Cons* as the second best album of 1978 in its end of year review.

The Jam's fourth studio album, *Setting Sons*, reached No 4 in the UK album chart. The sole single from the album, 'The Eton Rifles,' became the group's first top 10 UK hit, peaking at No 3.

Weller originally conceived *Setting Sons* as a concept album detailing the lives of three boyhood friends who later reunite as adults after an unspecified war only to discover they have grown up and apart. This concept was never fully developed, and it remains unclear which tracks were originally intended as part of the story.

It was ranked at No 4 among the top albums of the year for 1979 by *NME*, with 'Eton Rifles' and 'Strange Town' ranked at numbers one and five among the year's top tracks.

1979 was another very busy year for The Jam, with live dates taking them to Germany, France and Belgium at the start of the year, another North American tour in April and a full UK tour in May followed by a second 28-date UK tour in November and December.

> *"They had an enormous sound for a three piece. Sometimes you can get a better sound out of a three piece than a huge orchestra, and The Jam were a good example of that."*
>
> **Jools Holland**

GOING UNDERGROUND

'Going Underground' released in February 1980 went straight in at No 1 on the UK charts (the first of three instant chart-toppers for the group). The single's B-side, 'Dreams of Children', had originally been intended to be the A-side: but following a mix-up at the pressing plant, the single became a double-A-side, and DJs tended to choose the more melodic 'Going Underground' to play on the radio.

THE JAM

When 'Going Underground' their first UK No 1, was sitting at the top of the charts, The Jam found themselves across the Atlantic on tour in North America. They duly cancelled their last four concerts, jumped on Concorde and returned home to Blighty. Getting a No 1 record was a big deal.

The Jam were now riding high on their well-earned success and this was boosted even further when their next single 'Start!' also topped the UK charts. Having two No 1 records in the same year was a massive achievement for any band.

Recorded at The Town House, London, England during sessions in June and October of 1980, *Sound Affects* did even better, becoming a No 2 hit on the UK album chart. Weller is known to have opined that *Sound Affects* was the best album The Jam released throughout their career: freely admitting The Beatles' *Revolver* had been a major influence upon much of the material upon the album. The album spent

19 weeks in the UK album charts and, in the US, the album spent 11 weeks in the *Billboard* 200 album charts.

Record sales were indeed healthy, the concerts were selling out and The Jam toured the world taking in countries like Japan and Canada.

More singles followed, 'That's Entertainment', 'Funeral Pyre' and 'Absolute Beginners' (named after the Colin MacInnes novel of the same name).

The Jam would go down in rock history as being one of the greatest singles bands. Their B-sides would also get noticed, but then with brilliant songs like 'The Butterfly Collector' and 'Tales From The Riverbank' it's easy to appreciate why. The band's record company Polydor later stated that they believed 'Tales From The Riverbank' should have been released as the A-side to 'Absolute Beginners'.

All the time The Jam grew in popularity and success, they always maintained a special and unique relationship with their fans. There are countless stories of fans being allowed into sound checks. Paul, Rick and Bruce never shied away from giving the fans some of their time and signing a record sleeve or a poster for them. There was a mutual respect between The Jam and their fans and this loyalty would remain for decades after the band split up.

1981 saw constant touring with live dates in France, Sweden, Denmark, Germany, The Netherlands, Japan, North America and the UK.

In February 1982 The Jam had their third UK No 1 hit with 'Town Called Malice'. Their sixth studio album, *The Gift*, was released a month later. *The Gift* became The Jam's first No 1 album. This was

The JAM

Polydor

something The Jam had been aiming for since the release of their debut album *In The City* five years earlier.

The Jam were now the biggest band in the UK. However, on returning from their summer holidays, Rick and Bruce were called into a meeting with Paul and John Weller. During this meeting held in Red Bus Studios, London, the announcement was made that Paul wanted to leave The Jam, therefore breaking the band up. Both Rick and Bruce were stunned. It seemed a ridiculous thing to do, especially when they'd just had another No 1 single and No 1 album. John Weller was also disappointed with Paul's decision and attempts were made by all concerned (including the groups label Polydor) to change Paul's mind or at least present alternatives like having more time off or go and make a solo record. But Paul had made up his mind and no one was going to change it.

THE BITTEREST PILL

The Jam still had a contract to fulfil with Polydor Records and this meant they had to release more singles. 'Just Who Is The Five O' Clock Hero' was not released as a single in the UK but was a Dutch import. Despite this it still made No 8 in the UK Singles Chart in July 1982. 'The Bitterest Pill (I Ever Had to Swallow)' was released in September and reached No 2 in the UK Singles Chart and remained there for two weeks, unable to shift 'Eye of the Tiger' by Survivor and 'Pass the Dutchie' by Musical Youth from the top spot.

Then came the farewell single, 'Beat Surrender', which was released in November and became The Jam's fourth No 1 hit. A live album called *Dig The New Breed* was also

released and this satisfied the record label's demand for a final album.

BEAT SURRENDER

'Beat Surrender' was previewed live on the first episode of *The Tube*, on 5 November 1982. This appearance would also capture Paul Weller's last interview whilst still in The Jam. *The Tube* was broadcast on Channel 4 between 1982 and 1987 and whilst the show was running a plethora of diverse live acts performed on the show: these included U2, Madness, Wham!, Prefab Sprout, The Fall and of course The Jam, who in their set performed 'Beat Surrender', 'Ghosts', 'Modern World' and 'Town Called Malice'.

During its life the show was hosted by a mixture of presenters. These included Jools Holland, Paula Yates, Tony Fletcher, Leslie Ash and Muriel Grey. It was Grey who interviewed Paul back stage at the studios in November 1982. Paul, apparently unwilling to talk, was wearing a yellow crew neck jumper with a Dennis The Menace button badge on it, white jeans and holding a cigarette. But he responded to Muriel Grey's questions:
Presenter: "What is Paul Weller going to do next?"
Paul: "I'm not sure yet, I haven't got any definite plans."
Grey next starts to talk about Paul's other projects and refers to Respond his new record label, that Paul had recently got off of the ground. Paul takes advantage of the opportunity to plug Respond and seems to embrace the diversion away from having to answer questions about The Jam.
Paul: "It's funny you should mention that actually, we've got this one group called The Questions who have got a single out called 'Work And Play'."

THE JAM

2

Paul then continues by telling Grey that he wanted to get some more singles issued on the Respond label. Grey politely listens, picking up the interview with:

Grey: "Fanzines and poetry."

Paul responds by mentioning Riot Books and the Small Faces publication and he also refers to the forthcoming book on The Jam. This book was to be Paolo Hewitt's *A Beat Concerto*. Grey next steers the interview back to the topic of The Jam and their appearance on the show.

Grey: "Are you looking forward to doing the set live tonight on the show?"

Paul says that he is, adding that he's noticed people have been "moaning about music that's been on TV for the last five years."

Grey: "You're not going to give up music altogether are you?"

Paul: "I don't think any of us will. It's in our blood."

Grey attempts to push Paul to disclose information about what he's planning to do next.

Paul: "I haven't thought about it − sorry."

Grey gets the message and diverts her attention back to Paul's other interests, such as poetry and writing.

Grey: "Are you going to be famous and write a novel?"

Paul, shaking his head: "No, I don't think so."

It has since been said that at the time of the interview Paul had already secured a record deal with Polydor and that plans for The Style Council (The Torch Society was considered as the band's name too) were well under way.

Not long after The Jam's *The Tube* appearance and Grey quizzing Paul over his future plans, Paul found himself fielding more questions from an interviewer from the national UK evening news show *Nationwide* on a cold and blustery December afternoon in Brighton.

The *Nationwide* studio presenter said, "At 24 he (Paul) has become somewhat of a spokesman for the new beat generation. He has pronounced on politics, life and music to enthusiastic fans who receive his message. They've come from America and Japan to hear him."

Paul and the interviewer are then filmed standing on a promenade in Brighton beside a very rough sea.

The presenter with his back turned to the camera starts the interview: "The band is amazingly successful - why stop now?"

Paul, looking like he's freezing and wrapped in a beige trench coat and scarf. "I feel we have achieved enough. I think we've done all we can do as the three of us. And I think it's a good time to finish it. I don't want it to be going on, and for it to go on for the next 20 years and it become nothing. I want this to count for something. I want the past five or six years to count for something."

Paul continues sharing his feelings of dissatisfaction that he has about the class system and seeing people with power and wealth and how he'd like to see it "done away with", and "I'd like to see the power and wealth distributed properly."

The interviewer responds, "Is music going to help with this?"

Paul: "I don't think music can overthrow it directly but it can help communicate (the issues) to different people. Music is the only real culture that young people have got."

The interviewer: "You've done very well for yourself, aren't you being a bit self-righteous?"

Paul (quick to respond): "I think you've got

to try and work out what you're best at-so that's what I intend to do."

The programme then cuts to the 'Going Underground' video.

The interviewer talks about how Paul's apparent 'future appears to be mapped out'. Paul disagrees. "The Jam is a group regardless of me being portrayed as the front man. I think a lot of our fans think of it as being a group... as the three of us."

The interviewer pushes the point of Paul's future being 'mapped out' and asks, "What do the other two think? Some people might say you're dumping them."

Paul reacts, "Well that's a load of crap ain't it!" Paul explains again that The Jam is a group and it's not his responsibility.

The interviewer: "Are they happy about the break-up?"

Paul: "I wouldn't say they are happy but it's just something I felt inside me, and I have to go by my instinct. And I felt it's the right

THE JAM

2

thing to do. I thought about it. It wasn't like I just made up my mind overnight. What's nice about it is it's the first time for years that I haven't had any definite plans. I don't know what is going to happen - which I'm quite enjoying at the moment."

Paul, on a roll now, continues "whatever I do, I want to be successful or else there's no point in doing it".

'Beat Surrender' then begins to play and some photographs of The Jam playing live flash up. For many Jam fans, this was how they got hear about The Jam splitting up, even though rumours had been circulating already for weeks before The Jam's Fan Club's official announcement on 30 October.

FINAL TOUR

The Jam set off on the Beat Surrender Tour on 25 November 1982. On that tour they would also play five nights at Wembley Arena from Wednesday 1 December through to Sunday 5. Many of The Jam Army were still grappling with the news that their favourite band were splitting up and there were plenty of tears, amongst other emotions, when The Jam played their last ever concert on 11 December at the Brighton Centre.

The news of the band's demise had not been intended as a formal announcement, but after it was leaked, a hand-written press statement was distributed.

"Personal address to our fans,"wrote Weller. "At the end of this year, The Jam will be officially splitting up, as I feel we have achieved all we can together as a group. I mean this both musically and commercially. I want all we have achieved to count for something and most of all I'd hate us to end up old and embarrassing like so many other groups do."

> *"I want all we have achieved to count for something and most of all I'd hate us to end up old and embarrassing like so many other groups do."*
>
> **Paul Weller**

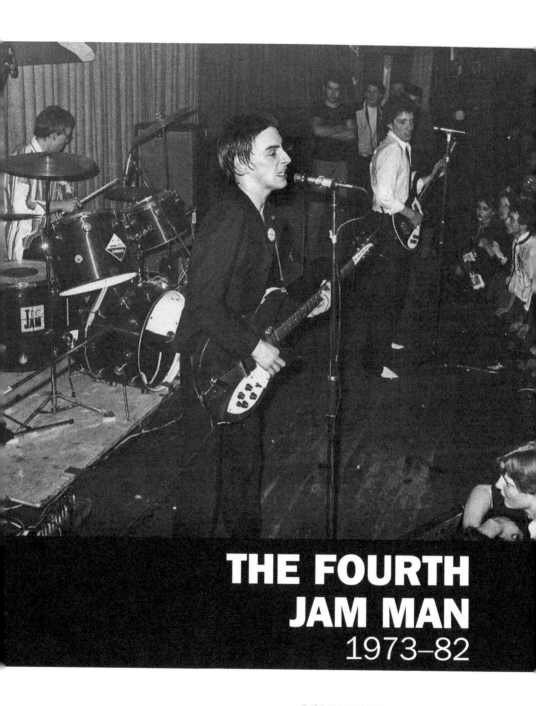

THE FOURTH JAM MAN
1973–82

THE JAM

3

"They are not imitators but upholders of a great British tradition ... This is Sixties music handled in an original and modern way which has given The Jam their distinctive and now truly distinguished style."

Philip Hall

THE FOURTH JAM MAN

3

Paul Weller always envisaged a four-piece band like his heroes The Beatles, Who, Kinks, Small Faces etc. But finding a fourth member proved a challenge and so it was when they were a trio that Paul moved to lead vocals and guitar and Bruce onto bass. Events moved quickly and a cast of key characters arrived to provide support...

In the first instance, there was Paul Weller and Steve Brookes, and then there was Neil 'Bomber' Harris. I think he was the first drummer that Paul and Steve worked with. It was their first attempt of trying to put a band together. Up until that point it had just been Paul and Steve working as a duo.

They worked towards doing some shows and it was at one of the organised events at the Sheerwater Youth Club that I got invited in because Neil couldn't make it.

I knew of Neil but I didn't really know him because he was one of the drummers around who was about our age. But he could actually play and I think even at the time when he was drumming for Paul and Steve he was also playing in some jazz band. I seem to recall he had a bit of reputation of turning up in a Dickie Bow tie.

It was always Paul's intention and desire to put together a four-piece band because that's what bands looked like - it was The Beatles and The Who and Small Faces model. All the best bands had four members. That's how 'proper' bands did it.

So, with this in mind and me now being Paul and Steve's drummer, it was a matter of finding

that fourth member, and this is where Dave Waller came into it.

Dave was a friend of Paul's and I knew him from Sheerwater School. He was in a younger year group than me. We hung around in the same group of friends - the musicians' gang - as kids do at school based on their interests. And Dave's interests and aspirations were about being a bit of a Bob Dylan type character. He liked the idea of playing a guitar and he liked poetry and he liked linking them together.

Dave really liked lyrics and the ideology of them and how they could portray something. Words he was good at but he wasn't a particularly good guitarist. It was all in good jest but on occasion he did take the brunt of some musical jokes.

I think Dave's limitations as a guitarist were frustrating for Paul and Steve. At this time it was Steve who was on guitar and although he was still learning, he was an able guitarist. He was also the lead singer.

We knew of other musicians. At Sheerwater we'd spend our break times hanging around the music room. This was where those who were interested in music or were learning to play the guitar, bass, drums

THE JAM

3

or whatever gathered. That's what this group of school kids connected with. I remember there was a really good guitarist named Richard Flitney. He was a real lead guitarist and he could play really well but he wasn't into the same kind of music as Paul and Steve were into so he wasn't asked to join the group. There was another drummer from the music room gang called Nigel Constable, but like Richard he wasn't into the same music as Paul and Steve so he didn't really fit in and so he didn't get asked to join either. Whether you fitted in was a big deal and if you fitted in, you connected on some level and that's how the musicians who became part of The Jam history arrived.

All the time the early days of The Jam were forming, Paul and Steve continued to play out as an acoustic duo. They worked hard at learning and adding new songs to their set list and these provided a foundation for myself and Dave Waller to build on.

Playing in a band wasn't for Dave though and he left. I think Dave struggled to keep up with us plus I think he just realised that poetry was more important to him than what playing guitar was. It wasn't like there was some meeting where Dave said he didn't want to play with us anymore or us asking him to leave - he just sort of wandered off.
With Dave now departed we were left as a three-piece, Paul on bass, Steve on guitar and me on drums. But we still wanted the band to be a four-piece.

It was during this time that we approached Bruce Foxton about joining but he didn't want to. He was busy playing with another band called Zita. I don't know what sort of music Zita played but maybe at that time Bruce just didn't like the sort of music we were playing - which was mostly stuff from the Fifties and Sixties. For a young band to

be playing songs from the Fifties and Sixties was all a bit too old hat for some people and was a fair enough attitude to take for someone in a band. It was maybe odd not being influenced by what music we were being surrounded by - which at that time was Bowie and Slade and rock and glam, music like that. We were playing music that our parents grew up with and liked, not the music that our older brothers and sisters and to some extent ourselves liked. There were times when I questioned if what we were playing was right. I mean - what was this Chuck Berry geezer all about?

But playing songs from the Fifties and Sixties got us work and Paul and Steve understood this and I think having work helped us when we approached Bruce the second time. We were able to say "look, we have gigs, we have bookings at this club". I think Bruce looked at Zita and what they were doing, or not doing, and looked at us and he accepted the invitation and he joined us as the rhythm guitarist.

In time Steve left too and this left the band looking like a three-piece again. It was after Steve left that Paul took on the role of lead singer, so Bruce was told that he should now play bass if he was to stay, as Paul moved onto lead vocals and guitar and that's how it stayed for the remainder of The Jam. But just before we settled as that three-piece, we did try again to recruit a fourth member. We put an advert in one of the local Woking newspapers saying we would be auditioning for the band. There was a pub in Woking called The Red House and it was in a room upstairs that we held those auditions. On the day there was about half a dozen guitarists that turned up, even a mate of mine called Brian Viner, who was an excellent lead guitarist, but in the end a keyboardist called Bob Grey got the job and

THE STORY: **THE FOURTH JAM MAN**

he became the fourth member of The Jam. He only ended up playing a couple of gigs with us and one of those was when we supported The Sex Pistols in Dunstable on 21 October 1976.

Once Bob left it returned to being just Paul, Bruce and myself and we continued to play gigs. Things just started to move very quickly and events just kind of over took us and our search for that fourth member just got pushed to one side. It was only a matter of months from when we supported The Sex Pistols to getting signed to Polydor and having our debut single released.

It was during those early days and getting signed that we had two guys who became involved with us as the road crew. These were Nicky Tredwyn and Alan Belchor and they were really The Jam's first road crew. I don't recall how we got to know Nicky and Alan. We certainly didn't know them from Woking. They were both from London. I think Nicky was a Streatham lad but I don't think I ever knew where Alan was from. What I did know was that Alan was an aspiring drummer. What we liked about Nicky and Alan was that they were into their music and they were of a similar age to us and they were keen to get involved in The Jam.

The other important thing was that both Nicky and Alan had no connections and this was important if you wanted the job as a member of the road crew. To work on the road you just cannot view it as being a nine to five job. Maybe it's different now but back in 1977 you couldn't. You had to be foot loose and fancy free and Nicky and Alan were just that. Joining The Jam as a member of the road crew was like joining the circus.

Being roadies suited Nicky and Alan. At the time Nicky was like some wild little

punk character. He loved it. He loved being a punk, the music, and The Jam. He loved the anarchy of it all too and the not being confined to having to live in one spot and have a boring job. He loved being constantly on the move, on the go. Being a roadie wasn't a normal job and I think Nicky found it to be really exciting. He got to travel, discover new places, see bands and he got paid for it.

Alan, like Nicky, also loved it. He picked it up as it went along. We were all learning. It wasn't like any of us had had any formal training anyway. They had their work cut out too. They had to carry all the gear around and set it all up, but we needed them to be doing this sort of stuff because we were off handling the press and doing photo-shoots.

I suppose I would describe Alan as being a bit more steady - a bit more reliable. You knew that if you asked Alan to do something he would do it. He could be very resourceful in finding ways to get a job done. To be fair to Nicky too, even though he was more of a wild card we could rely on him to also get the job done. Sometimes watching the pair of them was like watching *The Little and Large Show* though.

Nicky and Alan hung around throughout 1977. I think they came on our first trip to the States too.

Our first sort of tour manager was a guy called Adrian Enfield-Bance. He just seemed to pop up from nowhere. I have no recollection as to where he came from or how we got to know him. I was aware of a network of people who had an interest in wanting to get into the music industry, so maybe Adrian was one of those. Some of these people had already worked for other bands in some capacity. One might have

3

been the driver, the other a guitar tech or something.

Adrian was a very well-educated guy. I used to look at him and wonder why on earth he was trying to get involved in the music industry. He lived in Sudbury and was very well spoken.

Adrian and I became good friends and we'd often hang out. He was far from stupid and he was very articulate: which could be helpful at times. It was Adrian who drove The Jam around on our first proper North American tour in a Winnebago bus.

I think the other thing about being a roadie was that being one in the UK was different from being one in the US. In the US being a roadie is a very serious business. Roadies in the States were very professional and had a totally different mind-set. But then being a roadie for a band in the US has different demands. They have different issues to deal with. For instance travelling thousands of miles just to get from one city to the next is different to us in the UK where it might only be fifty miles.

Adrian wasn't with The Jam for too long. He just moved on. I'm not sure to do what - although I heard he went on to do some work with Phil Manzanera of Roxy Music. As 1977 came to a close we really started to realise that we needed more personnel around the band. It was like starting a new business. It was like having a list saying we need that, we need him, we need those and so forth. Some of them would only be required on a temporary basis and some full time.

As The Jam business became more serious and demanding we added Kenny Wheeler as our tour manager and as we needed more things we got them. For example, we needed a car. We bought a big three-litre Rover,

which sort of became the company car. Kenny drove the car and he'd come and pick us up and drive us all over the place - to gigs, to the studio, to press interviews.

In time we outgrew the car. We didn't miss its departure. It just wasn't comfortable trying to squeeze in Paul, Bruce, John and myself and of course Kenny, who was a big guy. We couldn't even sell the car. It was a mess. The front seat, Kenny's seat, had absolutely collapsed and the mileage was stupidly high. Once that Rover went we started to hire tour coaches from a firm called Busy Wheelers. We hired sixteen-seater coaches and they came with a driver. I think this was when Nicky and Alan moved on because they didn't have the correct licenses to drive these coaches.

The driver we got with the coach had mostly only driven punters on day trips to Margate and seaside resorts like that. Doing the band thing was a bit of culture shock for him.

Kenny Wheeler was one of the more experienced members of The Jam's crew. I think he'd worked with The Kinks and it was whilst they were on one of their 'break up' periods and so not touring that Kenny came to work with us.

Kenny knew how to play the role of road manager/crew boss/tour manager. This was useful because still at this time John (Weller) and Paul, Bruce and myself knew very little about taking an establishing band on the road. The job of the tour manager can be difficult and certainly involved. They have to liaise with a load of agents, the travel agents who sort out the hotels, flights and more. A band needs that somebody in the middle to pull it all together and make it work. It's a matter of them working out the logistics and saying "right, we need to do

3

THE JAM

this, so we need to get from here to there and we need this and that and we have to do it in this time".

Kenny was capable of doing this and his role also spanned several other jobs. For instance he was also a bit of a bodyguard. He looked out for Paul and when Paul was seeing Gill Price, Kenny would have to go everywhere they went. That was why he called him the 'gooseberry'. For example Paul and Gill would go and have a bite to eat at a restaurant and Kenny would also be there, sitting on a nearby table, all by himself. I liked Kenny, he had a good sense of humour and having a good sense of humour is a necessity when you're touring with a band. Getting too serious when you're on the road isn't always the best thing.

There were times when Kenny could be quite strict, especially with the fans. He was never too keen when we let people into the sound-checks. I suppose for Kenny it just interfered with the organisation of the shows. It was like he had a well-oiled machine and we were letting in all these fans with their spanners. But, fair play to Kenny, he dealt with it - he had to because us letting the fans in was something that Paul, Bruce and myself wanted to do and there are countless stories of fans being allowed into sound-checks. Some of the time they pushed though and sometimes we'd find a fan or two hiding away somewhere after the soundcheck. They'd have got into the soundcheck but didn't have a ticket for the concert so hiding away was one way of trying to see the show. If I think of Kenny, I also think about him playing cards on the tour bus. When we were on the road a bit of a card school developed. The players would usually be Kenny, John and Paul. I tried, lost my money and ducked straight out. Losing my hard-earned cash in

a game of cards wasn't for me. There were times when would I see some big handfuls of cash being either lost or won.

I understood why Kenny and the others played cards. It was a way of bonding and also a way of time wasting and, when you're on the road, there's often a lot of time to kill. After The Jam split, Kenny stayed with Paul throughout his Style Council and his solo years. I think in more recent years he's sort of taken a step back and now his son has taken over that job. I don't think the fans get allowed in anymore though. Things have changed on that matter.

As The Jam started to really establish themselves we got another tour manager. Having Dickie Bell freed Kenny up to concentrate on the other things that the band needed and this included acting as a sort of personal assistant to John.

I think Dickie had previously worked with bands like Iron Maiden. He had very extensive experience of tour managing. Having Dickie's expertise helped because The Jam's tours were getting bigger and more international and the demands were changing and becoming more challenging. I mean we were now into the realms of sending the road crew and often the gear ahead in advance and we'd turn up a few days later sometimes. Dickie really came into his own when it came to organising all this stuff and he did it well. Dickie came across as being extremely worldly when it came to the whole rock and roll world. Dickie also knew a lot of people in the music industry. He always seemed to know someone at the venue, the next promoter and band members and crew from other bands.

I know Dickie use to freak John out sometimes. When we were on the road Dickie and John would sometimes share a hotel room. In those sort of situations you'd see the side of Dickie that had been influenced by being on the road with the likes of Iron Maiden. There'd be antics. Whenever I got into trouble it was usually down to Dickie Bell. He and I were out on the piss one afternoon and we ended up at some studio where The Cure just happened to be recording. I couldn't get through the door so ended up kicking it. Only it was made of glass and I cut my leg. When I was pissed and got into a fight at the Pink Pop Festival, I was with him then too.

Dickie was a very lively sort of character and he was good fun to be around. He also knew people in America and when we toured there I would hang out with him and he'd take me to see the best places and people. He took me drinking at Barney's Beanery on Santa Monica Boulevard, West Hollywood. The bar had been frequented by actors, musicians and writers since it had opened in

the late Twenties. The likes of Errol Flynn and Rita Hayworth had spent many a night in the place. Dickie wanted to show me the place where he told me Janis Joplin drank her last drink before dying the following day and it was also where Jim Morrison allegedly pissed up against the bar whilst being drunk. I was fascinated by the place. I don't know if Paul or Bruce ever visited it when we were on tour there.

Dickie took me to see all kinds of rock and roll motels and hotels and bars and clubs such as the Rainbow Bar and Grill, Gazzarri's and lots more on Sunset Boulevard.

When The Jam were touring the States there were still hotels that catered for rock bands and who tolerated certain rock and roll behaviours. There'd be furniture in the rooms that had basically been stuck back together, having been destroyed by some band that had stayed there just before us. Dickie would say, "You smash that up - the owners won't mind

THE JAM

- they expect it." Every table in those rooms seem to rock and wobble as soon as you put your bag on it.

Another notorious hotel The Jam stayed at was the Hyatt House, also on Sunset Boulevard, which was where John Bonham supposedly rode a motorbike in the hotels hallways and Keith Moon tossed a TV out of his bedroom window. It landed on Sunset Boulevard.

The Hyatt House, also endearingly known as 'the Riot House', had served as a party place for most of the big rock bands of the Sixties and Seventies - Led Zeppelin, The Who and The Rolling Stones had all stayed there. The end-of-tour party scene in the film *This is Spinal Tap* was filmed on the roof of the hotel. They had all left their mark on the place in one way or another. And Dickie Bell knew the stories.

Of course from the very early days there was John Weller. He is a huge part of The Jam's history. I have a vague memory of the first time I met John. I was round Paul's house. After the Sheerwater Youth Club gig we would rehearse in Paul's bedroom. It would be Paul, Steve and me, sitting around working out how to play the songs.

John liked his music. Born on 28 November 1931 he had been brought up in London. He was from Lewisham and he was around when rock and roll had started. He was a bit of a Teddy Boy. He'd also been a bit of an amateur boxer and had worked hard at it. He started when he was about twelve and when he joined the RAF he continued to develop it there. John had been a featherweight champion as a younger man.

I think John helped to steer Paul in a direction to do something he wanted and something that perhaps didn't need to be a solid job, like an office job. For instance John

tried to get Paul to play football. But football wasn't for Paul. Instead he showed an interest in music, so John encouraged that.

Once John got behind Paul he started to get the gigs. At first when it was just Paul and Steve, and then when it became The Jam. He was very well placed to get us gigs because he was a taxi driver and he used to pick punters up from those clubs that he'd then approach to get us gigs.

John was a gregarious guy and he would talk to the club owners about bookings and he'd talk to punters about where the better clubs were. And thankfully for us John was willing to do his sort of thing. He liked that Paul was in a band and what we were setting ourselves up to do.

At this time we were still just young lads. We still had to prove ourselves at a time when most of the other acts getting bookings

THE STORY: **THE FOURTH JAM MAN**

were people who had been around a lot longer and were a lot more established. The club owners would often be sceptical and ask John questions like "will they behave themselves? Do they have enough material?" John fielded all of these questions and more and got us the bookings. As we got more and more serious we then organised photo shoots and press releases and John used these to hustle us gigs.

John knew a lot of people around town and from a lot of different backgrounds. He'd worked several jobs, some all at the same time. These included bricklaying and being a taxi driver. It was through his connections that John managed to borrow vans for us to use to get our equipment to the venues. We had a lot of different vans in the early days. One of those vans even came with its own security system, and that was a lioness cub. John knew a guy called Ronnie. I think he got to know him from going to Michael's Club. Ronnie used to take the lioness to Michaels Club. It was dark in there so at first the punters thought it was just a big dog. It wasn't until it growled that they realised what it was. Ronnie would also take the lioness for walks around Woking and the locals sort of got used to it.

John asked Ronnie if we could borrow his Luton van and Ronnie agreed. What we didn't know was that he kept the lioness in the back of the van. This meant that when we borrowed the van and went to gigs, the lioness came with us too. She would be in the back of the van, along with the drums, guitars and amps.

Ronnie would drive and we'd sit in the front. I remember the lioness pushing her giant paw through the partitioning window one time, as we returned home after a gig. She placed her paw on John's shoulder, which

naturally worried him. Ronnie just punched the lioness on her nose and she retreated to the back of the van.

There was another occasion when we used Ronnie's van to play a gig at the Tumbledown Dick in Farnborough. When we had finished the gig, we set about breaking down the gear and getting it ready to load it back into the van. One of the people who'd been in the audience kindly offered to help us carry it to the van.

We failed to mention that there was a lioness living and guarding the van and when the shutters went up he dropped whatever he was carrying and ran away. You can't blame him.

Ronnie's lioness eventually ended up in some safari park because she simply got too big for him to keep in the van. There'd also been an incident where she'd scared some old woman who had been wearing a fur coat and that helped to seal her fate.

Another thing that John was really helpful with was collecting the money from the club owners at the end of the night. We were just kids and we were still insecure and none of us liked having those discussions about money. No one wanted the job of having to approach some seasoned club owner and ask for our fifteen quid. But John could do this and he had a way about him that meant that getting paid wasn't a problem. John was also well-liked and that helped in all sorts of ways.

One of John's contacts had been Rick Parfitt's dad. Of course Rick went on to have huge success with Status Quo. The Parfitts were members of the Woking Working Men's Club in Walton Road, just like John Weller, and they too would spend many evenings in there. When the Wellers moved to Stanley Road, they only had to walk a few feet and

THE JAM

they'd be at the entrance to the club. John was able to speak to Rick and borrow some of his gear.

Another time John got us a gig at Stamford Bridge - the home of Chelsea Football Club. This came about because John knew someone who had a connection with both Woking Football Club and Chelsea Football Club.

These sort of gigs were good to do because they helped raise our profile and they gave us a break from playing the usual clubs and pubs. I think John enjoyed being involved with the band and getting us gigs. It took up a lot of his time, as it did ours. Ann resented being left at home at the weekends. We were out playing a lot of Friday and Saturday nights and John would be with us on most of these nights.

Once The Jam signed to Polydor and we were going into the studio, John wouldn't get involved with that so much. He'd sat in on some of the very first studio sessions we'd done, like at Bob Potter's place, but I think he found that quite boring really because for him it meant mostly just sitting around. He had no role in the studio, other than to keep encouraging us, which he did and which we were grateful for. He certainly didn't sit in the shadows of the studio making suggestions or telling us what or how to play.

In the early days John was also still holding down jobs to make his living, so sometimes he'd just drop us off somewhere and then go and be a taxi driver or lay some bricks. Personality-wise, people would describe John as being one of those people who had the gift of the gab. This helped when it came to 'bigging up' the band and hustling gigs for us. He was an approachable man and that also helped, but he could have a short temper - which wasn't a bad thing. I saw times when the boxer in him would come out and I saw

people back off and be careful not to cross him. I viewed John as being quite a sociable man and friendly and you could see how being a taxi driver suited him.

Ann Cradock had met John whilst she was working in an office at the Lion Works in Woking. At the time John was working as a tarmacer for a firm called Morris and Rose and they had a contract to do some work in the Lion Works grounds. Ann caught John's eye and he chatted her up. They started to date and within a year they were married and a year later Paul was born.

As The Jam got bigger and they collected more fans, Paul's sister Nicky took it upon herself to manage the band's fan club. When the Wellers moved from Stanley Road to Balmoral Road John converted the coal bunker into the offices of The Jam Fan Club. It would be in there that the fan mail was opened and read and often replied to. Polydor would sometimes suggest that Paul, Bruce and myself say a few words about the up and coming tour or the release of a new record, or something like that. We'd then do that and this would get its release via the fan club. Out of the three of us Paul was the best at responding to this. He would write a whole page that was often very detailed, informative and insightful. Bruce and I weren't so good at it. I think we saw it as being homework and that turned us off.

During the fan club's life lots of things were sent out, even a letter that officially announced The Jam splitting up. There were times when Ann and Nicky needed to recruit some neighbours just to help out with sticking letters into envelopes. It was like this until the franking machine at Polydor got appropriated for such things.

Nicky was still quite young when The Jam started to really take off. Sometimes John

THE STORY: **THE FOURTH JAM MAN**

would let her have the day off school so she could come along to see us on *Top of the Pops* or get to a gig somewhere. When we were breaking into the London music scene and playing at places like The Red Cow and the Nashville Rooms, Nicky would be there weaving her way in and out of the audience trying to sell the button pin badges we had made up with the venue's name on them. And of course she was one of the people included in the 'Art School' video that we made. The whereabouts of The Jam Fan Club reached Jam fans. This was partly because Nicky placed adverts in the music newspapers and these included the Wellers' home address. This meant that fans could go knocking on the Wellers door and ask if Paul was in (which happened many times). And on many occasions Ann would let the fan inside, make them a cup of tea and even allow them to have a nose around Paul's bedroom. When The Jam split up several fans even camped out on the green in front of the house. For some

Jam fans, making the often long journey to the Wellers' home was the equivalent of a Beatle fan making the journey to Liverpool and knocking on the door of Mendips (John Lennon's childhood home).

Ann and Nicky were proud of Paul and The Jam and in their own way did what they could to support them and it stayed like this for the duration of The Jam's life. After The Jam split up, Nicky worked at Solid Bond Studios whilst Paul was with The Style Council.

In 2015 and 2016 Ann and Nicky both agreed to participate in Q&A sessions at Jam-related events and they were more than happy to talk about their experiences of being involved in and around The Jam. Their stories thrilled the audiences.

As The Jam got bigger it became clear that Kenny Wheeler couldn't manage all the band's needs. Extra personnel were hired to help out with security. Chris Adoja was one of them.

Chris had worked in security. One of his jobs involved acting as security for a wealthy Arab when he visited the UK. Chris struck me as being a sensible guy: he had his head screwed on. He was a big guy too so you'd think twice about messing with him. He had a presence about him that suited the work he did.

I think Chris came from London. He certainly lived in London when he started working for The Jam. He knew the score. When it came to security he knew exactly what needed to be done. On the times when we'd get hassled by fans after gigs he knew how to manage the situations. He was a good guy to have around.

The other security guy we pulled in to help out was Joe Awome. Joe was another big guy and, like Chris, you'd think twice about

THE JAM

3

messing with him. Like John Weller he had a history with boxing too. Joe had even faced Muhammad Ali in an exhibition fight. He had lasted for two rounds.

We knew Joe from the days of playing in Michael's Club. He'd worked as the doorman there: he was that big he blocked the door at the top of the stairs. But being a doorman for a club in Woking was different to working as security for a band that was playing big venues and having fans trying to grab us. I mean, there was one occasion when Paul, Bruce and myself were exiting some venue and trying to get on the coach, when someone grabbed an end of Paul's scarf. But then someone else grabbed the other end - which meant Paul's scarf tightened around his neck and started to choke him. The security had to deal with that and quickly, which they did, and Paul managed to get bundled onto the bus and was okay. He was shaken up by it though. But these were the risks that Chris and Joe had to deal with and which Joe had to learn about when he was hired.

I think Joe must have lived in the Woking area because that's where he worked. I remember that I would see him running around the streets of Woking when he was training - he was a very fit man.

In one of my attempts to give up smoking Joe said he could help me. He suggested that I go running with him. Stupidly I agreed to go with him and we met up one morning in the hotel lobby where we were staying. So, me with my tracksuit and trainers on we set off. I had no chance of keeping up with him. On another occasion I only got as far as the street outside the hotel. I think we were on tour in Germany and it was freezing. I got outside the hotel and thought 'no' and just went back inside and let Joe go for a run by himself.

The Jam were privileged to have had Joe and Chris and most of the time it was okay work for them. There was an incident in Sweden though that caused some upset. Some guy got beaten up outside the venue. He went to the local police station and told them that he'd been beaten up by Joe. The police showed up and arrested Joe and took him down to the police station. Of course Joe had had nothing to do with beating this guy up and thankfully some fans stepped in and told the police what they'd seen and how they'd seen some other guys commit the assault. With this information the police had to drop all the charges and let Joe go free.

After The Jam split up I stayed in contact with Joe. The last time we met up was two months before he died.
On 4 December 1994 a memorial gig was organised for Joe at the Shepherd's Bush Empire. Paul Weller performed on the night. Joe had been suffering from a brain tumour and had tragically died on the operating table.

Another key player in The Jam's story is Chris Parry. Chris was an A&R man employed by Polydor. Chris was from New Zealand but had moved to the UK and got a job with Polydor. I think he had played in a band whilst being in New Zealand. He was a drummer, so he liked his music. I remember he loved sailing too - as all New Zealanders seem to.

I got the impression that Chris was quite an ambitious guy. When he became involved with The Jam he quickly placed himself in the position as also being the band's producer and he was very hands-on with the first album. To his credit, after having a go at producing, I think Chris was able to be honest with himself and accept that he couldn't quite cut it as a producer.

It was at one of the gigs in the Nashville in

THE STORY: **THE FOURTH JAM MAN**

the early part of 1977 that Chris showed up. He watched the gig and, at the end, he came and introduced himself. He told us that he had liked what he had heard and he was going to talk to his superiors at Polydor about us. He more or less promised us some studio time, which we just took with a pinch of salt. But then Chris did return for another show and he told us that he'd booked us into some studios - that turned out to be Anemone Studios. Our relationship with Chris really took off from there.

Once Polydor signed us Chris was given the role of acting as the man who worked in the middle. He was a sort of mediator between the record label and us, and he did a great job. He understood the music industry and what was happening. He genuinely wanted The Jam to do well and he invested in us. I feel that we learnt a lot from Chris in those early days of being signed to a label and he introduced us to ways of thinking that would help to make the band a success.

Paul, Bruce and myself spent many nights out with Chris after doing recordings. He'd often take us to one of the burger joints just around the corner from the Polydor offices in Stratford Place. We were happy with that, after all Chris would pick up the bill as a Polydor expense. I remember he'd often ferry us about in his Volkswagen Scirocco, which totally impressed us. Chris eventually left Polydor to start up his own label. His label was called Fiction. One of the biggest acts he signed was The Cure who went on to have considerable success.

Once Chris realised that an experienced producer was needed he brought in Vic Smith. Vic had worked for Polydor since the early Sixties and cut his teeth working with the likes of The Rolling Stones and Joe Cocker. Around the time of working

with The Jam, he changed his name to Vic Coppersmith-Heaven.

It had been Chris who had taken Vic to see The Jam. He said he felt it was a "great show with amazing spirit and energy". He ended up working on all of The Jam's albums except *The Gift*.

Vic was a very meticulous guy. He also made a point of keeping everything that we recorded on tape. This could be useful because there'd be times in the studio when we'd record multiple takes of a certain track we'd be working on, but then decide it wasn't happening and we'd go back to an earlier take and that would be the one that was working after all.

Being in the studio is like building something. You get the drums and bass down; then you start to add other instruments and sounds. Vic encouraged this and he was very good at remembering what we had laid down in a previous take and he would refer us back to it and we'd go "oh yeah, that works". Vic had that discipline that's needed in the studio and we learned from him. It would be Vic who'd remind us that time is money and

THE JAM

3

that we only had a certain amount of time and budget to work with.

Another thing that Vic was really good at was being able to make that call and tell us to stop. He'd say the song has reached a point where it's just right. And we needed someone around us like that.

Vic also had a really good understanding of what works on vinyl, as opposed to playing live, and on the running order on an album. He understood the importance of the first track and what this would mean for the listener. He understood that the first few bars on the opening track would be the ones that leave the impression. For example, take a song like 'Jailhouse Rock'. From the very first snare beat and piano/guitar strikes you are grabbed. Vic encouraged this with us and especially by the time of recording the *This is the Modern World* album he'd encouraged an attitude of cut the crap and cut out the faffing about - and we listened.

I found Vic to be quite dry and very professional and he knew how to get the best out of us. He was also fairly tolerant with us. On one occasion I set his shirt on fire and this was whilst he was wearing it. I don't know why I did it! Years later I saw him in Liverpool and I apologised. I told him that the incident had played on my mind for many years and I was really sorry. He was like "that's really cool man" but I know at the time he was really annoyed. I recall that he'd brought the shirt back from a trip to Bali. I think he had a shop or stall in Bali that he ran with his wife and because of that he would bring us back ties. I've still got a couple at home.

The other guy we used in the studio was Pete Wilson. He certainly knew his way around the equipment in the studio. He was very useful to have around and very easy to get on with. Pete was a dab hand at being a studio engineer. He was tuned into everything - he heard every buzz that shouldn't be there.

Pete was a quiet man. He could take instructions and act upon them. When it came to recording *The Gift* we decided to ask Pete if he'd produce it. By that time we knew what sound we wanted and we had a better idea of how the studio equipment worked. We knew we could communicate our wishes and thoughts to Pete and he'd help us get to where we wanted to be. Sometimes this was just a physical task - knowing where to plug what lead into what hole.

By the time of *The Gift* Paul, Bruce and myself had learnt a great deal from Chris Parry, Vic Smith and Pete Wilson. We took our educations into our new lives after The Jam.

It was when Chris Parry stepped down that Dennis Munday took over that role. I don't know what Chris went on to do. By the time Dennis came in The Jam were pretty well established. We had a good track record with records that had achieved good chart positions, we had built a loyal fan base and we had toured a lot.

My first impression of Dennis was that he was a man who knew his way around the music industry. He understood it and the people that drove it and what their expectations of us were. I think Dennis found himself fighting our corner on many occasions. I think he was a genuine Jam fan. He possibly saw something in us that reminded him of his teenage years. In the Sixties he'd been a Mod and had gone to see the Mod bands of the day like The Who and Small Faces and he'd seen them in the best clubs like The Marquee and 100 Club. So there he was a little over a decade later, seeing another Mod-looking band who were also playing in the 100 Club and The Marquee. I guess in some ways history was repeating itself for Dennis.

I wouldn't describe Dennis as a company man. He had a foot in both camps and was able to see things from our point of view. Because of this we felt well represented. There were many times when Paul, Bruce, John and I would find ourselves faced with the hard-nosed types that Polydor employed. The topic usually related to money and how the budget they were offering to cover something just wasn't enough. In these moments Dennis would step in and handle the situation to try and resolve something or find an outcome that suited everyone.

One example that comes to mind was when the sleeve for *Setting Sons* was being worked on. Our idea was to have the rosary around the outside to be embossed. We thought this would look really good. The hard-noses knocked our suggestion back saying it would cost too much money to manufacture. Discussions were held and in the end with Dennis's intervention the first 100,000 were embossed but all the others thereafter were not. This was a compromise that worked for everyone.

Dennis would often attend meetings held at Polydor and be that mediator type person in the room. When any press or photo shoots were arranged he'd sometimes be present for those too. He kept an eye on most things Jam-related.

And Dennis would often pop his head around the door in whatever studio we were working in at any particular time. His job included providing us with reminders of things like dates when something needed to be done by, such as the master tape of *Sound Affects* being submitted to Polydor. This was

when he was representing the record label and making sure we were on target.

I think a good A&R man has to be dedicated to the job and to the band that they are working with and, I think we had that in Dennis. Like Chris Parry and Vic Smith we learnt from Dennis too. Even today I find it fascinating talking to Dennis because he still has an insight into how the music industry operates and the changes that have happened to make it what it is today. One of those conversations Dennis and I had was how labels today are less interested in the artists but are more interested in just the product - it wasn't like that back in The Jam's day!

When The Jam started to release records there was a push in the record industry to issue records in sleeves that had artwork on them. There had been a period of time when the big labels just put records out in plain sleeve bags that only had the record labels name and logo on it, for example Polydor's red sleeves with their name written in black. But for The Jam Polydor brought in Bill Smith. Bill was a designer who worked for Polydor. He had worked with bands like The Who so we were impressed.

Like Dennis Munday Bill had been a Mod in the Sixties and he had too had visited the Mod clubs and seen the Mod bands. He was a Londoner so he'd been well placed to witness the birth of Mod.

Bill had lots of ideas, which he was able to present to us whilst also keeping the bosses at Polydor happy. Bill would organise the photographers, for example Martyn Goddard, who worked on a few Jam records. Martyn would take lots of photos and then we'd sit down with him and Bill and go through all these photos on the contact sheets. Then we'd choose which ones we liked and cross off the ones that we didn't. Bill would pitch

3

THE JAM

3

in too because after all it was him that would be needing to do something with the photo. Bill was very good at providing the reasons why he wanted a certain photo and we trusted his judgment.

Having Bill onboard was another asset for The Jam because his sleeve designs helped to promote and market the band. Sleeves like *All Mod Cons* were fantastic. I think Bill did all The Jam sleeves, singles and albums except for *The Gift*.

But there were posters too that helped market The Jam. Posters would often be designed using the photos that didn't make it onto a record sleeve. Such posters would find their way into shops windows and on walls, into venues and also as give-aways in magazines or sent out via the fan club. They would also be used as adverts in the music newspapers like *Sounds* or the *NME*.

Bill was very instrumental in helping to create and promote that first Jam logo and the monochrome look. He was there when we were photographed for *In The City* against the white tiled wall: it had been Bill's idea and that photo shoot took place in Martyn Goddard's studio. I remember that Bill had built this tiled wall for the purposes of the shoot and I remember that at the end he invited us to smash it up - which we happily did. I don't know if Martyn took any photos of that.

It was Bill who marched us out of the Polydor offices to find a wall and spray paint *In The City* on it. The image of The Jam on a wall with the M being underlined came later. Keeping everything in black and white really worked for that period.

Martyn came with a good reputation. We listened to him and took our direction from him. Over The Jam's years he got some really good pictures of the band.

As The Jam got bigger so did the demand from the fans and one of the ways to satisfy the demands was to produce merchandise. A guy called Brian Hawkins was responsible for handling the merchandise that included things like t-shirts and badges. Brian ran a business with his dad in London and somehow had gotten into producing merchandise for bands.

Brian was a very lively character, very funny too. He certainly liked a party, which suited us. He'd also produce limited edition items such as tour jackets for certain members of the crew. Those sort of things also doubled up as a backstage pass. Those jackets were quite exclusive really. I remember that he gave Paul, Bruce and myself dressing gowns with our initials on them. They were useful actually because we could wrap them around ourselves when we came off stage and were all sweaty. There were two designs, one was black and white and the other was red, with some piping. I've still got mine.

It's also important to mention some of the road crew. For example there was Dave Liddle. Dave took care of the guitars and absolutely loved the status of being a guitar roadie for a successful band and to be fair to him he did it very well. After The Jam split Paul kept him on as his guitar tech.

Dave took his role very seriously. He was very protective of the guitars. He didn't like it when they were being abused - which could be quite a lot. It would be Dave's job to tune the guitars on stage and swap them when a change was needed. Dave would also be with us when we went into the studio. He was a good guitarist himself and there are some jams recorded that Dave is playing on.

It was Dickie Bell and myself who interviewed Dave for the job. I would sit in on many of the interviews when we were recruiting for the road crew. The interviews were really just a matter of finding out who the person had worked with, what they were capable of doing and things like that. I can't remember who Dave had worked with before The Jam.

Another guy we interviewed was Ian Harvie. He was my drum tech but also took on the role of crew boss. When Ian left a

Scotsman called Wally Miller took over the drum tech role and he looked after my drums both on the road and in the studio.

Wally was great to be around and I socialised a lot with him. He was always filled with stories that were interesting. What used to make me laugh about Wally was that as soon as he'd set up the kit that would be his job done. He would sit down with a newspaper. The trouble was if John

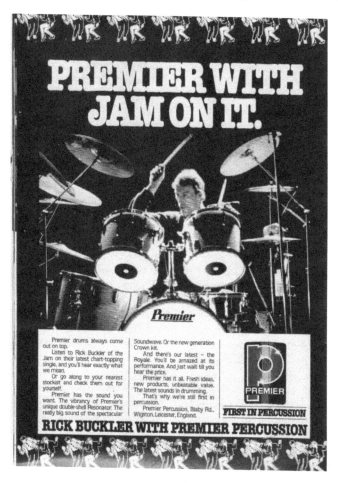

THE JAM

saw someone sitting around doing nothing he would have to have a word. So whenever John appeared Wally would get out a duster that he kept in his pocket and start dusting the kit with a "I'm just finishing off the kit John" remark. And then as soon as John disappeared he'd put the duster back into his pocket and sit down to read his paper again.

We would often socialise with the road crew because we'd meet up in some hotel after the concert. They didn't always stay in the same hotels as us, but on the occasions when they did it seemed the obvious thing to have a drink in the hotel bar. We sort of had a ready-made party who were willing to have a drink.

Once a concert was over it was always hard to come down from it. By the time you get changed and jump on the coach and get to the hotel, you're still riding on the adrenalin. Youcan't just go straight to bed, so you make a bee-line for the bar. In the bar we'd have a drink and wind down and tuck into the sandwiches that John would have had the hotel staff prepare for us.

Being on the road is all about building up for the concert that night. You do the travel, the sound check, you hang around for a bit, then you play, then you return to the hotel. There are high and low points throughout the day. Even the moment before you step on stage can be nerve-wracking. We all got nervous. I think we considered it a good thing to get nervous before a performance. It gives you edge. I think when you step onto a stage with a sense of complacency then mistakes can happen. Paul really suffered from nerves. Out of the three of us he was the most nervous. He would vomit before stepping onto stage but that would sort him out and he could perform. For me, my nerves would calm after I had got through the first song. By that time I knew

that everything was working okay, like the monitors and we had nothing to worry about. As soon as I knew Paul was alright and Bruce was alright it was like lighting the touch paper and off we'd go. The concert then flowed.

The Jam was never one to faff around. Paul rarely spoke between songs and when he did he would only say a few words, so it was mostly start one song, finish it and straight into the next one. Paul, Bruce and I worked together as a band. We were like a machine that worked well live and The Jam had a good reputation as being a really good live band and our road crew contributed to making the whole thing work.

Another thing that helped make the whole thing work was the sound and we had Bob Jeffries and Alan Wick to thank for that. We used company called Muscle Music that Alan owned and we bought the company off him. This meant we owned our own PA system which we could use for our UK dates. Bob and Alan stayed with us after we bought Muscle Music and managed our out-front sound.

It was Bob who got it in the neck when there was trouble with the monitors. On one occasion Alan had to have words with Bruce. This was because Bruce threw his bass at Bob. Luckily Bob saw the bass hurtling through the air and managed to duck out of the way. The following day Alan went out a bought an American footballer's outfit, a shirt with large shoulder pads and helmet and Bob turned up at the venue dressed up in it. This was to make a point to Bruce that it wasn't acceptable to launch bass guitars at the crew.

Names (and there are many more), to also mention as playing a part in The Jam's story also include George McManus, George Chambers, Simon Rickman, Mike Benson, Mike Brady, Ray Salter, Alan Wick and Maurice Gallagher.

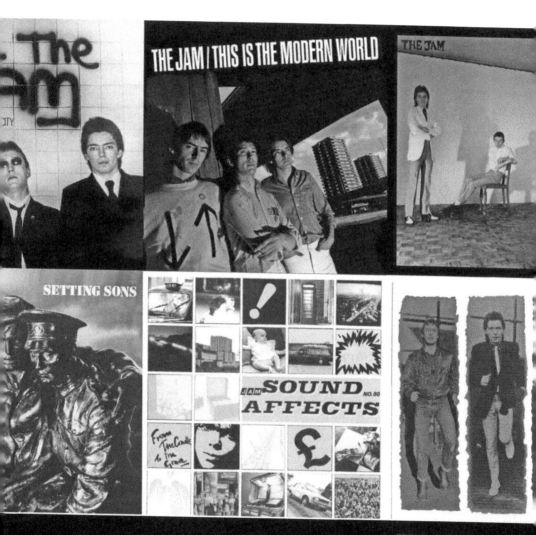

THE ALBUMS

4

> *"Sound Affects is a truly stirring record ... It brings the necessary orthodox of The Jam to a peak ... The balance is magnificent, classical in design ... A celebration of a liberating force in rock and roll."*
>
> **Dave McCullough**

THE ALBUMS

4

Two LPs packed with classic tracks within a 12-month period ensure that The Jam have a place at the top table of new wave bands. In total six studio and one live album during The Jam's relatively brief existence are a testimony to how extraordinary the output of the band was. What follows is a complete listing of all their recorded output.

IN THE CITY

Polydor. Released 20 May 1977. Peak UK Chart Position No 20.

Art School/I've Changed My Address/ Slow Down/I Got By in Time/Away from the Numbers/Batman Theme/In the City/Sounds from the Street/Non-Stop Dancing/Time for Truth/Takin' My Love/Bricks and Mortar/The Modern Word/The Gift

The debut studio album by The Jam featured the hit single and title track 'In the City' which had been released the previous month showcasing Weller's punchy, direct songwriting. The album was recorded in 1977 when the three band members were aged between 18 and 20. This was an era that preached attitude over musicianship. *In The City* is a raw and unfinished introduction to The Jam. They were well dressed and skilled at their instruments, taking most of their cues from Sixties Mod, rock and soul.

Weller recalled writing 'In the City' to Q magazine: "It was the sound of young Woking, if not London, a song about trying to break out of suburbia. As far as we were concerned, the city was where it was all happening: the clubs, the gigs, the music. I was probably 18, so it was a young man's song, a suburbanite dreaming of the delights of London and the excitement of the city. It was an exciting time to be alive. London was coming out of its post-hippy days and there was a new generation taking over. The song captured that wide-eyed innocence of coming out of a very small community and entering a wider world, seeing all the bands, meeting people, going

THE JAM

4

to the clubs, and the freedom that it held."

The new wave of punk was dominating the music press. At the start of the year, The Clash headlined the opening of London's only punk club The Roxy. *Leave Home*, the second studio album by American punk rock band the Ramones, had been released. Sid Vicious had replaced Glen Matlock as the bassist of the Sex Pistols who, after signing to A&M Records in a ceremony in front of Buckingham Palace, were then dropped by the label and had now signed to Virgin Records. The Buzzcocks had released their debut EP *Spiral Scratch*, The Damned had their debut album *Damned Damned Damned* and Television had released their debut album *Marquee Moon*. And six weeks before *In The City* hit the shops, The Clash released their self-titled debut album.

In The City hit a real nerve with the new wave of Mod kids. The Jam bettered the competition with good pop sense and strong melodies. A fitting illustration is the cover, where the band's clean-cut Mod portrayal belies their youthful rebellion while the hasty rendering of their name in graffiti contradicts the development and precision of their tight musicianship.

'Art School' opens the album with Weller strumming four chords, before counting in the rest of the band with a Ramones-style '1234.' The band launch into the song with Rick and Bruce driving it along. The title track is a tribute to the young commoner which also serves to castigate authority and condemn police brutality: "You still think I am crap But you'd better listen, man, Because the kids know where it's at, In the city there's a thousand men in uniforms, And I've heard they now have the right to kill a man."

'Away From The Numbers', is still a favourite with Jam fans, with its obvious Who sound. The 'ooh oohs' in the backing vocals are reminiscent of The Who, along with the guitar, drums and bass which also create a Sixties Who feel.

The album includes two cover songs. 'Slow Down' is a 24-bar blues written by Larry Williams which was first released as a single in 1958 and a rhythm and blues hit that influenced the growing rock and roll movement of the time. Both 'Slow Down' and the single's flip-side, 'Dizzy Miss Lizzy', were covered by The Beatles, in 1964 and 1965 respectively. Williams died at his home from a gunshot wound to his head on 7 January 1980, aged 44, in a suspected suicide. The second cover is the theme to the Sixties television series, *Batman*, which had also been previously covered by The Who, The Kinks and Link Wray.

Rick Buckler:

The Jam's version is certainly a unique take that's full of punk energy. The song was a fun thing to do. We just played around with it one day in the studio – we certainly sped it up."

'Non-Stop Dancing' is a joyous tribute, both lyrically and musically, to the Northern Soul dance parties of the late Sixties and early Seventies. 'Time For Truth' sees Paul vent his political views with an attack on British Prime Minister James Callaghan (between 1976 and 1979): 'And the truth is you've lost Uncle Jimmy, admit your failure and decline with honour while you can.' The final song on the album, 'Bricks and Mortar', also sees Weller taking a well-aimed swipe at authority and lays into politicians and their destructive decisions.

When Paul was growing up in Woking he would have noticed the old town getting the once over from the "Yellow bulldozers, the donkey jackets and JCBs", and as he toured the UK he would have witnessed so many other towns affected by the blight of development: "While hundreds are homeless, they're constructing parking spaces.

4

The album sleeve was designed by Bill Smith, a former London College of Printing art student who had been employed at Polydor Records as their art director since 1976. His idea for the album was to depict three guys that are in a band. They've just done a gig and are on their way home and have popped into an underground toilet. Then someone shows up and say's "Oh, aren't you The Jam?" to which the band members reply, "We are," and then they spray paint the band's name onto the wall.

Smith and photographer Martyn Goddard hired a studio and built a wall upon which they put the white tiles. Goddard took about 36 shots in total from which they chose the one, which ended up on the album sleeve.

Upon its release, the four major UK music weeklies all gave the album positive reviews. Reviewing the album in the *NME* Phil McNeil said Weller's songwriting "captures that entire teen frustration vibe with the melodic grace and dynamic aplomb of early Kinks and Who". In the *Record Mirror*, Barry Cain wrote, "Armed and extremely dangerous The Jam stalk the decrepit grooves. If you don't like them, hard luck they're gonna be around for a long time. It's been a long time since albums actually reflected pre-20 delusions and this one does." Chas de Walley in *Sounds* said: "The Jam are more widely accessible than just about anybody sheltering under the New wave umbrella... and for boys who insist that nothing stronger than Vic goes up their noses, Messrs Paul Weller, Rick Buckler and Bruce Foxton certainly operate close to the speed of light... yet this album creates grave misgivings... it's a fine album but despite the high energy, Weller's raucous untreated voice, *In The City* shows The Jam at times so close to the beat groups they're aping that they end up like Flamin' Groovies." Brian Harrigan of *Melody Maker* was equally impressed, proclaiming that "Weller-composed songs are anything but an

embarrassment. He has a deft touch that places his material on a much higher plateau. Lay down your prejudices and give them a try – they're guaranteed not to disappoint."

Rick Buckler:
I think *In The City* showed The Jam to be at our most raw. It represents a time when we were coming out of the working men's clubs and pubs but managed to capture the heat and intensity that often built up in those venues. 'In the City' was identifed as the song that should be our debut single and 'Takin' My Love' was to be the flip side. We were happy with the decision too. It was one of our newer songs and we felt it showed who we were and what we were intending.

> *"Weller's chording is inspired, he skitters in early Townshend feedback licks with ease, he layers his guitar in a way that should be an object lesson to Wilko Johnson – he's just amazing, his songs capture that entire teen frustration vibe with the melodic grace and dynamic aplomb of early Kinks and Who."*

Phil McNeill, *NME*

4

THIS IS THE MODERN WORLD

Polydor. Released 18 November 1977.
Peak UK Chart Position No 22

*The Modern World/London Traffic/Standards/
Life from a Window/The Combine/Don't
Tell Them You're Sane/In the Street Today/
London Girl/I Need You (For Someone)/Here
Comes the Weekend/Tonight at Noon/In the
Midnight Hour/The Gift*

The hasty follow up to *In The City* (released
less than seven months after their debut
album), finds Weller with a shortage of
material. Like all the six studio albums by
The Jam, it is short — 12 tracks and 31:19
minutes. But the album revealed a lyrical
progression and maturity with songs such as
the impressive 'Life From A Window' and the
blazing single, 'The Modern World', Weller's
powerful statement of intent. The album is a
snapshot of a day in the life of the declining
British Empire during the late Seventies. With
eight Weller originals, plus a co-write with
former Jam guitarist Dave Waller, two songs

penned by Bruce Foxton ('London Traffic'
and 'Don't Tell Them You're Sane'), and a
cover of the Wilson Pickett 1965 Soul classic
'In The Midnight Hour', *This Is The Modern
World* was the product of The Jam gigging
relentlessly during 1977.

During July 1977 the group released 'All
Around The World', (with 'Carnaby Street' as
the B-Side) which peaked at No 13 on the UK
singles chart - The Jams highest placing to date.
A brilliant single with an unforgettable chorus.
Polydor needed to fill the gap between
their debut album, *In the City*, and *This Is the
Modern World*. It would be another two years
before The Jam placed a song in the UK top
10 again with 'The Eton Rifles' in October
1979 reaching No 3.

English photographer Gered Mankowitz (who
had worked with worked with The Rolling
Stones, Small Faces and Jimi Hendrix amongst
others), took the cover image under part of
the Westway in London. Although the shoot
was taken during the day, lights helped to give
those very hard looking black shadows with
the band coming out of them. It provided an
abstract type background.

Rick Buckler's stiff, unpretentiously
forceful drumming and Foxton's hyperactive,
bubbling bass lines make for punk rock's
greatest-ever rhythm section. Bill Smith
told *Uncut*; I was responsible for all the Jam
covers – singles and albums, from 'In the
City' through to 'Absolute Beginners'. For
the cover of *This Is the Modern World* I wanted
to produce a very Post-Modern image, with
a small nod to Situationism. I wanted an
urban/modern setting for the band that
firmly rooted them into London culture, so
we found the location for the shoot under
the Westway near North Kensington. The
Mod influence was very much down to
Paul, he had seen Pete Townshend wearing

a jacket or something with arrows on, so we put the arrows using gaffer tape onto his jumper. Having used the suits for the first *In The City* shoot, we quickly moved into the more Mod/Carnaby Street look from then on. The shoot was done using daylight and then added flash to give heavy shadowing and emphasise the concrete monoliths of the Westway support columns and the feeling of claustrophobia from the road above. We were all pleased with the resulting images.

Although the title track is still its best known, 'Life From A Window' and 'Tonight At Noon' display a more mature, observational side to Weller's songwriting than anything on *In The City*. The trio's clothes, haircuts, and tunes reflected an obsession with the mid-1960s Mod style, and some termed the band the new Who.

The closing track and the only cover on the album is 'In The Midnight Hour'. The song was composed by Pickett and Steve Cropper at the historic Lorraine Motel in Memphis where Martin Luther King, Jr. would later be assassinated in April 1968. The track which gave Pickett his first hit on Atlantic Records has also been covered by the likes of Them, Roxy Music, Tina Turner, the Young Rascals and the Righteous Brothers.

The US album release had a different track order, included the 'censored' single version of 'The Modern World', and added the UK single 'All Around the World'.

Rick Buckler:
The Modern World album was our first proper studio album. I feel we jumped in feet first and with still very limited studio experience we did alright. Despite what the critics said I think the songs are strong and it's a good album that we only really appreciated much later.

> *"It's not that Weller is softening, it's just that he's learning."*
> **Barry Cain, Record Mirror**

ALL MOD CONS

Polydor. Released 3 November 1978. Peak UK Chart Position No 6

All Mod Cons/To Be Someone (Didn't We Have A Nice Time)/Mr. Clean/David Watts/English Rose/In The Crowd/Billy Hunt/ It's Too Bad/Fly/The Place I Love/A Bomb In Wardour Street/Down In The Tube Station At Midnight/The Modern World/The Gift

The Jam returned to the UK dispirited after supporting Blue Öyster Cult in North America in 1978. The tour did not go well, with fans booing the three-piece off the stage on more than one occasion. Back

THE JAM

4

home and to make matters worse, Weller was suffering from writer's block. The demos they recorded were rejected by Polydor A&R man Chris Parry, who suggested they return to their home town of Woking and write a new set of songs.

Weller later said; "Initially we were annoyed and hurt that our songs were panned by the label. On reflection it was a healthy thing to have an 'outside-the-bubble' objective view. It made us re-think our approach and we raised the bar. Once in RAK studios, we knew we had a great album in the making. I guess we had a point to prove. We were a great band with great songs and three great players."

Maybe Weller turning 20 had something to do with it. On *All Mod Cons* Weller had taken that great leap forward as a songwriter and produced a set of songs that draw inspiration from, rather than merely imitate, his idols. The musicianship here is as good as it gets – Weller, Buckler and Foxton are locked into each other, the breakdowns and codas on 'In The Crowd' and 'Down In The Tube Station At Midnight' are clearly the result of years of playing together soaked in sweat.

A double-A-side single preceded the album's release. With a cover of the Kinks 'David Watts', and the Weller-penned fury of 'A'-Bomb In Wardour Street' it reached No 25 in the UK chart when issued on 26 August 1978.

The phrase 'all mod cons' stands for 'all modern conveniences,' but Weller was flexing his sarcastic wit when he used it as the name of The Jam's third album. Engineer Vic Coppersmith-Heaven had them delve deeper into their beloved Sixties influences and introduced the band to double-tracking and phasing, adding to the psychedelic feel during recordings.

The quintessentially English *All Mod Cons* kicked off a simply amazing run of three superb albums. This and the follow-ups - *Setting Sons*, and *Sound Affects* have all rightfully achieved classic status. *All Mod Cons* is a record still brimming with a ferocious hunger today.

The title track and 'To Be Someone (Didn't We Have A Nice Time)' – is a surprisingly effective exploration of the dark side of stardom, but Weller is careful not to get too insular. Songs like 'Mr Clean' and 'In The Crowd' offer a view of Weller's world, while most startling is 'English Rose' (still a staple of Weller's solo shows), his first ballad – which has a tenderness about it way beyond its writer's years. Weller developed a third person commentary, honing a talent for narrative and storytelling. "Class issues were very important to me at that time" said Weller. "Woking has a bit of a stockbroker belt on its outskirts. So I had those images – people catching the train to Waterloo to go to the city. 'Mr Clean' was my view of that."

The Kinks became Weller's new benchmark, and the album includes a faithful, forceful rendition of their 1967 class-conscious 'David Watts' (sung by Bruce Foxton). Along with Watts, the lacerating class resentment of 'Mr. Clean', the everyday-life 'In The Crowd', and the grittily detailed social commentary of 'Down In The Tube Station At Midnight' showed the ability of Weller to create songs that illustrated English suburban life. This sustained their popularity, and continued the tradition of Pete Townsend, Steve Marriot, Ray Davies and of course, Lennon & McCartney.

The album's masterpiece though, and arguably the best thing The Jam ever recorded 'Down In The Tube Station At

Midnight' bristles with furious energy. Sharp and simple and all the more arresting because of it the track weds Weller's seething narrative and siren-like leads to Foxton's alternately chunky and supple bass.

The track finally confirmed Weller's arrival as a major lyrical talent. The lyric, which tells the story of a young man attacked on the underground, managed to tap superbly into the violent tension of the times. A heady mix of scathing resentment and fluctuating harmonies towards the end, the track careers out of control toward a shambolic crescendo of emotion.

All Mod Cons was the turning point in a journey that would see The Jam become one of the most revered British bands of all time.

Rick Buckler:
Writing and recording *All Mod Cons* was like stepping through a new door into a new world. It was like we'd discovered something new about ourselves and it was a turning point for The Jam. Things seemed to come together for us with this album.

Bruce Foxton:
All Mod Cons was a great time for the band and the fans who stayed with us to this day. When I hear the album now I just think, Yeah, it's a great album!

Charles Shaar Murray:
This is a good a place as any to point out that bassist Bruce Foxton and drummer Rick Buckler are more than equal to the new demands that Weller is making on them: the vitality, empathy and resourcefulness they display throughout the album makes *All Mod Cons* a collective triumph for The Jam. *NME*

SETTING SONS

Polydor. Released 16 November 1979.
Peak Chart Position No 4

Girl On The Phone/Thick As Thieves/Private Hell/Little Boy Soldiers/Wasteland/Burning Sky/Smithers-Jones/Saturday's Kids/The Eton Rifles/Heatwave/The Modern World/ The Gift

Back in November 1979, Paul Weller was still only 21 years of age. Margaret Thatcher and the Conservatives had just assumed power and a major recession was just around the corner. Punk rock had burnt itself out and new bands like Joy Division, and the Teardrop Explodes had arrived championed by Radio 1's John Peel.

Having already released three albums over an 18-month-period between May of 1977 and November of 1978, The Jam's status as one of the most prolific bands since the Sixties was already assured. The Jam had maintained their course, as other groups fell by the wayside. For The Jam, the only way was up and their chart placings in the British charts were confirming the fact.

THE JAM

4

Setting Sons features a much harder, tougher production, and arguably, this is the Jam's most thematically ambitious album. Weller originally conceived *Setting Sons* as a concept album detailing the lives of three boyhood friends who later reunite as adults after an unspecified war only to discover they have grown apart. This concept was never fully developed, and it remains unclear which tracks were originally intended as part of the story, 'Thick As Thieves' and 'Burning Sky', and the ambitious mini-rock operatic 'Little Boy Soldiers' are the most explicit survivors of the original album concept.

The albums opening track 'Girl on the Phone', starts with the Townhouse Studio receptionist's phone ringing. The two-part harmonies, complex structure and long, twisting instrumental break were a clear new step. The title was taken from a Roy Lichtenstein pop art painting from 1964, the one with a blonde-haired girl speaking into a white telephone saying, 'Oh Jeff ...I love you, Too...but...'

Bruce's bass introduces 'Private Hell' and the pace picks up at this point in the album. 'Private Hell' about a stereotypical bored housewife simply sounds gigantic with its slashing rhythms, harmonies and ominous bass part. 'Saturday Kids' might be Springsteen's 'Glory Days' describing the small pleasures and constricted lives of working class youth following the footsteps of their parents.

'Little Boy Soldiers' demonstrates Weller's increasing sophistication as a songwriter, with a good multi-sectioned structure.

The attack on public school education referenced in 'The Eton Rifles' proved something of a pivotal moment for the band. The single gave them a well-deserved top three singles chart placing, and laid the foundations for the string of No 1 hits that followed. The inspiration for 'The Eton Rifles' was a march by the unemployed that had set off from Liverpool and took in Eton College en route. Flush-faced Etonians jeered, "Hello, hooray" as the marchers passed by and they, in turn, reacted strongly. What Paul saw was a class war being played out before him.

More recently Weller questioned British Prime Minister David Cameron's claim that he was a fan of 'Eton Rifles'.

Cameron, who was a student at the prestigious Eton College, had previously insisted that he had great affection for The Jam's 1979 track. "I was one, in the corps. It meant a lot, some of those early Jam albums we used to listen to," he had said in the past. "I don't see why the left should be the only ones allowed to listen to protest songs." Speaking to *Mojo* about Cameron's fandom, Weller declared: "The whole thing with Cameron saying it was one of his favourite songs... I just think, 'Which bit didn't you get?'" People say, 'Why don't you write any more political songs?' But I would just write exactly the same fucking things I wrote thirty-odd years ago."

'Smithers-Jones' is Bruce's reaction to events he'd witnessed in his own life. He knew how it felt when his father was made redundant. This is arguably the best song that Bruce wrote for The Jam and he sings it over a backing of woodwind instruments. Although other versions were available, the album version was the one with strings that were arranged by Pete Solley.

Following the dissolution of the Jam, Foxton regularly performed 'Smithers-Jones' with Belfast-based punk band Stiff Little Fingers, whom he subsequently joined in 1990.

'Heatwave' is essentially a cover of The Who's cover of the Martha Reeves and the Vandellas hit, featuring future Style Council member Mick Talbot's first keyboard work with Weller. Weller later said of the track's inclusion; "It's the 'Yellow Submarine' of *Setting Sons*, but I didn't have any more songs!"

Setting Sons was ranked No 4 among the top Albums of the Year for 1979 by *NME*, with 'Eton Rifles' and 'Strange Town' ranked at No 1 and 5 among the year's top tracks.

Uncredited on the album sleeve the cover art features a photograph of Benjamin Clemens' bronze sculpture, The St John's Ambulance Bearers. Cast in 1919, this sculpture depicts a wounded soldier being carried by two ambulance workers. This sculpture is currently in the possession of the Imperial War Museum in London, England. The shot on the back of the sleeve of the bulldog and the Union Jack was taken Andrew Rosen who Weller knew. He liked it and wanted to use it with the album sleeve design.

Rick Buckler:

I think *Setting Sons* is a very confident and proud album. I think this album was The Jam saying we are here now. By 1979 I believe we felt established and we felt confident in our ability to come up with good songs.

Paul Weller:

I think there's some great songs on *Setting Sons*, with 'The Eton Rifles' as the stand-out. 'Private Hell' I really like as well. I was concentrating more on my lyrics at that time, and quite a few of the songs, like 'Burning Sky', started off as prose or poetry.

SOUND AFFECTS

Polydor. Released 28 November 1980.
Peak UK Chart Position No 2

Pretty Green/Monday/But I'm Different Now/Set The House Ablaze/Start!/That's Entertainment/Dream Time/Man In The Corner Shop/Music For The Last Couple/Boy About Town/Scrape Away/The Modern World/The Gift

This, their fifth effort, is often said by fans to be their best; the other candidate of course being 1978's *All Mod Cons*. *Sound Affects* with its jangly guitars, harmonies and mid – Sixties brass is a superb mix of funk and psychedelic rock. Weller has said that he considered the album a cross between Michael Jackson's *Off the Wall* and The Beatles' *Revolver*. In BBC Radio 6 Music's documentary *The Jam: Made in Britain*, Weller cited this as his favourite Jam album.

At the time, Weller was reading *Histories of Camelot* alongside the romanticism of Percy Bysshe Shelley and William Blake, (Weller works in his literary flair with

4

a Shelley quote in the liner notes). His lyrics were also more human and approachable. Several times he makes self-deprecating reference to his 'star' status ('Boy About Town') and also the acceptance of the healing power of love ('But I'm Different Now').

The band had opened their ears to more than just the Kinks, Beatles and The Who. 'Monday' all but directly quotes David Bowie's early single 'Love You Till Tuesday' while 'Boy About Town' and 'Man In The Corner Shop' has echoes of every great swinging Sixties power pop single.

Sound Affects begins with 'Pretty Green' with Foxton playing bass notes which he repeats three times. Then a single strike of a snare drum from Buckler and the hi-hat kicks in. The production is full of reverb – you already know this won't be anything like their previous album, *Setting Sons*. Paul revealed that he pinched the name 'Pretty Green' from an American TV game show host who would say, "Here's a big barrel of pretty green for you, folks!", whilst watching TV during an North American tour. In 2009, Liam Gallagher launched his own clothing label and called it Pretty Green after the song.

The Beatles' *Revolver*-era 'Start!' is 'Taxman' in all but name, but done so wonderfully as to negate any gripes. The eleventh UK single release by the group and their second No 1, following 'Going Underground/Dreams of Children'. On its release on 15 August 1980, it debuted at No 3, and two weeks later reached No 1 for one week. Polydor had pushed for 'Pretty Green' to be the first single released, but Weller insisted on 'Start!' and consulted a few of the band's friends as to what they thought the best release would be. Heated discussions ensued and the decision was left until the last moment, to the point that sleeves for both possible singles sat waiting at the printers. The groups friends backed Weller and they chose 'Start!'

The gripping acoustic 'That's Entertainment's backwards guitars fairly reek of incense. Weller has freely admitted that *Revolver* had been a major influence upon much of the material on the album. Weller told Absolute Radio; "I was in London by the time I wrote 'That's Entertainment', writing it was easy in a sense because all those images were at hand, around me. I wrote it in 10 minutes flat, whilst under the influence, I'd had a few but some songs just write themselves. It was easy to write, I drew on everything around me.'"

The simple acoustic instrumentation is stripped down to basics. However, even this monster tune is not without influences. The lyrics take inspiration from a poem by the young poet Paul Drew called *Entertainment* and Weller favourite the Small Faces' 'Itchycoo Park' lends the spinal chords to the intro.

Never officially released as a single, 'That's Entertainment' remains one of the two all-time biggest selling import singles in the UK, alongside The Jam's 'Just Who Is the 5 O'Clock Hero?', which hit the charts at No 8 as an import in 1982.

'Boy About Town', sees Weller busying about London's Oxford Street and is not unlike the 'mod anthems' of The Jams earlier records. The title may have come from a London-based commuter mag at the time called *Girl About Town*, but could just have easily have been lifted from the lyric of The Kinks' 'Well Respected Man.'

All of the songs on *Sound Affects* were credited to Weller as the writer apart from 'Music For The Last Couple' an instrumental apart from a couple of lines that was credited to all three members of The Jam.

You can hear the soul influences of James Brown and Sam Cooke and late Seventies post punk all over this album. 'Scrape Away', the last track, resembles 'Shout', with Weller, Foxton, and Buckler gleefully jamming on the chorus in the last few minutes.

The cover art is a pastiche of the artwork used on various *Sound Effects* records produced by the BBC during the Seventies. It was Wellers idea to produce a sleeve that looked like one of these albums. It was also Paul's idea to change sound effects to 'sound affects', a clever play on words.

Sound Affects stands up superbly over many of its now-dated contemporaries. On this album you get to hear the Jam at their absolute peak, the infusion of soul and dance music is what makes *Sound Affects* still a unique wonder of rock n' roll.

Sound Affects spent 19 weeks on the UK album charts, rising to No 2 in late 1980

Rick Buckler:
Sound Affects was the album we really let ourselves free to experiment and indulge in. The Jam had success by this time so we had permission to experiment more. We also felt confident to push the boundaries too and we still felt we had something to prove to our fans.

VINYL REVIVAL

UK Supermarket chain Tesco started stocking vinyl records for the first time in its history in December 2015 in a bid to cash in on the craze for vinyl and the revival of record players.

The chain got more than it bargained for when in the summer of 2016 it offered limited edition pink vinyl pressings of classic albums including *Sound Affects* as Father's Day gifts. This resulted in Jam enthusiasts driving to Tesco stores around the UK searching for a copy of the LP sparking searches and tipoffs on Facebook and Twitter.

Keith Lewington, who moderates the Jam Society Facebook page, bought 12 copies and mailed them to members for the cover price plus postage. He also posted the barcode for *Sound Affects* for fans to take and show to staff at the Tesco stores.

It was reported that some fans were met by bewildered Tesco employees, with one asking if vinyl was like a CD and another mistaking calendars for albums.

THE JAM

4

THE GIFT

Polydor. Released 12 March 1982. Peak UK
Chart Position No 1

*Happy Together/Ghosts/Precious/Just
Who Is The Five O' Clock Hero/Trans-
Global Express/Running On The Spot/
Circus/The Planner's Dream Goes
Wrong/Carnation/Town Called Malice/The
Gift/The Modern World*

In February 1982, The Jam had their third
UK No 1 single with 'Town Called Malice/
Precious'. The single went straight in
at No 1 achieving something only The
Beatles and Slade had done previously in
the UK charts. In March their sixth and
final studio album, *The Gift*, was released
and became The Jam's only No 1 album.
The album was largely recorded during
1981 to 1982, assisted by producer Peter
Wilson, and is generally regarded as
the culmination of the smoother, more
adult-oriented sound of the band's later
work. When the Jam finished recording
The Gift, none of the members knew the

band would cease to exist by the end of
the year.

On *The Gift*, Weller's message was also
changing in his songwriting. Themes of unity
pervade the usual disenchantment; along
with his social commentary – seemingly
more confident in his political leanings.
Weller stated; "I was thinking about the
times we were living in. It wasn't the height
of Thatcherism but she was well into her
stride by that time. The country was being
depleted and the working classes were being
shat on. It was a very desolate time. You
couldn't help but be touched by the politics
of the time, you were either for or against it
and I was reflecting what I saw around me."

The 'Town Called Malice' lyrics lament
disappearing aspects of stereotypical
working class life in Margaret Thatcher's
Britain. The track is an unstoppable and
unforgettable Motown tribute with some of
Weller's most incisive lyrics about small-
town life. Weller was passionately vocal in
his opposition to Thatcherism throughout
his career. Before she died he said, "I
hope she rots in her own hell." He firmly
believed Thatcher and her government had
tried to destroy traditional working class
communities and he channeled his anger
into music. 'Town Called Malice' has since
been used in the movie *Billy Elliot* and *John
King's The Football Factory*. It's also a favourite
of Ray Davies from The Kinks who said he
especially liked the sound of the snare drum
and the Tamla Motown style riff.

'Precious' was a lashing love-struck
funk workout. Nothing The Jam had done
previously compared to 'Precious'. It may
have been a brave thing for the band to
include on the album. But Paul was on the
move and he wanted Jam fans to move on up
with him.

One of the quintessential 'state of the nation' songs in the band's catalogue it is still frequently performed by Weller in concert as a rousing finale to the set is 'Just Who Is the 5 O'Clock Hero?', (which was released as a 7-inch vinyl single in the Netherlands only). Weller is writing about his Dad but also reacting to something that Prince Phillip had said about the ordinary man needing to pull his socks up and make a bit more effort that obviously got beneath Paul's skin. "My dad had been a hod carrier most of his life. It was tough work. He'd come home looking like he'd been sandblasted, covered in cement. I liked the irony of that. But he always had a smile on his face. You could hear him arriving home, whistling down the alleyway that ran beside our house in Woking. He was the '5 O'Clock Hero'. He made the money and fed and clothed us."

The Gift has some undeniably Jam-esque moments, such as the opener 'Happy Together' which is introduced by somebody saying, "For all those watching in black and white, this one's in technicolour." Paul is letting everyone know there's absolutely nothing outdated about The Jam's new album – which he knew would be their last.

'Trans-Global Express' is the snappiest song on *The Gift* with some cultured brass and fine drumming from Buckler. Paul once said of Rick, "He was absolutely the right drummer for The Jam."

'Running On The Spot' begins with Paul's "1, 2, 3, 4" count in and it's another full-throttle surge. Rick impresses with some sassy snare, reminiscent of 'Funeral Pyre'. Twenty-five years later 'Running On The Spot' became a regular feature in Weller live sets.

'The Gift' is the most aggressive track on the album. It's forceful with swirling Hammond sounds that complement Paul's angry guitar and no-nonsense vocals. Soulful with bubbly lyrics full of moving and grooving, topped off with a riff-lift from the Small Faces' 'Don't Burst My Bubble'.

Other musicians who played on *The Gift* included Steve Nichol on trumpet, Keith Thomas on saxophone and Russ Henderson on Hammond and steel drums.

The original release of the album was on 12-inch vinyl, and initial copies came with a paper bag stating 'The Jam... A Gift'. These copies are increasingly difficult to find, especially in good condition. Other issues included the regular vinyl issue, the Japanese vinyl issue (with a bonus lyric book), the CD issue, the re-mastered issue, and a recently issued Japanese version in a mini-LP style sleeve.

Rick Buckler:

The Gift was us returning to the rawer side of The Jam. We were aiming for something simple and straightforward and we went into the studio with this approach. We were trying to be a live band in the studio again but a band that had gained a lot more experience since 1977.

Paul Weller:

We got into soul again. We started backtracking. I was into soul as a kid. I was on a big learning curve. The influence of soul music pointed in the direction of where I was going to go after that, but it was very much our sound, we were trying to expand it and do something else with the Jam sound.

4

THE JAM

4

DIG THE NEW BREED

Polydor. Released 10 December 1982.
Peak UK Chart Position No 2

*In The City/All Mod Cons/To Be
Someone (Didn't We Have A Nice Time)/
It's Too Bad/Start!/Big Bird/Set The
House Ablaze/Ghosts/Standards/In The
Crowd/Going Underground/Dreams Of
Children/That's Entertainment/Private Hell/
The Modern World/The Gift*

Dig The New Breed is a collection of live
performances recorded between 1977 and
1982 at the 100 Club, London, The Rainbow,
London, Hammersmith Palais, London, Bingley
Hall, Stafford, Reading University, Edinburgh
Playhouse, and the Glasgow Apollo. The album
spent 16 weeks on the UK album charts.

As a unit the three players shine, tightly
wound, explosive, giving the melodies the full-
bodied roar they deserved and with the mix of
songs, these live numbers confirm what made
The Jam such a great band.

SNAP!

Polydor. Released 14 October 1983. Peak
UK Chart Position No 2

Disc 1
*In the City/Away from the Numbers/All Around
the World/The Modern World (Single Version)/
News of the World/Billy Hunt/English Rose/
Mr. Clean/David Watts (Single Mix)/'A' Bomb
in Wardour Street (Single Version)/Down in the
Tube Station at Midnight (Single Edit)/Strange
Town/The Butterfly Collector/When You're
Young/Smithers-Jones (Single Version)/Thick
as Thieves*

Disc 2
*The Eton Rifles (Single Edit)/Going
Underground/Dreams of Children (US
Edit)/That's Entertainment (Demo Version)/Start!
(Single Version)/Man in the Cornershop/Funeral
Pyre (Remixed Version)/Absolute Beginners/
Tales from the Riverbank/Town Called Malice/
Precious (Single Edit)/The Bitterest Pill (I Ever
Had to Swallow)/Beat Surrender*

Snap! is a greatest hits album released in 1983, one year after the group disbanded. The double-album includes all sixteen of the band's UK singles, plus some B-sides, album tracks and rarities. When released the album spent 30 weeks on the UK chart.

Initial quantities of the album included a limited edition four-track EP, *Live*, recorded at Wembley Arena during the farewell tour of 1982. Featuring the tracks 'Get Yourself Together', 'Move On Up', 'The Great Depression' and 'But I'm Different Now'. The EP is notable for the fact that these songs were never re-issued on any other Jam compilation.

Beginners/Town Called Malice/Precious/Just Who Is the 5 O'Clock Hero?/The Bitterest Pill (I Ever Had to Swallow)/Beat Surrender

The Jam – Greatest Hits spent 22 weeks on the UK album chart and includes all of the band's eighteen hit singles plus 'Precious' (which was released as a double A-side along with 'Town Called Malice'). The album also includes two singles, 'That's Entertainment' and 'Just Who Is the 5 O'Clock Hero?', which made the UK charts without ever being released there, when they charted after being imported from Europe.

THE JAM – GREATEST HITS

Polydor. Released 1 July 1991. Peak UK Chart Position No 2

In the City/All Around the World/The Modern World/News of the World/David Watts/Down in the Tube Station at Midnight/Strange Town/When You're Young/The Eton Rifles/Going Underground/Start!/That's Entertainment/Funeral Pyre/Absolute

THE JAM – EXTRAS

Polydor. Released 6 April 1992. Peak UK Chart Position No 15

The Dreams of Children/ Tales from the Riverbank/ Liza Radley (Demo)/Move On Up/ Shopping/ Smithers-Jones/ Pop Art Poem (Demo)/Boy About Town (Alternate version)/A Solid Bond in Your Heart/No One in the World (Demo)/And Your Bird Can Sing/ Burning Sky

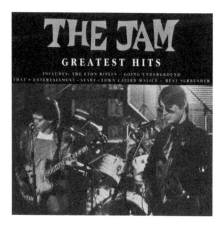

THE JAM

(Demo)/Thick As Thieves (Demo)/Disguises/ Get Yourself Together/ The Butterfly Collector/ The Great Depression/ Stoned Out of My Mind/ Pity Poor Alfie/Fever/ But I'm Different Now/ I Got You (I Feel Good)/ Hey Mister/ Saturday's Kids (Demo)/We've Only Started/ So Sad About Us/ The Eton Rifles (Demo)

Extras includes 26 B-sides, rarities and unreleased tracks. 11 of these songs (tracks 1,2,4,5,6,14,16,17,18,19,25) were released on the box set *Direction Reaction Creation,* making the other 15 tracks exclusive to this album. The album also features a demo of 'A Solid Bond in Your Heart' which was later released as a single by The Style Council plus a demo version of The Beatles' 'And Your Bird Can Sing' and a demo of 'Get Yourself Together' originally recorded by the Small Faces.

Jones/Little Boy Soldiers/The Eton Rifles/Away from the Numbers/Down in the Tube Station at Midnight/Strange Town/When You're Young/A' Bomb in Wardour Street/Pretty Green/Boy About Town/Man in the Corner Shop/David Watts/ Funeral Pyre/ Move on Up/Carnation/The Butterfly Collector/Precious/Town Called Malice/ Heat Wave/The Gift

The inclusion of nine songs from two December 1979 shows in London is the best portrait of what an actual specific show must have been like.

LIVE JAM

Polydor. Released 25 October 1993

The Modern World/Billy Hunt/Thick as Thieves/Burning Sky/Mr. Clean/Smithers-

THE JAM COLLECTION

Polydor. Released 22 October 1996. Peak UK Chart Position No 58

Away from the Numbers/ I Got By in Time/I Need You (For Someone)/ To Be Someone (Didn't We Have a Nice Time)/ Mr. Clean/English Rose/ In The Crowd/ It's Too Bad/The Butterfly Collector/ Thick as Thieves/ Private Hell/ Wasteland/Burning

Sky/ Saturday's Kids/ Liza Radley/ Pretty Green/ Monday/ Man in the Corner Shop/ Boy About Town/ Tales from the Riverbank/ Ghosts/ Just Who Is the 5 O'Clock Hero?/ Carnation/ The Great Depression/ Shopping

The Jam Collection includes only one of the band's singles ('Just Who Is the 5 O'Clock Hero?' which was unreleased in the UK), as it focuses on the group's album tracks and B-sides.

DIRECTION REACTION CREATION

Polydor. Released 26 May 1997. Peak UK Chart Position No 8

CD one
In the City/Takin' My Love/Art School/I've Changed My Address/Slow Down/I Got By in Time/Away from the Numbers/Batman Theme/ Sounds from the Street/Non-Stop Dancing/ Time for Truth/Bricks and Mortar/All Around the World/Carnaby Street/The Modern World (Album Version)/London Traffic/Standards/Life from a Window/The Combine/Don't Tell Them You're Sane/In the Street Today/London Girl/I Need You (For Someone)/Here Comes the Weekend/Tonight at Noon/In the Midnight Hour

CD two
News of the World/Aunties and Uncles (Impulsive Youths)/Innocent Man/David Watts/ 'A' Bomb in Wardour Street/ Down in the TubeStation at Midnight/ So Sad About Us/The Night/All Mod Cons/To Be Someone (Didn't We Have A Nice Time)/Mr. Clean/English Rose/ In the Crowd/Billy Hunt/It's Too Bad/Fly/The Place I Love/Strange Town/The Butterfly Collector/When You're Young/Smithers-Jones/The Eton Rifles/See-Saw

CD three
Girl on the Phone/Thick as Thieves/Private Hell/Little Boy Soldiers/Wasteland/Burning Sky/Smithers-Jones/ Saturday's Kids/ Heat Wave/Going Underground/ The Dreams Of Children/Start!/ Liza Radley/Pretty Green/Monday/But I'm Different Now/Set the House Ablaze/That's Entertainment/Dream Time/Man in the Corner Shop/Music for the Last Couple/Boy About Town/Scrape Away

CD four
Funeral Pyre/Disguises/Absolute Beginners/ Tales from the Riverbank/Town Called Malice/ Precious/Happy Together/Ghosts/Just Who Is the 5 O'Clock Hero?/Trans-Global Express/Running on the Spot/Circus/The Planner's Dream Goes Wrong/Carnation/The Gift/The Great Depression/The Bitterest Pill (I Ever Had to Swallow)/Pity Poor Alfie/ Fever/Beat Surrender/Shopping/Move On Up/Stoned Out of My Mind/War

CD five
In the City (Demo)/Time for Truth (Demo)/ Sounds from the Street (Demo)/So Sad

THE JAM

4

About Us (Band Demo)/Worlds Apart (Demo)/Billy Hunt (Alternate Version)/It's Too Bad (Band Demo)/To Be Someone (Band Demo)/David Watts (Band Demo)/ Best of Both Worlds (Band Demo)/That's Entertainment (Band Demo)/Rain (Demo)/Dream Time (Demo)/Dead End Street (Demo)/Stand By Me (Demo)/Every Little Bit Hurts (Demo)/Tales from the Riverbank (Alternate Version)/Walking in Heaven's Sunshine (Demo)/Precious (Demo)/Pity Poor Alfie (Swing Version)/The Bitterest Pill (I Ever Had to Swallow) (First Version)/A Solid Bond In Your Heart (Band Demo)

Direction Reaction Creation is an anthology issued in 1997 and includes 117 tracks over five discs, including all of the songs from their singles (although, where applicable, the A sides are present in their album versions only) and six studio albums.

With a strict adherence to chronological order, the box presents each single followed by its B-sides, (six of which appear on CD for the first time, including the brilliant 'See Saw').

Disc five offers over an hour of studio demos, 22 previously unreleased tracks of considerably different takes of better-known material. *Direction Reaction Creation* comes with a lavish 88-page booklet with great liner notes, an extensive band chronology and discography, and the band's complete gig list, along with plenty of rare photos and memorabilia.

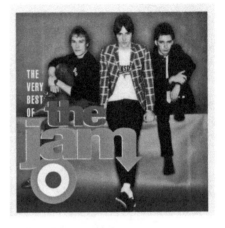

THE VERY BEST OF THE JAM

Polydor. Released 25 October 1997. Peak UK Chart Position No 9

In the City/All Around the World/ The Modern World/ News of the World/ David Watts/ 'A' Bomb in Wardour Street/ Down in the Tube Station at Midnight/ Strange Town/ When You're Young/The Eton Rifles/ Going Underground/ Dreams of Children/ Start!/That's Entertainment/ Funeral Pyre/ Absolute Beginners/ Town Called Malice/ Precious/ Just Who Is the 5 O'Clock Hero?/ The Bitterest Pill (I Ever Had to Swallow)/ Beat Surrender/

The Very Best of The Jam is the third greatest hits package (fourth including *Compact Snap!*). The compilation features all of The Jam's singles in chronological order. It has the same tracks as *Greatest Hits*, but with two more tracks.

'The Bitterest Pill (I Ever Had to Swallow)' was released as a single in 1997 to promote the album, it was previously a single 15 years before, and again four years later in 2001.

45RPM: THE SINGLES, 1977–79

Polydor. Released 2 April 2001.

Disc one
In the City/Takin' My Love/In the City (Video)

Disc two
All Around the World/Carnaby Street

Disc three
The Modern World/Sweet Soul Music (live at the 100 Club)/Back In My Arms Again (live at the 100 Club)/Bricks & Mortar (live at the 100 Club)

Disc four
News of the World/Aunties and Uncles (Impulsive Youths)/Innocent Man/News of the World (Video)

Disc five
David Watts/'A' Bomb In Wardour Street

Disc six
Down in the Tube Station at Midnight/So Sad About Us/The Night

Disc seven
Strange Town/The Butterfly Collector/Strange Town (Video)

Disc eight
When You're Young/Smithers-Jones/When You're Young (Video)

Disc nine
The Eton Rifles/See Saw

This is a box set compilation which contains the first nine singles released by the band between 1977 and 1979 in remastered formats with original artwork and reproduction sleeves.

45RPM: THE SINGLES, 1980–82

Polydor. Released 30 April 2001

Disc one
Going Underground/Dreams of Children/ Away from the Numbers (live at the Rainbow)/Modern World (live at the

THE JAM

Rainbow)/Down in the Tube Station at
Midnight (live at the Rainbow)/Going
Underground (video)

Disc two
Start!/Liza Radley/Start! (video)

Disc three
*That's Entertainment/Down in the
Tube Station at Midnight (live)/That's
Entertainment (video)*

Disc four
*Funeral Pyre/Disguises/Funeral Pyre
(video)*

Disc five
*Absolute Beginners/Tales from the
Riverbank/Absolute Beginners (video)*

Disc six
*Town Called Malice/Precious/Town Called
Malice (video)*

Disc seven
*Just Who Is the 5 O'Clock Hero?/The
Great Depression*

Disc eight
*The Bitterest Pill (I Ever Had to Swallow)/
Pity Poor Alfie/Fever/The Bitterest Pill (I
Ever Had to Swallow) (video)*

Disc nine
*Beat Surrender/Shopping/Move on Up/
Stoned Out of My Mind/War*

This set contains nine singles released
by the band between 1980 and 1982 in
remastered formats with original artwork and
reproduction sleeves.

THE JAM AT THE BBC

Universal International. Released 21 May
2002 – 3 CD Set. Peak UK Chart Position
No 33

Disc one
*In the City/Art School/I've Changed
My Address/The Modern World/All
Around the World/London Girl/Bricks
And Mortar/Carnaby Street/Billy Hunt/In
The Street Today/The Combine/Sounds
From The Street/Don't Tell Them You're
Sane/The Modern World/'A' Bomb in
Wardour Street/News of the World/Here
Comes The Weekend/All Around the World*

Disc two
*Thick As Thieves/The Eton Rifles/Saturday's
Kids/When You're Young/Absolute
Beginners/Tales From The Riverbank/Funeral
Pyre/Sweet Soul Music/The Gift (Live)/Down in
the Tube Station at Midnight/Ghosts/Absolute
Beginners/Tales From The Riverbank/
Precious/Town Called Malice/In The Crowd/
Circus/Pretty Green/Start!/Boy About Town*

Limited edition bonus disc
Girl on the Phone/To Be Someone (Didn't We Have A Nice Time)/It's Too Bad/Burning Sky/Away From The Numbers/Smithers-Jones/The Modern World/Mr. Clean/The Butterfly Collector/Private Hell/Thick As Thieves/When You're Young/Strange Town/The Eton Rifles/Down in the Tube Station at Midnight/Saturday's Kids/All Mod Cons/David Watts

The Jam at the BBC includes songs from John Peel sessions recorded in 1977 and 1979, the first Radio 1 *In Concert*, from 1 June 1977 and a second hour-long concert recorded at The Rainbow Theatre on 4 December 1979 and The Hippodrome, Golders Green on 19 December 1981. This collection focuses on what many saw as the most vital aspect of the group: its live output, The Jam were always at their core a blistering New Wave band throughout their live career and this collection proves that above any doubt.

Completed by a booklet rounding up the band members' own recollections of both the band and the BBC, The Jam at the BBC captures a side of the Jam that their core catalog has long cried out for. It might well be the best album they've ever released.

as Thieves/Smithers-Jones/Saturday's Kids/Going Underground/Start!/Liza Radley/Pretty Green/Boy About Town/That's Entertainment/Tales from the Riverbank/Town Called Malice/Ghosts/Carnation/Beat Surrender

The Sound Of The Jam was released to mark their twenty-fifth anniversary. It contains a remixed version of 'That's Entertainment', featuring only the guitars and vocals of the demo version and without the bass, drums and percussion. When released *The Sound Of The Jam* spent seven weeks on the UK album chart.

THE SOUND OF THE JAM

Polydor. Released 21 May 2002. Peak UK Chart Position No 3

In the City/Away from the Numbers/The Modern World/David Watts/Down in the Tube Station at Midnight/It's Too Bad/To Be Someone (Didn't We Have a Nice Time)/Mr. Clean/English Rose/The Butterfly Collector/The Eton Rifles/Private Hell/Thick

FIRE AND SKILL: THE JAM LIVE

Polydor. Released November 2015

I've Changed My Address/Carnaby Street/The Modern World/Time For Truth/So Sad About Us/London Girl/In The Street Today/Standards/All Around The World/London Traffic/Heat Wave/Sweet Soul Music/Bricks And Mortar/In The City/Art School/

THE JAM

Back In My Arms Again/Slow Down/In The
Midnight Hour/Sounds From The Street/
Takin' My Love/In The City (Encore)

Live At The Music Machine 2nd March 1978

*The Modern World/London Traffic/I
Need You/The Combine/Aunties And
Uncles/Standards/Here Comes The
Weekend/Sounds From The Street/News
Of The World/London Girl/In The Street
Today/Bricks And Mortar/In The Midnight
Hour/Carnaby Street/All Around The
World/Slow Down/News Of The World
(Sound-Check - Bonus Track)*

Live At Reading University 16th
February 1979

*The Modern World/Sounds From The
Street/Away From The Numbers/All Mod
Cons / To Be Someone/It's Too Bad/
Mr. Clean/Billy Hunt/In The Street Today/
Standards/Tonight At Noon/Down In The
Tube Station At Midnight/News Of The
World/Here Comes The Weekend/Bricks
And Mortar/ Batman/The Place I*

*Love/David Watts/Heat Wave/A Bomb In
Wardour Street*

Live At Newcastle City Hall 28th October
1980

*Dreamtime/Thick As Thieves/Boy About
Town/Monday/Going Underground/Pretty
Green/Man In The Corner Shop/Set
The House Ablaze/Private Hell/Liza
Radley/Dreams Of Children/The Modern
World/Little Boy Soldiers/But I'm Different
Now/Start!/Scrape Away/Strange Town/
When You're Young/The Eton Rifles/Billy
Hunt/Down In The Tube Station At
Midnight/To Be Someone/A Bomb In
Wardour Street*

Live At Hammersmith Palais 14th
December 1981

*The Gift /Down In The Tube Station
At Midnight/Man In The Corner
Shop/Ghosts/Absolute Beginners/Town
Called Malice/Set The House Ablaze/
That's Entertainment/Tales From The River
Bank/Precious/Happy Together/In The
Crowd/David Watts/Boy About Town/Pretty
Green/Funeral Pyre/Circus/Going
Underground/Big Bird/Little Boy Soldier*

Live At Wembley Arena 2nd
December 1982

*Start!/It's Too Bad/Beat Surrender/Away
From The Numbers/Ghosts/In
The Crowd/Boy About Town/Get
Yourself Together/All Mod Cons/
To Be Someone/Smithers-Jones/The
Great Depression/Move On Up/When
You're Young/David Watts/Private Hell/
Down In The Tube Station At Midnight/*

*Mr. Clean/Trans-Global Express/Going
Underground/The Butterfly Collector/
Dreams Of Children/The Gift*

The title of the collection refers to a
motto inscribed on Paul Weller's guitar
amplifier. This 6-CD box set offers almost
an alternate history of The Jam, tracing
their career through live outings as
opposed to their classic studio albums.
From an early gig at London's iconic
100 Club, held on 11 September 1977, to a
stand-out 2 December 1982 show, held at
Wembley Arena (one of their final shows,
part of the Beat Surrender '82 tour), it sees
the band grow from their raw beginnings
to becoming an arena-filling act.

THE JAM

VIC COPPERSMITH - HEAVEN

During the mid Seventies Smith was working at Polydor's old studios in Stratford Place, London, and was pleased to get involved with The Jam's recordings. "I remember that first gig Chris Parry took me to. It was a period of real excitement and although there were only between 15 and 20 people there, it was a great show with amazing spirit and energy."

Later when The Jam slimmed their team of two producers down to one, the then-renamed Coppersmith-Heaven had developed the group's sound with harmonised guitars and acoustic textures. He worked on *In the City* (1977), *This is the Modern World* (1977), *All Mod Cons* (1978), *Setting Sons* (1979) and *Sound Affects* (1980).

After leaving school in 1961, Smith worked in the recording studios at Polydor and by 1967 found himself working as the engineer on the Cat Stevens' album *Matthew and Son*. He also worked on The Rolling Stones *Let It Bleed*, engineering such tracks as 'Honky Tonk Woman', and Joe Cocker's 'With a Little Help from My Friends'. In early 1968 he produced the Nashville Teens' version of 'All Along the Watchtower', the earliest cover version of Bob Dylan's song, which was released as a single in the UK and Europe on Decca Records some six months before Jimi Hendrix's hit version. Later credits include working with Black Sabbath, Vinegar Joe and Judas Priest.

> *"It was a great show with amazing spirit."*
>
> **VIC COPPERSMITH**

Interviewed in *Sound on Sound* magazine in 2007 Vic talked about working with George Harrison: "It was a real turning point for me when I engineered Billy Preston's 'That's the Way God Planned It'. George Harrison was producing a great line-up that included Klaus Voorman on bass, Ginger Baker on drums and Eric Clapton and George on guitar. At an early stage of the session, while I was trying to create the sound mix, George came into the control room and said, 'Look, get away from the desk, come into the studio and listen to the song.' That was the first time a producer had ever allowed me to get that musically involved as an engineer. Billy got on the piano and just started jamming the song, and while we had tea and chatted, Eric and George played acoustic guitars and you could really feel the song developing. I then engineered the track pretty much on my own from the control room, while everybody else performed in the studio, until we got the best take. That session was an incredible and creative experience for me."

Smith also produced The Vapors track, 'Turning Japanese', which reached the top three in the UK Singles Chart, at the same time that The Jam's 'Going Underground' was at No 1. In September 1980, when 'Start!' reached No 1 it was Coppersmith-Heaven's second production credit on a chart topping hit single. By the end of 1980 Coppersmith-Heaven's term with The Jam ended. 'Funeral Pyre' was their first single to be produced by Pete Wilson instead of Heaven.

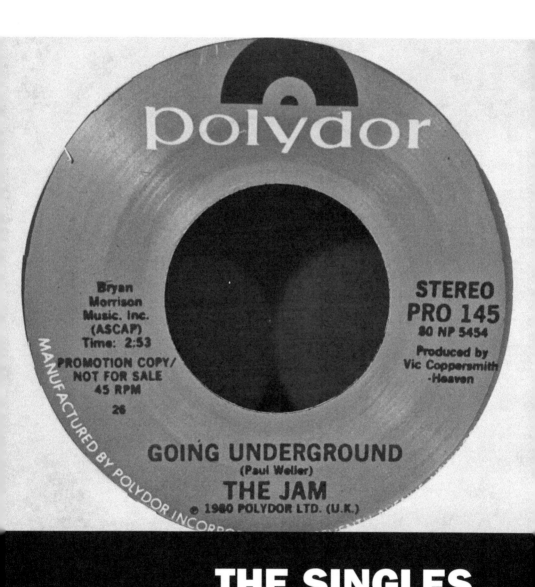

THE SINGLES
1970–79

THE JAM

5

"*The best Jam songs mix an angry kitchen-sink realism with a surging desire for a change.*"

Mark Cooper

THE SINGLES

In The City/Takin' My Love

Polydor. Released 29 April 1977.
UK Chart Position: 40

The Modern World/Sweet Soul Music/Back In My Arms Again/Brick And Mortar

Polydor. Released 28 October 1977.
UK Chart Position: 36

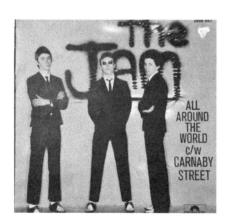

All Around The World/Carnaby Street

Polydor. Released 15 July 1977.
UK Chart Position: 13

News Of The World/Aunties And Uncles (Impulsive Youths)/Innocent Man

Polydor. Released 3 March 1978.
UK Chart Position: 27

David Watts/A Bomb In Wardour Street

Polydor. Released 18 August 1978.
UK Chart Position: 25

Strange Town/The Butterfly Collector

Polydor. Released 9 March 1979.
UK Chart Position: 15

Down In The Tube Station At Midnight/So Sad About Us/The Night

Polydor POSP8. 13 October 1978.
UK Chart Position: 15

When You're Young/Smithers-Jones

Polydor. Released 17 August 1979.
UK Chart Position: 17

5

The Eton Rifles/See-Saw

Polydor. Released 26 October 1979.
UK Chart Position: 3

Start/Liza Radley

Polydor. Released 15 August 1980.
UK Chart Position: 1

Going Underground/Dreams Of Children

Polydor. Released 14 March 1980.
UK Chart Position: 1

That's Entertainment/Down In The Tube Station At Midnight. German Import-Metronome

Released 30 January 1981.
UK Chart Position: 21

THE JAM

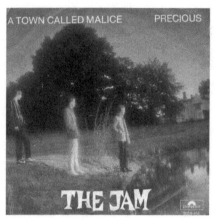

Funeral Pyre/Disguises

Polydor. Released 29 May 1981.
UK Chart Position: 4

Town Called Malice/Precious

Polydor. A 12" was also issued that
included a live version of *A Town Called
Malice*. Released 29 January 1982.
UK Chart Position: 1

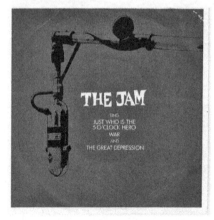

*Absolute Beginners/Tales From The
Riverbank*

Polydor. Released 16 October 1981. UK
Chart Position: 4

*Just Who Is The Five O' Clock Hero/War/The
Great Depression.* Dutch Import

Polydor. Also issued as a 12". Released 21
June 1982. UK Chart Position: 8

The Bitterest Pill (I Ever Had To Swallow)/Pity Poor Alfie/Fever

Polydor. Released 6 September 1982. UK Chart Position: 2

Beat Surrender/Shopping. Also issued as a double pack that included *Beat Surrender/ Shopping/Move On Up/Stoned Out Of My Mind/War*

Polydor. Released 22 November 1982. UK Chart Position: 1

The Jam recorded 'Pop Art Poem' specially for *Flexipop!* and also did an exclusive remix of 'Boy About Town'. The double track Flexi disc appeared on the cover of the second issue of *Flexipop!* Magazine at the end of November 1980.

US EPS
The Jam EP – 1981, No 176
The Bitterest Pill (I Ever Had to Swallow) EP – 1982, No 135
Beat Surrender EP – 1983, No 171

US SINGLES
Start – 1980, No 75 Dance Music/Club Play Singles
A Town Called Malice – 1982, No 31 Mainstream Rock
Precious/A Town Called Malice – 1982, No 45 Dance Music/Club Play Singles

VIDEOS AND DVDS
Transglobal Unity Express (1982)
Start! (1983)
Greatest Hits (1991)
The Very Best of the Jam (1997)
The Complete Jam On Film 1977–1982 (2002)
The Complete Jam (2002/2003)

5

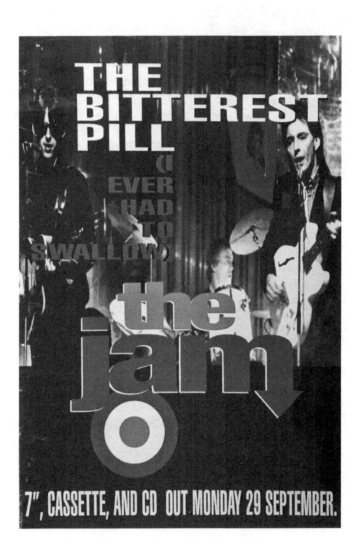

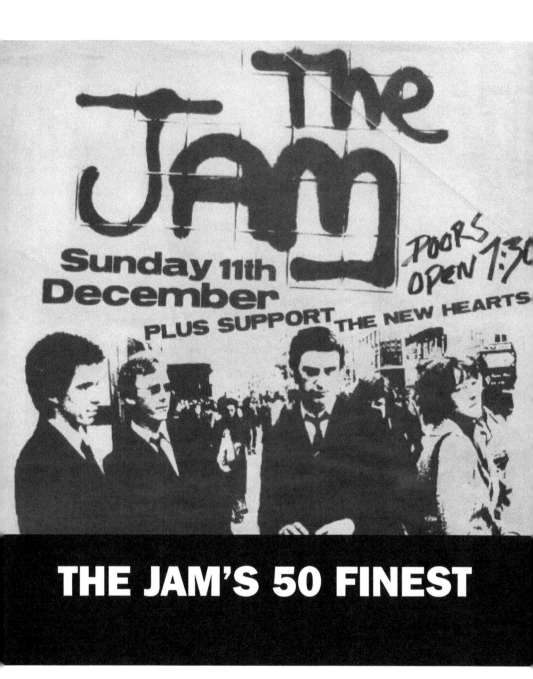

THE JAM'S 50 FINEST

6

*"The Jam obviously
had a big effect on my
life as well as Bruce's
and Paul's, but when I
talk to Jam fans there's
this real connection
that it had an effect on
them as well."*
Rick Buckler

THE JAM'S 50 FINEST

6

AND THE STORIES BEHIND THEM

1. THAT'S ENTERTAINMENT (PAUL WELLER)

Recorded October 1980, Townhouse Studios, London.
Studio versions available on *Sound Affects, Snap, Direction Reaction Creation* and *The Very Best Of The Jam: About The Young Idea.*

According to Paul he wrote 'That's Entertainment' "whilst under the influence". Paul had been to a pub and had returned home to his Pimlico flat that he shared at the time with his girlfriend Gill Price. He'd been drinking: something which Rick recalls was a favourite pastime in The Jam and something that Paul would himself continue with for many years after The Jam's splitting up. To Paul's credit (although he admitted that he missed the "chaos and madness of it sometimes") he stopped drinking on 1st July 2015 and at the time of writing this book, seven years later, he hasn't had a relapse.

By the time Paul wrote 'That's Entertainment' his *Riot Stories Publications* had been up and running for several months. Riot Stories had included a poem called *Entertainment* in its *Mixed Up, Shook Up* (which

was a small book with a collection of poems by different poets). *Entertainment* had been sent to Riot by Paul Drew. Weller had read it and admitted that he drew inspiration from the poem's content and title, influencing his song. Paul said he wrote to Paul Drew asking if he could 'nick' a bit of his idea.

There are comparisons that can be detected between the poem's words and the songs lyrics. Both describe a landscape and a world as seen through the eyes of the authors. On the one hand there's a rape before a mug of Horlicks and on the other there's breathing in petrol as the window is opened. Both poem and song also paint a picture of everyday life: there are mentions of everyday murders, Marks and Spencer, the *Daily Express* and watching ducks, watching the news and travelling on a bus. In 1980 the reader or listener would certainly have been able to relate to both and three decades on, what's changed?

'That's Entertainment' was the first Jam song where an acoustic guitar was used as the up-front instrument. Paul strums his way through the song, maintaining a level that

6

avoids much light or dark shading. Paul drives the song along, accompanied by Bruce's bass and minimal drumming from Rick. But it works, it's all that the song requires. The song's charm is in its simplicity. But also listen from two minutes and eight seconds because a psychedelic-sounding backwards guitar is introduced. It lasts for less than twenty seconds. It's like a cameo part played on a Rickenbacker guitar.

'That's Entertainment' was produced by Vic Coppersmith-Heaven. Although never released as a domestic single in the UK during the band's lifetime, an import version from Germany peaked at No 21, which was a huge achievement for an imported single at the time and stood as a testament to the popularity that The Jam had achieved. (The song remains one of the two all-time biggest selling import singles in the UK, alongside The Jam's 'Just Who Is the 5 O'Clock Hero').

And who hasn't looked at their life and where they are and in that moment wished that they were far away? But that's life for some and that's entertainment for others. It was the perfect title for Rick Buckler's autobiography *That's Entertainment: My Life In The Jam*.

For many years after The Jam split up Paul didn't perform 'That's Entertainment' live, but in his solo years he started to re-introduce it. Some of these performances were shared with his friend Noel Gallagher, much to the delight of Jam and Oasis fans.

In 1991 'That's Entertainment' was re-issued (for a second time) and reached the top 50. Former Smiths frontman Morrissey also covered the song featuring 'Chas Smash' aka Carl Smyth of Madness on backing vocals. Put out on the B-side of 'Sing Your Life' in April 1991, the single reached No 33 in the UK charts.

The same year the British alternative rock band The Wonder Stuff covered the song.

In 2001 Paul released his second live album. He lifted lyrics from 'That's Entertainment' and used them to call his album *Days Of Speed*.

Rick Buckler:

We recorded 'That's Entertainment' about two or three times. We certainly ended up with various versions. One of those versions had more drums on it, like the version on *Direction Reaction Creation*, but although we mucked about with it, it was never a song that we felt needed much or any drums on it. As we got deeper into the recording process of the song, the percussion just got stripped back more and more, until there was hardly any on it at all. As a band we were always doing and trying different things with our songs. This was no different for 'That's Entertainment', it was just that for this song - we were working with something that was more of an acoustic number. But we were mindful, to not do it just like 'another' acoustic song. So we tried different things but in the end felt the song stood up on its own - with just the acoustic guitar.

During the recording it just got to a point where we resigned ourselves to agreeing that it just needed to be kept simple. An important attitude that Paul, Bruce and I shared was that whatever we did, we did for the benefit of the song. This was our ethos when it came to recording songs and it was like this for the whole of The Jam's recording career. Doing what was best for the song was a mentality that we just felt we needed to have. For us we were trying to achieve a well-recorded song and, this was above anything else. For example, from a drummer's point of view it wasn't a matter of trying to get down as many drum fills and percussive sounds as

6

possible, just because the drums were there. It was never a matter of showing off the skills of the drummer. For us it was more a matter of trying to achieve a good song by being inventive. Ringo Starr is a good example of this. Sometimes what's needed is to do just the right thing - what the song needs - not what the drummer needs. We always wanted to find the right sounds and use the right instruments that suited the song. We learnt a lot about what a song needs from listening to The Kinks. We liked that storytelling aspect. We always tried to link this to the approach we took to our songs. What we aimed to do was make the song the most effective that we could. We understood that a song is about sound and it's the sound that matters.

The other important element about 'That's Entertainment' was the strength of the lyrics. I believe someone sent Paul a poem and he liked what he read. I don't recall there being much conversation about the poem or the person who had sent it at the time. I think as far as Bruce and I were concerned Paul was simply providing us with another set of lyrics that he'd written.

One of the things with The Jam was that once a song was finished we never really sat around and formally agreed on it being the finished product. Things flowed in their own way.

Another thing about 'That's Entertainment' was that this was one of the very rare occasions when Paul presented Bruce and me with a finished song. When he put 'That's Entertainment' on the table it was already an acoustic song that had lyrics. It just needed some finishing touches that got sorted out in the studio.

The Jam were always working. We were on the road a hell of a lot. This restricted the song-writing to some extent. This also meant

that we got to a point where songs were written in the studio or sometimes in sound checks. Paul had ideas and riffs and so on, but the only times we could all be together was in those rehearsals or at sound checks, these were good places to try things out.

Songs didn't get written on the tour bus. This was not how The Jam's songs came about. The tour bus was purely for playing cards and having a drink. For us the tour bus wasn't a working space. The Jam's tour bus wasn't like you see in the rock and roll films, where there's someone strumming along on a guitar in one area, whilst someone is drinking and taking drugs with a bunch of groupies in another. That's a very American rock and roll band perception. The Jam's tour buses were not like *Summer Holiday* either, where every now and then we'd all burst into song. The tour bus for us was more about cards and recovery time. We could have called The Jam tour bus ward eight or something along those lines.

When it came to making the video, there's just a few shots of me making a few tapping noises. We made the video in some room in Soho. I remember the room being very dark. It was a very different style of video compared to what we had made up until that point. I mean previous videos had had us performing live, like 'Art School', 'When You're Young' and 'News Of The World', or we'd be running out of tube stations, like in 'Strange Town'. I thought the video worked because we felt the song was more of a reflective song. It didn't need a full throttle energetic video.

Doing the video in this room was different to doing other videos in places like Townhouse Studios, which basically meant that we didn't have to relocate to some other place or venue. We liked Townhouse, which was pretty familiar to us and it was easy to

THE JAM

get to. Plus we already had all our equipment set up because we were still in the middle of some rehearsing or recording session.

On the day of the filming we just turned up like it was a usual day at the office. The film crew spent some time moving things around to suit their purpose and switched on a few spot lights.

I don't recall the filming for 'That's Entertainment' taking too long, unlike some of the previous video shoots. In the same way that the song was kept simple, so was the video and it's all that was needed.

2. GOING UNDERGROUND (PAUL WELLER)

Recorded December 1979, Townhouse Studios, London
Available on *Snap, Direction Reaction Creation* and *The Very Best Of The Jam: About The Young Idea*.

'Going Underground' was produced by Vic Coppersmith-Heaven and was to be The Jam's first of three No 1 records (a double A-side with 'The Dreams Of Children'). Getting a No 1 record was where the band had been heading and it was certainly welcoming news for Polydor. When news reached Paul, Bruce and Rick that their song had hit the top spot, they were, of course pleased. They also needed to celebrate it and perform on *Top of the Pops*, so they cut short their current tour of America and headed home.

The Jam presented themselves at the BBC's television studios to record 'Going Underground'. During that period of *Top of the Pops* life the show was broadcast every Thursday evening. On the show Paul is seen wearing an apron that is back to front. The reason it's turned back to front is because it

had the Heinz Beans logo on it. Paul wanted to wear the apron just for a bit of fun but was told that because of the UK's advertising laws the BBC would be infringing them if they showed Paul wearing the apron. Paul's reaction was to still wear the apron but wear it back to front. When the show was broadcast it certainly raised a few eyebrows.

Talking about recording the track Vic Coppersmith-Heaven told *Sound on Sound* magazine: "There were songs like 'Going Underground' where I never achieved a vocal performance that I was really happy with — I remember going up to Paul in the canteen when I was trying to mix that track after we had completed the recording and explaining to him that the chorus section of the song just didn't quite make it. I couldn't mix it. I don't think he really understood what I was talking about at the time, and he was quite reluctant to re-vocal the chorus section of the track, but he did end up coming back into the studio and really getting into it, which was great. He gave the track the energy it needed. The final vocal performance really carried the song and helped turn it into the hit track it became.

Paul and Bruce used to work really well together for vocal overdubs. I would stand them in the studio facing each other about three or four feet apart, so they had eye-to-eye contact, and they'd record their vocals together. They were often recorded together as a joint vocal just to retain that live excitement.'

Thirty-six years later that apron would reappear and eyebrows were raised again. At the time Nicky Weller was touring the *About The Young Idea* exhibition and it had landed in Liverpool. The original idea for the exhibition had been conceived by Den Davis a few years earlier and Nicky helped his dream become

THE JAM

6

a reality. On one of the Q&A events being held there Paul's mother Ann Weller wore the apron as she served cups of tea from behind the make-shift tea stall - you can take a girl out of Woking but you just can't take Woking out of the girl. The sight put a smile on many people's faces -especially those that had the opportunity to wear the apron. The public gets what the public wants right?

'Going Underground' deserved to be a No 1 record: it's full of attack and energy but retains a melody that The Jam were so skilled at capturing. A perfect example of a perfect pop song - it comes in at two and half minutes too. It's punchy and to the point, and the points that a twenty-two-year old Weller wanted to 'scream and shout' about related to the threat of a nuclear attack and what seemed like World War Three could actually happen.

By the time 'Going Underground' was released on 14 March 1980, Paul was already declaring his support for the Campaign for Nuclear Disarmament (CND). The Jam would play a series of pro-CND concerts in 1981. Paul had something to say about how much of the British tax - payers money was being spent on 'rockets and guns', rather than kidney machines and he knew that Jam fans would listen to him, and they did - and The Jam were certainly responsible for boosting the CND's ranks of supporters.

The Wellers decided it would be a fitting tribute to have 'Going Underground' played at John Weller's funeral: Paul's father died on 22 April 2009. He had managed The Jam and steered his son's career for thirty years. It was a fitting tribute indeed.
POW! POW! POW!

Rick Buckler:

I have a vivid memory of the day on which 'Going Underground' was released. We were on tour in the States at the time. The fact that we released a single knowing we wouldn't be in the UK at the time was very unusual. I mean record labels would tend to base all of their promotion around the band and having the band available to help promotion was essential. The Jam played many concerts and tours because that's what we knew worked to promote our latest single or album.

Being in America at the time of the release had its problems. Trying to find out what was happening with 'Going Underground' was one of them. We were caught off guard because I remember that we thought that on its release it would chart and work its way up the chart, and by the time we had finished the American tour and returned home, it would have crept its way up the chart and we could give it a boost by some UK promotion. But we got completely caught out because 'Going Underground' was released on March 14 1980 and went straight in at No 1. The day before we'd been at the Showbox, Seattle and the remainder of the tour was meant to take us to California and Texas, but we didn't finish the tour. Instead we flew immediately back to the UK on Concorde. I recall that the Concorde tickets were outrageously expensive. The price was staggering, a small fortune by anybody's standards. It was a luxury to travel on Concorde, but it was a nice way for us to celebrate having our first No 1 record. Also the thought of only spending just over three hours on a plane compared to eight was an attractive proposition.

Making our exit from that States tour didn't bother us too much. They just didn't get us at that time. And having a No 1 in the UK did little for them. Even up until that point

6

of getting a No 1, we were the unknowns in America. We were travelling from state to state and playing to people that had little or no idea who we were. It often felt like we were back at square one again and really having to fight for our audiences.

It was that particular American tour that we also supported Blue Öyster Cult and their fans didn't get us at all. But during that visit to the States we were also jumping on and off of various tours. The Blue Öyster Cult's tour was just one of them.

The thing I admired about America was that they had touring right down to a fine art. Take Blue Öyster Cult, they had three road crews. Those crews worked a system that meant that one crew would set up in some city or town, whilst the band were already set up and playing somewhere else. The crew then moved on to another place and the band slotted in to where the crew had been. There was a sort of overlapping, leap-frogging thing that went on, but it meant that everything worked really well. The reason for the road crews and operations and systems like that was because of the logistics of trying to get a band performing around such a vast area - and the States are huge.

As much as we didn't like it, touring America was accepted as being a much needed opportunity. We knew it would do us no good, or limit us, just playing to the converted in the UK all the time. The Jam understood that we needed to find new audiences and that this was going to be a continual thing. America, because of the size of the country, offered us that. And sometimes trying to convert people and turn them on to the music of The Jam was a challenge. We played at venues and in towns where the people had never seen or heard of us. At best some might have read something

about us in one of the music papers or magazines. But The Jam were just a small part of a much bigger picture in the States. But there were some areas that seemed more turned on than others. This may have had something to do with the British Invasion of the Sixties.

America was just such a massive place. And music was a big thing for the Americans. It was big business. Regarding the size of the place, when a band released a single it could take up to three months for it to penetrate all the shops and radio stations. But in the UK this can all be achieved in the space of a week. America had more music papers and magazines and lots of radio stations. Plus they had the college radio thing, which the UK didn't have. And in the States college radio is a big deal.

Another thing about the difference between the UK and America is that in the UK you may get five or six bands releasing a single at the same time. When 'Going Underground' was released bands like Blondie with 'Call Me' and Dexy's Midnight Runners with 'Geno' were also climbing the charts and both of them went to No 1 in the weeks following 'Going Underground' being at the top of the chart. But in America you have major bands releasing their singles in one state, another band in another state and so on and none clash, because the vastness of the states means that they could do this. You have to remember that America has six different time zones. It just can't be stressed enough how taking on America was a whole different ball game to taking on the UK.

Being in America at the time of 'Going Underground' being released also meant that we were still only the support act and this came with all sorts of limitations. Not being in control was one of them. For the

THE JAM

6

North American tours we had American management who felt that to play in front of large audiences was what needed to happen. I don't think we disagreed with this, but large numbers in the States means large numbers. I think when we supported the Blue Öyster Cult we were playing in thirty thousand capacity venues.

What the Americans call club gigs are very different to what we know as club gigs - especially when it comes to the sizes of the clubs. A club for them would still have a capacity of four to five thousand people. In the UK a club would hold four or five hundred. The numbers game in the States becomes a very different game on so many levels and The Jam had to learn to accept this.

Having one of our records go straight to No 1 was just incredible. We couldn't have predicted it. We'd hoped it would get there and we were pleasantly surprised when it went straight in to No 1. But certainly when we were in the studio recording 'Going Underground' we didn't think we had a No 1 record on our hands. That way of thinking just didn't come into it.

There was a time when the song might not even have ended up as a single. 'Going Underground' was just another song that The Jam were writing and recording. It went into the pot of single contenders along with others. When any album was being recorded there'd be songs that us and Polydor would think could suit as a next single. There'd be all sorts of opinions flying around when it came to choosing a song for a single release. In the beginning Paul, Bruce and my opinions were considered to a lesser degree, but as we got more successful our opinion became more important and we had more of a say.

Choosing a single was rarely an easy process. We'd have our idea and the label

theirs and they'd come back and say our choice wasn't a goer because it wouldn't get the radio airplay needed because it may be too long or too raunchy or too noisy or too something. There were times when I think Paul felt badgered into having to come up with a song that suited the agenda of the record label and not The Jam. At times this was a point of conflict between The Jam and Polydor.

Having a No 1 record also meant that we had to do *Top of the Pops* because that's what you did when you got a No 1 record. On the show Paul wore a Heinz baked beans apron turned inside out. He wanted to wear it for a laugh, but the bods at the BBC told him that he couldn't because of advertising laws in the UK. So, Paul's compromise was to still wear it, but the way he did on the performance. That same apron reappeared thirty six years later when Ann Weller wore it as she manned the tea stall at the *About The Young Idea* Jam exhibition in Liverpool. Fans then queued up to get their photographs taken, either with Ann wearing it, or wearing it themselves.

The other side to the story of getting to the top of the charts was the feeling of relief that Polydor had. They had been waiting for it and for a record company to have this means a great deal. At the time they also understood the benefits much more than we did. Before we came along Polydor had been the label for some big acts, The Who and Slade amongst them, and they were selling records in big numbers throughout the Seventies.

Polydor had suspected The Jam would get a No 1 at some point. They, like Paul, Bruce and me, had watched our singles as each new release achieved better sales and got to higher positions in the charts. I suppose Polydor had reason to assume that it was only a matter of time until their latest successful band was going to get this.

Polydor had been doing their bit, which included getting the records out and getting the distribution right and we had been doing our bit by producing the songs, getting them recorded, playing gigs and all the time our fan base was increasing. We were all doing our best and this culminated in 'Going Underground' being our first No 1 hit single.

Keeping an eye on how records moved about was something we kept a close eye on. We'd stay in contact with a plugger called Spanner. We'd speak to him and get an idea as regards to what he thought the predictions would be for the next single or album release. They had means of finding this sort of stuff out - or at least get a sense. As a plugger he knew what shops were stocking our records and where they were and in what sort of numbers they were ordering the records in. It was this sort of information that helped them predict where the record might get to in the charts.

The record label would also keep an eye on who else was about to release a single. So when 'Going Underground' was going to be released this was also a consideration. The music industry was a bit of game when it came to this. It would be a matter of saying 'Going Underground' can't be released on that week because Rod Stewart or Elton John are going to put a record out and those guys were expected to get a No 1 or at least chart very high". The record label couldn't always get this right and The Jam did fall foul of this a couple of times. I think there was one occasion when David Bowie prevented us getting a record any higher. It could be very competitive at times. I mean the charts is a numbers game and another act might only have to sell ten more records than you and they'd get to No 1 that week and you

wouldn't, someone like Bowie would just suck all the sales for a record release that week.

All the time we'd been with Polydor, we had been learning how the industry worked and what was needed to be a successful band and sell records. For example, to get to No 1 a record would need to sell a certain amount. So if, at the time, a record could get to No 1 by selling 100,000 copies, then the record label would only release 100,000 to the shops. This meant that some people wouldn't be able to get the record in the first week of it being released. What this meant was that in the second week the label would release another 100,000, so the people that had missed out could then buy a copy. And this meant there'd be a good chance of the record staying at the No 1 position. If the label had pressed up 400,000 records and released all of them at the same time and it got to No 1, there'd be a chance that the record might drop off the top spot the following week. But by releasing only 100,000, it kept the demand high and it helped the record sustain a good chart position. We learnt about these sorts of games that the industry and record labels played and it's understandable why.

Nowadays the music industry has changed so much that this sort of scenario doesn't apply anymore. Back in the days when The Jam were releasing singles it was a big deal for the band, the record label and the fans. Fans would save up their money to buy our records - they would go out of their way to pre-order the records. Some fans wanted our record on the day of its release just to ensure that they got a copy. Securing The Jam's latest release was important and The Jam was always very privileged to have such loyal and keen fans.

That's another thing that has changed in

6

6

VIDEOS

Generally speaking Paul, Bruce and I hated having to do videos. One of the things we detested doing was having to mime along to the songs. This was one of the reasons why the three of us weren't particularly keen on doing *Top of the Pops*. The thing was we felt The Jam were a live band. That's what we enjoyed the most and everything else seemed a bit false.

I think when it came down to it I just accepted videos as being a necessary tool to promote our records.

I don't think any of The Jam's videos are particularly great. I think it was hard to pin down what our songs were about in the videos, especially Paul's songs where the lyrics can be interpreted in many different ways.

The Jam were not like, say Duran Duran, who just wrote songs about lying around on a beach or something. Making videos for bands like Duran Duran would have been a lot easier than making videos for The Jam. The things Paul wrote about were often important subjects and Paul took his lyrics very seriously.

When we did the video for 'Going Underground', the band video concept was still relatively new. This of course all changed a couple of years later when *MTV* came along. Another thing that bothered us about making videos was that it sometimes cost more money to pay for the video than what it had done to record the song in the first place and it was The Jam that was footing the bill, not Polydor.

'The Bitterest Pill' was a good example of making a video that cost a fair chunk of money. For that video we hired a house for the shoot. I think it was in Fulham. One room was set up to look like a scene from *Great Expectations*. It had a large table that was covered in plates and glasses and a wedding cake. Everything was covered in cobwebs. There was a model used in the video too and she wore a wedding dress.

Throughout the video Paul was required to act out various parts. As he is seen 'singing the story' of a relationship falling apart he had to kiss the model 'the promise of your kiss', bang his fist on a table and angrily push a cup off the table. One of the rooms in the house had a nice fire burning away in the fireplace. I'm in that scene talking to the model. The idea is that we are friendly and Paul sees this as he spies on us through the window. Our acting skills were really put to the test on the 'Bitterest Pill' video.

I also remember how the film crew on the day seemed to take forever to do anything. The crews for the shoots always seemed to be overstaffed and too many people seemingly doing very little. Our patience was tested on many occasions. I can remember several

conversations with the film makers where we'd be saying "why can't we just film that bit?" Some things seemed simple to us.

When The Jam were recording we were the ones in control, we sat in the control seat. But when it came to making videos someone else had that control and we didn't always like it. We weren't great at being told what to do, especially when it came to someone telling us that we weren't needed for two hours, but can you sit there and just wait to be called. I found this sort of thing really frustrating. It was on the 'Bitterest Pill' video that Bruce got so frustrated that before it was finished he decided to just go home.

We'd been at this house all day, it was approaching midnight and Bruce had had enough. In Bruce's absence Dennis Munday was brought in. He had a similar haircut to Bruce, so Dennis

became Bruce for a few seconds!

I don't think Paul, Bruce or myself felt we were very good at making videos. I think some of the video makers lacked a certain experience too. Again, the concept of the music video was still in its infancy and there didn't seem to be a great deal of creativity

about the content.

Sometimes it felt like we were just turning up on the day of the shoot and there hadn't been much thought or planning put into what would be happening. It was a bit like facing someone scratching their head and coming up with something like "how about we film you running down the street?" But on other occasions we

were presented with storyboards because the producers and directors had taken the trouble to script out and plan what would happen. I think the video for 'That's Entertainment' was one of the better-organised and scripted out shoots.

I think it was due to the hit and miss experiences that The Jam had had when it came to making videos that we felt on edge whenever it was suggested that another one get made.

We didn't like being told to act either. You can see the unease that's on our faces in the videos for 'Strange Town', 'Absolute Beginners' and 'When You're Young'. Acting wasn't one of our talents. I think Paul had more fun with this sort of thing when he was in the Style Council, but whilst in The Jam I think he felt as uncomfortable as Bruce and myself.

THE JAM

modern society - the hunger in fans just isn't the same. Kids can now download records from their phones or computers, whilst they hang around their bedroom or are walking to school. You just don't see queues of fans waiting outside record shops or Woolworths on the day of their band releasing their latest record anymore.

Having 'Going Underground' going to the top of the charts had an impact. Whilst some things didn't change, some things did. The live shows started to get bigger. Having a No 1 was one way of reaching new fans and these people would start coming to our shows. We played bigger and better venues and we could see that the audience numbers had swelled.

By the time of 'Going Underground' the Mod thing had really grown, so the audiences would be full of kids in parkas and Sixties styled suits and haircuts. Kenny (Wheeler) called them the Muppets. Not all of our fans were Mods, but a vast number were. At the time bands like The Chords, Secret Affair and The Merton Parkas were all attracting the same fans as The Jam and for a few years, this revivalist Mod thing was very active. I suppose for some it never really stopped.

One thing that didn't change as we played in bigger and better venues was the nerves we felt before we went on stage. Nerves were always there and it didn't matter whether we played in front of two hundred at the Nashville or two thousand at Hammersmith.

Having this massive hit meant the hotels got better too. It reached a point where I no longer needed to share a room with Bruce, or John Weller with Kenny Wheeler. 'Going Underground' was a huge success and The Jam just carried on doing shows, appearing on various radio and television shows, doing interviews. Looking back I think Paul, Bruce and I got quite blasé at times and took for

granted that we'd be featured on the front cover of this or that magazine. But for us three we were experiencing things very differently from our fans or the record label. We were on the inside looking out and everyone else was on the outside looking in. For us at times it seemed hard to gauge what the changes were, whereas the fans probably noticed it more.

Alongside the surge in band interviews and new media interest came the awards. One of the music papers that kept an interest in The Jam was the *NME*. This had started in 1978 when *All Mod Cons* was awarded Best Album. The Best Album Award was repeated with *Setting Sons*, *Sound Affects* and *The Gift*.

The *NME* had all sorts of awards and this was important stuff for bands and the fans. Other *NME* awards included: Paul getting best songwriter in 79, 80, 81 and 82. He also won Best Guitarist in 79, 80, 81 and 82. Bruce got the award for Best Bassist in 79, 80, 81 and 82. I got Best Drummer in 79, 80, 81 and 82. The Jam got Best Group in 79, 80, 81 and 82. Paul got Best Male singer in 1980 and 1982, alongside the Most Wonderful Human Being in 80, 81 and 82. 1980 was also the year that the Creep of the Year award went to Margaret Thatcher, which also shows what else was going on at the time and what else was influencing a song like 'Going Underground'.

The *NME* had some silly awards too such as the Farce of the Decade which in 1979 was awarded to the Mod revival. That year the Best Film went to *Quadrophenia*. Paul got the award for the Best Dressed Male and Best Haircut in 82. In 1982 The Jam got the awards for Best Group, Best Longplayer (*The Gift*), Best Live Act, Best Single ('Town Called Malice') and The Event of the Year-The Jam Split. I also got Best Drummer, Bruce Best Bassist and Paul Best Guitarist.

I remember when Paul, Bruce and myself

were invited to an awards event in some theatre. This was for 'Going Underground'. When it was time to accept the award for our No 1 single, Paul refused to go and pick it up. This left just Bruce and me to do it. I think the person handing over the award was American singer Suzi Quatro. It was quite embarrassing really because the expectation was that all three of us would go and accept the award. At the time Bruce and I had no idea that Paul wouldn't get up. I didn't know what Paul's reasoning was. I don't think I ever found out. I've since learned that Paul asked our A&R man Dennis Munday to take his place. It just happened and he just stayed in his seat with his girlfriend Gill beside him and my missus Lesley beside her.

On the approach to the awards event, I remember there being a feeling that there was a good chance that 'Going Underground' was in the running for something, but we didn't know for certain. I also recall feeling badgered by Polydor into making sure that we attended the event. It was very much a case of "you must go!" I guess Polydor had got wind of something and getting any award was a big deal.

There was also a video made for 'Going Underground'. We were filmed playing our instruments in a white room. I'm playing my white Rogers drum kit and Bruce and Paul have their black and white Rickenbackers. Black and white is a theme that continues in the video. Bruce wears a black and white tie and he also wore his black and white Jam shoes (often endearingly called the Badger shoes).

Throughout the video there are numerous references relating to war and patriotism. The video begins with the image of Uncle Sam and there's also a poster of Lord Kitchener, both doing the finger pointing and inviting 'You'

to join the army. These images connected to the political and military themes contained in the 'Going Underground' lyrics. At one point there are several photographs of Tory politicians and atom bombs exploding. It was 'Going Underground' that really propelled The Jam into the realms of being included in such campaigns as CND and Ban the Bomb marches. It was around 1980 that The Jam performed at a number of CND-organised events. The very last image in the video, as Paul's guitar rings off, is of an atom bomb exploding. Such images of the mushroom clouds produced by atom bombs were all over the place going into the Eighties. I think The Jam were one of the earliest bands to align ourselves with organisations like the CND. I think we certainly helped promote awareness for CND and introduce young people to the threats that their generation were being faced with. Such issues were probably more important to Paul than they were to Bruce and me, but we were more than happy to support it.

One of the things Paul's lyrics and The Jam were good at was producing records that had an observational view. I don't think Paul wrote from a point of being judgemental but

6

he was saying "look, this is what is going on". I don't recall ever offering up solutions to problems or preaching in any way.

The Jam didn't rally to any particular political view. However some people tried to push us in that direction. I think in Paul's Style Council years the political thing was much more defined than what it had been in The Jam years. Paul was certainly more vocal about his political leanings in the Style Council years, what with the whole Red Wedge thing. I suppose The Jam were political with a small p.

The Jam were also very aware and very conscious of not aligning ourselves to any particular political party because we knew that as soon as that happened we'd be restricting ourselves. This restriction would then impact on what could or couldn't be written about and even what sort of concerts could or couldn't be played. And then there'd be added problems like the audiences we would attract to the concerts. I know bands like The Specials and Madness had these sorts of problems. I mean this was the late Seventies and there were skinheads active again and right wing organisations like the National Front would show up, sometimes in force, at concerts and basically spoil what was going on.

The Jam took the position that having an independent view would be better for the band's career and we could still write songs with certain messages contained within them and we could play those songs as we wanted to and to whoever would listen.

I think we learned early on about the problems that saying something to the press about politics can create. There was that time when Paul was speaking to Steve Clark and said, "All this 'change the world' thing is becoming a bit too trendy. We'll be voting Conservative at the next election." There was a whole backlash about this. *Sniffin' Glue* really pulled us up on it and used Paul's words to really have a dig at us. In response Paul burnt a copy of the fanzine on stage one night at the 100 Club.

Later Paul did neutralise his comment by putting his hands up and declaring "that was really fucking stupid". In the end I don't think it did too much damage to our career but at the time it was heated and important to some people. Rock and roll history is littered with examples of comments that have caused troubles for a band. Think of The Beatles and John Lennon's "we're more popular than Jesus now" remark and how much trouble that created. I mean the Fabs got death threats over that. At least when Paul said the Conservative thing the worst we had to put up with was being spat at on stage a bit more!

What I liked about Paul's often willingness to speak his mind was that he was also reminding people that we were "pop stars not politicians, for fuck's sake". I think I took the view that whatever my political view happens to be, why should that matter to the songs that I'm drumming on? I've always taken the view that I'm a musician and not a politician and I have no power over anything. I use to find it uncomfortable when people asked me questions about my opinions on the threat of atomic war. But it didn't mean that we couldn't campaign for certain causes or lend our support - which The Jam did.

Also looking back on the subject of politics I don't think we were that informed about issues anyway. Paul had to take more flak about being a spokesman for his generation than Bruce and me did. It was something he was never comfortable with or promoted in himself. Back in 1976 he'd been labeled

6

a 'revivalist' by Caroline Coon who was writing for the *Melody Maker* at the time. Paul responded with the "how can I be a fucking revivalist when I'm only eighteen?" comment.

The whole Mod revivalist thing was a strange one. Around late 78 and 79 there was an explosion of bands that appeared who all had similar sounds and interests. Mostly they harked back to the clothes and bands of the Sixties. The difference was whereas the Mods were born out of the Fifties, the attitudes, fashions and music that were around then and that their older brothers and sisters were into, the Mod thing of the Seventies was based on what happened with the Sixties Mods. For example in the Sixties the Mods spent their bank holiday weekends invading places like Brighton or Margate and in the Seventies they did the same again.

Bands like The Chords, Secret Affair and The Lambrettas all listened to the same music that The Jam did and they too put their influences into their songs. They also liked to wear button-down shirts and three-button jackets and desert boots, just like we saw the Mods in the Sixties do. The look wasn't unique to The Jam but people did look up to us to see what we were wearing.

This became evident in the new burst of life that shops in Carnaby Street saw. You had places like Shelleys and Melanddi's selling items that Paul, Bruce and I wore. There was the whole Jam shoes thing, that included the bowling, cycling and badgers from Shelleys Shoes and then shirts from Melanddi's. That shop was owned by two guys Mel and Andy - that's where the shop's name came from. And for a few years business in Carnaby Street was great again.

However, all the time this was going on, we were getting free shoes and clothes from those shops. I mean after all we were the best

place to promote their goods. We were still very conscious that we wanted to create our own identity and set ourselves apart from what else was going on. We also wanted to create a sound that would be unique to us. We wanted people to hear a song on the radio and know that it was a Jam song. And I believe we achieved this.

We were also aware that there were other bands trying to copy us, look like us and write songs like us. It didn't annoy us as such but we were alerted to it. This sort of thing has happened often in the music business. In the Sixties you had loads of bands copying the way The Beatles structured their songs and then they wore the same style suits. In the Seventies you had bands all looking like The Rolling Stones. In America you'd have all these band members wearing leather 'pants' and styling their hair the same way. It was sometimes hard to see who was who and what band they were in.

The Jam tried to buck such trends. We didn't consider it to be a good idea to follow trends. When The Jam released *In The City* we got lumped in with the punk thing, but we didn't dress like punks. It was one of the things we liked about Dr. Feelgood. They went on stage wearing knackered old jackets and suits and they looked anything but pop stars. They were a unique band in many ways.

I think The Jam saw our look as being based on everyday fashions and being individuals and not following trends. I think we wanted our dress sense to reflect our music too, just like the smart look of the Sixties Mods bands reflected their songs - smart and sharp!

Another thing that The Jam had on the other 'Mod' bands from that revivalist period was the ability to be consistent with releasing good songs. It seemed to me that those

6

other bands struggled to keep the standard up. They'd have one or two good songs, but then struggle. But it's only an opinion and I think The Jam were able to be different and survive because we were hungrier than those other bands. We had a drive that pushed us on and we loved what we were doing. Even after 'Going Underground' went to No 1 we still retained that hunger and we still felt like we wanted to prove ourselves and improve ourselves as a band. Paul, Bruce and myself all pushed each other to be better. This had been the same since we started. One of our aims was to not become boring. It was important to us to keep things fresh and always moving on. Our intention was to make our next album better than the last and this was always in the forefront of our minds. I think this is an attitude that Paul has sustained throughout his career, even though not all of his fans can understand it with each new album.

It even reached a point in The Jam's career where we didn't really need to put ourselves under such pressure to keep on being better and improving and pushing ourselves, but it was as if we didn't know or want to be any different. The Jam worked hard throughout the whole of our career and that helped make us who we were.

I recall having a conversation with Dennis Munday from Polydor one day about how the music press liked to be able to pigeon hole a band. It basically helps them out. Historically most bands feel uncomfortable being labeled. For some it doesn't matter – "we are a Mod band", "we are a Heavy Metal band", "we are Goths" or whatever. The Jam never put ourselves out there as a Mod band. That just happened. We were just writing songs and playing them the way we wanted. It just so happened that our influences included bands like The Kinks, Who and Small Faces,

who had strong Mod links. The bands in the Nineties like Oasis and Ocean Colour Scene were lumped into something called Brit Pop and they hated that. It's all to do with what makes the lives of the music press easier. The Jam were lumped into the punk thing, then the new wave thing and then the Mod thing. We just did what we did.

Something that didn't change for us following 'Going Underground's success was our wanting to get back into the studio. Recording was important to us and the desire to work on new songs. Having a No 1 record meant that getting a new album out was a necessary next step. After 'Going Underground' we worked towards *Sound Affects*.

3. START! (PAUL WELLER)

Recorded June 1980, Townhouse Studios, London

Available on *Sound Affects, Snap, Direction Reaction Creation* and *The Very Best Of The Jam: About The Young Idea.*

'Start!' was released seven months after the No 1 hit 'Going Underground' and became The Jam's second UK No 1 hit. Upon its release on 15 August 1980, it debuted at No 3 and two weeks later reached the top of the chart where it stayed for one week. The track was the lead single from the band's fifth album, *Sound Affects*. The single's B-side was 'Liza Radley'. Throughout the song Bruce provides a catchy, melodic bass line which, yes, does have similarities to The Beatles' 'Taxman'. This has never been denied.

It was during this period that Paul used his Pop Art designed Rickenbacker guitar (the one with Whaam written on it in yellow), that provides those chord strikes that cut through the verses. That guitar contributes to that jagged edge feel that the song has. Paul makes further use of his guitar a minute and a half into the song when he delivers one of his finest guitar solos. It's a really good addition to the song.

'What you give is what you get' is a mantra for Jam fans and one which is well worth taking note of and, when the record was purchased what you got was a pink sleeve with the words 'Start!' written on it. It was simple and effective and - like The Jam at that period - it stood out!

Rick Buckler:

'Start!' was a song that we recorded during the sessions that led up to the *Sound Affects* album. There had been discussions about what should be the next single and it was

felt that 'Start!' would be a suitable song. I remember 'Pretty Green' was also a contender and our discussions were about what would be best to release, 'Start!' or 'Pretty Green'. These discussions often included several people. These would be John Weller, Dennis Munday, Polydor, Vic Smith. Everyone had an opinion which would all be listened to and considered but there was also an element of choosing the next single based on intuition too. Sometimes we just knew what should be released as a single and it really was a matter of agreeing on 'that is the one'.

Choosing a next single never fell into the realms of examining some analytical reasoning for it. Often it would be more about asking ourselves what we should use for the B-side. Sometimes we just agreed to put something on the B-side that wasn't on the album. The Jam have gone down as one of the bands to have had some really good B-sides. Songs like 'Tales From The Riverbank' and 'The Butterfly Collector' have become classic songs amongst Jam fans.

Even the point of keeping songs that we wanted to be issued as singles but kept off albums was often a contentious thing when it came to the record label. The label often struggled with this. They understood that people wanted to hear that song on the album. It's a formula that worked and that bands had always done. Think how many songs from The Beatles' 'A Hard Day's Night' ended up as A and B-side issues.

Record labels understand that songs sell albums and so to release a good single is a sure way to sell albums. And if that single is included on the album, even better. But The Jam stood our ground on many occasions. We wanted to be different to other groups. The Jam had some good songs like 'When

THE JAM

You're Young', 'Strange Town' and 'Going Underground' that were all issued as singles but didn't get included on any of our albums. We were pleased with this, but the record label wasn't always.

Another thing that The Jam tried to avoid after *In The City* was issuing singles that were also the title of the album. Sure there were songs like 'All Mod Cons' and 'The Gift' that also appeared on the albums *All Mod Cons* and *The Gift*, but we also had albums like *Setting Sons* and *Sound Affects* that had no relevance to individual songs. The Jam were quite unique in that way.

Personally I never really liked the way that a record label releases an album then plunders it to issue a bunch of singles from it. I have always felt this was a bit of a cheek and unnecessary but it went on and still does.

The Jam's way of wanting to give the fans something extra was to release songs that didn't appear on albums and also if they did then we'd try to include a B-side that was new and not on the album.

What The Jam wanted to do was keep our singles special. I know this was very important to Paul and I know that he really liked it when we had singles released that weren't songs lifted from albums.
For us, and I think our fans, releasing a single was a special event. We tried to avoid detracting from this special feeling because people had already had it on an album. We considered each single as a unique piece of work - an entity in its own right.

The B-side to 'Start!' was 'Liza Radley'. Paul played an acoustic guitar and piano on this and Bruce, alongside his bass, also played accordion. We recorded the song in Townhouse Studios in the April. I wrote some of the lyrics but I never got

credited for it. Something had happened to a recording of it that we weren't happy with. I recall that it had something to do with the amount of verses. But we seemed to be short with the amount of lyrics we had to work with and we didn't feel the song deserved to have some lyrics repeated, so Paul just looked at me and asked me to have a go. I grabbed a pen and some paper and wrote some lyrics down and handed them to Paul and he sung them. I liked the song and always felt it was one of the most interesting Jam songs.

At the time 'Liza Radley' wasn't recorded with the intention of having it as a B-side - it could have easily turned up on *Sound Affects*. But after discussions it was felt that it would suit as the B-side for 'Start!'. I think people compared 'Liza Radley' to The Beatles' 'Eleanor Rigby', but then by the time 'Start!' was released people had heard how important The Beatles had been to us and especially to Paul. You cannot underestimate how influential The Beatles were on Paul and how much they informed Paul's own songwriting.

I think we felt that 'Liza Radley' fitted with 'Start!' well as a single. 'Start!' was a good song and at that time very different to anything that The Jam had done. It took some people some time to get their heads around it. One music journalist, Paul Du Noyer, wrote a review of *Sound Affects* in the *NME* in November 1980 saying "it's neither escapist nor revivalist, whatever impressions 'Start!' might have given" adding "it's every bit an album of this decade, a point which won't need labouring after the release day". But I have no idea what 'impression' 'Start!' had had on some people.

6

"I mean 'Liza Radley'? Are you serious? Most bands would lop off a limb to have that as their best single. That was just one of many gems lurking on the flip side that still sounds timeless..."

Martin Freeman

We liked that that track was very different to all of our previous single releases. It also sat nicely on *Sound Affects* and certainly wasn't a song that just padded the album out. I've always felt that having to pad out albums was a dreadful thing.

The song got the spotlight and received the recognition that it deserved when it became our second No 1. I liked recording the song too and this was a good example of how Vic Smith contributed his studio skills. I remember how he worked on the backing vocals and especially making the 'T' sound at the end of the word start. He did something with it so that the T made its presence felt and it enhanced that part of the song.

We didn't appear on *Top of the Pops*. I can't remember why because we weren't on the road much on the month (August) when it was at No 1. We had another video made though. The video wasn't very inspiring really but it was straight forward. We were filmed playing our instruments in Townhouse Studios. We're mostly just surrounded by studio clutter-leads, stands and unused drums.

The only variation in the video is when Paul's psychedelic guitar solo comes in, for this bit they altered the colours, which gave it a slight psychedelic visual affect. In the video we are all dressed in quite casual ways. Paul wears some Lennon-esque style sunglasses.

'Start!' and The Beatles connection didn't get lost either. This related to Bruce's bassline and The Beatles' song 'Taxman', which was on their *Revolver* album. But in the studio at the time no one made a big deal about it. As far as Bruce, Paul and myself were concerned it wasn't a straight lift from McCartney's bassline at all, but there were similarities, which was understandable because at the time of recording we were listening to *Revolver* quite a lot. *Revolver* is such a great album, with tracks like 'Taxman', 'Eleanor Rigby', 'Got To Get You Into My Life' and 'And Your Bird Can Sing' - which Paul and Pete Wilson recorded a cover of just as a bit of fun really whilst they were in Polydor's Studios. *Revolver* had also been released in August, but fourteen years earlier.

Bruce's bass sounds really good, there's a really rounded sound to it, which wasn't always the case when it came to bass sounds on Jam tracks. Bruce used an old Sixties bass called a Epiphone Rivoli and that's what created that sound.

It's only been as the years have gone by that the issue of the bass line has become bigger. Someone started that ball rolling and as times gone by it's just become something to talk about. I can't really see any problem. Musicians are borrowing and nicking stuff from the people they admire all the time. And it's always been that way. The Beatles had their influences, The Who, The Kinks, The Jam, Oasis and so on, and all bands songs are influenced by the people they like and look up to. It's inspirational.

THE JAM

6

Like most Jam songs we recorded several versions and 'Start!' was no different. Some had different drums going on. Now I had 'Killer Queen' by Queen in mind at the time. On the song Roger Taylor uses his hi-hats to fatten the sound of his snare drum. He managed to create a certain sound by opening the hi-hats as he hit the snare. I used that Queen song - or Roger's drum sound as inspiration for the sound I got on 'Start!'. I really liked the way this approach added some extra punch to the drum pattern. I think it really stands out.

One thing about The Jam was that we were very self-intuitive when it came to finding ways to play our instruments. Once Paul presented us with a riff or some melody, somehow we knew what to do and because of this most of the time things came together quite quickly. It was only after that we'd develop the songs structure and sounds and so on to make it the final product. But you have to remember that by the time we recorded 'Start!' Paul, Bruce and I had been together for a long time. This can happen in bands and between musicians.

I can't recall my reaction to the single reaching the top of the charts. It wasn't that many months after 'Going Underground', so we were still feeling the benefits of that.

The process for issuing 'Start!' had been like all the other times. I suppose the difference this time was that we were in the UK rather than being in America like we had been with 'Going Underground'. Being in the UK did mean we were closer to what was happening, so we knew the shops stopped counting for the chart placing on a Saturday night. In those days shops weren't allowed to open on Sundays, which meant nothing moved and there'd be no record sales after Saturday night. And then on Monday all the

figures would get collected, which meant that by Tuesday the record labels knew what the sales had been and how the record was progressing regarding its positioning in the charts. Then the BBC could work out who they wanted to appear on *Top of the Pops* and whilst all this was going on, we had someone from Polydor reporting all this stuff back to us.

If we were going to make an appearance on *Top of the Pops* this had to be dealt with too. There'd be times when bands were on the road or even out of the country. It was in these situations that having the videos available helped. Also if the band or label had spent say thirty grand making a video they wanted it to be seen. So videos also became the excuse behind which bands hid so they could avoid having to do *Top of the Pops*. As important as *Top of the Pops* was, there were times when appearing on it was just an inconvenience. Appearing on the show meant stopping whatever else you was doing and blocking the whole day out to be in BBC studios to build up to the performance being filmed. This was a lengthy process because you wouldn't be the only band on the show and they were also all awaiting their turn.

The *Top of the Pops* staff didn't really like bands sending in videos rather than turning up themselves. They preferred bands to actually appear on the show. It had been happening since the Sixties. *Top of the Pops* had been going since 1964. It wouldn't be until *MTV* arrived that the way music fans accessed their favourite music and bands changed.

The other difference with 'Start!' as compared to 'Going Underground' was that it didn't go straight to No 1. It was released on August 15 and went in at No 3. It took a further two weeks to get to No 1. So for those two weeks we kept watch on its progress and it was looking like it would get to No 1. So unlike 'Going Underground' which was straight in at pole position, 'Start!' was gradual. It was still exciting though, and still a brilliant achievement to have a second No 1 record.

The period between 'Going Underground' and 'Start!' had also seen the re-release of all The Jam's singles to date. What 'Going Underground' had helped do was increase our fan base. So this extra push helped our latest single too. Polydor re-released all of our singles again when we split up. We had all of our singles in the top 100 at the same time on three occasions, an achievement that no band other than The Beatles had ever done apparently.

We had no say in re-releasing records but we could see why the label would do it. Over The Jam's career we were gathering new fans each step of the way. We had people getting into us only because of *All Mod Cons* or they were too young and only became music fans at the time of *The Gift*. And in cases like this the fan would then start going back through The Jam's catalogue and collect the records from there.

4. ENGLISH ROSE (PAUL WELLER)

Recorded August 1978 at RAK Studios, London
Available on *All Mod Cons, Snap, Direction Reaction Creation* and *The Very Best Of The Jam: About The Young Idea.*

Undoubtedly 'English Rose' is one of The Jam's finest works. It's understandable that it was considered as a potential B-side for 'David Watts'. The fact that the song is performed only by Paul doesn't matter -The

Jam were a collective. They also trusted the song enough to leave it in its purest form and include it on *All Mod Cons* (although the title didn't appear on the album sleeve - the true reason has never been confirmed). This was the first song to only include one member from the group playing a song on a Jam album.

Written as a ballad with Paul's girlfriend Gill Price in mind, the song's legacy some thirty years later has meant that many an English female has been called an English rose by their lover. It's meant to be a loving tribute to someone you love and maybe you miss. When Paul wrote the song he was on tour in North America, a place that he wasn't really connecting with at the time and when all he yearned for was to be back home with Gill.

It was Vic Coppersmith-Heaven's idea to add the sounds of the lapping waves against a shore and the boat's horn. It worked, in effect serving as the backing band, and certainly helped to tease the listener's imagination. The waves are still lapping as Paul begins to play his acoustic guitar. It's gentle, soothing and beautiful.

The very sentiment contained in the opening lyrics evoke that sense of longing and wanting and desire to 'return' to that loved one after all the 'roaming' of the 'seven seas' has been done.

'English Rose' is one of those songs that simply stops a person in their tracks. It demands that you stop and listen and enjoy and although not included in Jam concerts, it certainly found its place in Paul's sets on numerous occasions during his solo years. He even performed it in his first live appearance a few months after The Jam split up, it was at an Everything But The Girl concert at the London ICA on 5 January 1983. Tracey Thorn on vocals and Paul and Ben Watts shared

THE JAM

6

guitar duties. When *Fire And Skill: Songs of The Jam* was produced it was the Everything But The Girl version that was included.

The song draws to a close, leaving the listener feeling reflective and it serves a reminder to remember the people we love most from our own lives. For Paul, in 1978 it was Gill.

Rick Buckler:

The song title didn't get listed on the *All Mod Cons* album sleeve because the final decision to include the song was made too late to get the art work changed. I think the final cover may have even been with the printers by that point. The process of putting an album out involves working to strict timelines that marries up the printers, the vinyl pressing company, the marketing, press and so on. Any delay in any area can cause a huge problem. We had a similar problem when it came to *Setting Sons*. There were sleeves that were printed that didn't have the tracks written on them. Some sleeves had to have stickers stuck onto them that listed the tracks that were on the album. This was a big cock up at the time that had to get dealt with.

There was talk about 'English Rose' not even being included on the album at all. I recall that Paul was somewhat reticent about the song. I think he'd written it as a real, from-the-heart love song about his girlfriend Gill Price. He'd written it whilst we were on tour in the States but it was almost like he'd not written it for public consumption. I believe the song was quite personal to him.

When 'English Rose' was put out there it did get mixed opinions because it was the first song to be released that didn't include Bruce or me. It was also an acoustic song. Up until that point Jam fans had only heard Jam songs performed by the three of us and our songs weren't really ballads.

But the song was added to the album and I don't recall Bruce or I having any issues with it. I suppose Paul could have released it as a solo song, but I doubt that would have gone down too well with the record label because at the time the brand name of The Jam was the pull rather than any solo ventures. Personally I'm not a big lover of acoustic love songs, so I wasn't overly knocked out by the song, but I liked it and it fitted well on *All Mod Cons*. It also showed our fans what The Jam were capable of and that we didn't need to smash our way through three minute songs every time.

I also don't think Paul was entirely sure of the song either. I think it may have reminded him of the sort of songs that he'd written with Steve Brookes when they were both younger. Those songs were love songs and maybe a bit weak. I mean a good love song has to have content and that's where it gets its strength from. When Paul and Steve wrote those songs, they didn't have much experience of love, so the content was a bit thin.

My recollections of the conversations at the time are that it was Paul who out of the three of us was most hesitant about it being included on the album. Apart from it being so personal to him and Gill, maybe he didn't see that it fitted alongside songs like 'Billy Hunt', 'In The Crowd' and 'Mr Clean'. Those songs all captured a certain mood, a mood that was around the band and around Paul, which was influencing his songwriting, so 'English Rose' didn't really sit beside them as comfortably. It's a song that has gone on to stand the test of time. Paul has performed it countless times in his solo years and it's a song that often serves a bond between male Jam fans and their partners.

5. FLY (PAUL WELLER)

Recorded August 1978, RAK Studios, London

Available on: *All Mod Cons, Direction Reaction Creation.*

'Fly' is another song that reflects where Paul was with his lyric writing in 1978. The track can be found as the third song on side two of The Jam's third album *All Mod Cons*. 'Fly' is another love song about young love, in the sense of those first steps in a new relationship and how it feels fresh, captivating and can feel like it's so important that nothing else matters. Only a few months earlier, nothing other than Paul's relationship with Gill had mattered and his songwriting had suffered, and so The Jam were suffering.

This is one of The Jam's softer sounding starts to a song. Paul's using his acoustic again which he plays whilst describing his loved one and declaring his hope that they will 'always be around'. When Paul was writing for *All Mod Cons* he was still only twenty years old.

Rick and Bruce then join in, which elevates the song into a whole new dimension. After the initial explosion the song quietens down, Rick discarding his snare skin, choosing to use rim shot instead. The choruses and middle eight in 'Fly' are creative and are not without employing some Who-esque 'oohs' and then the song returns to its formative quieter and softer arrangement until it ends.

Rick Buckler:

I remember that Vic had to really work with Paul when it came to the guitar solo. Paul didn't feel that comfortable playing lead guitar, which he shouldn't have done really because he is an absolutely fine guitarist and the part he plays on 'Fly' works very well. But in the studio Vic had to encourage this out of Paul. The lead that Paul played suited the song too and it wasn't like it was a drop to your knees solo like a Jimi Hendrix or Jimmy Page type guitar break.

I saw Vic work with Paul a lot when it came to coming up with ideas for lead guitar parts. At times I think this was a bit of a struggle for Vic too. It's possible that Paul had a bit of a hang up when it came to playing lead guitar and thought lead guitarists were only the Richie Blackmores of the world. However, Paul was fully aware of the George Harrison-style lead guitar approach and he would have this in mind when it came to adding lead guitar to Jam songs. Paul was more interested in melodic lead guitar rather than showing off.

You have to remember too that Paul wasn't a natural lead guitarist. When The Jam was starting off it was Steve Brookes who played the lead guitar whilst Paul played rhythm. As time passed Paul did

6

become more confident playing lead and there are many Jam tracks that reflect this.

The Jam songs recorded reflected what we played live but not all Jam songs suited being performed live. 'Fly' was one of them. We never played that song live. We liked experimenting with a song like 'Fly' in the studio, but it wasn't what we were about live - and The Jam were really a live band and it was what we loved doing most.

Playing live is a completely different beast to working in the studio. There were things that could be done in the studio that just couldn't be done live and vice versa and 'Fly' was a good example of this. I mean Paul couldn't play the acoustic part and the electric guitar part on stage at the same time.

In many ways *All Mod Cons* was very different to *In The City* and *Modern World* because *All Mod Cons* was the first Jam album where not all the songs came from the live set or would ever be included. The first two Jam albums were really an extension of our live sets at the time.

> *"The Jam were now! Gigging now! Recording now! Singing about now!"*
> **Graham Coxon**

6. TO BE SOMEONE (DIDN'T WE HAVE A NICE TIME). (PAUL WELLER)

Recorded July 1978, Eden Studios, London
Available on: *All Mod Cons; Direction Reaction Creation; The Very Best Of The Jam: About The Young Idea.*

With its Who-esque introduction, Paul, Rick and Bruce all crashing in together, the second track on *All Mod Cons*, 'To Be Someone (Didn't We Have A Nice Time)' is one of The Jam's most melodic tunes and one the most jerky at the same time. The guitar riff keeps it that way.

Paul's lyrics evoke a tone of reflections and dreaminess - Can I be someone? Could I be someone? What would it be like to be someone? What are the advantages of being someone? What would it be like to be liked by everyone? What Would it be like to have wealth and lots of girls? This song throws up all these questions and more and what teenage boy or girl didn't explore such musings while they lay on the bed listening to their favourite records?

Paul said that the song wasn't about him. He wasn't reflecting on his own life. At this point he still only had twenty years of life experience to draw upon. Having said that, the last three years of Weller's life had probably been the most intense.

The chorus is the section of the song where Paul ramps up his vocals. The aggression is back, sticking up two fingers is back and the band are hard. But they are soon back to that gentler verse and more reflections.

Another two and half minute perfect pop song, ending with a wistful Paul reminding the listener of the song's title and an urge to keep those questions coming.

Rick Buckler:

Generally when I think of Jam songs what springs to mind first is playing them live on stage, rather than recording them in the studio. More often than not I laid down the drums for a track in a single take. The rest of the song was built on that and that bit took time. We often did other versions too, but they wouldn't take long to do. So I don't have many in depth memories of the recording of our songs.

I liked 'To Be Someone' because it was sort of taking the piss out of your own situation really. It's one of those Jam songs that had humour in it. I liked the lyrics and the way they paint a picture of someone pondering on what it would be like to be a 'rock singer' or a 'big film star'. I liked the tongue-in-cheek aspect of it all really which had meaning to Paul, Bruce and myself, because by the time of 'To Be Someone', we were better informed regarding what it was like being in the spotlight. By the time of *All Mod Cons* we no longer had to fantasize about "what would it be like to be rock singers". We had a pretty good idea and it wasn't all what we had expected. I mean being in a successful band was very demanding, we weren't rolling in money and there was a lot of hanging around studios and driving up and down the country. It was a rollercoaster ride most of the time.

'To Be Someone' was another Kinks/Ray Davies-influenced type song. It was that story telling approach as seen through somebody's eyes. Paul Weller, like Ray Davies, got very adept at writing songs in this style. It also takes skill to tell those stories in a two to three minute song.

I always liked playing 'To Be Someone' live and thought the audience connected with the song and its lyrics. I felt that they felt part of the song because they were seeing themselves in the story too.

7. "A' BOMB IN WARDOUR STREET' (PAUL WELLER)

Recorded August 1978, RAK Studios, London
Available on: *All Mod Cons; Snap; Direction Reaction Creation; The Very Best Of The Jam: About The Young Idea.*

''A' Bomb In Wardour Street' was released as a double A-side with 'David Watts', and was the band's second single release in 1978 and reached No 25 in the UK charts.

Rick's first use of a cowbell is heard on this song. He uses it wisely alongside his snare to help build up what sounds like an aggressive and scolding song.

Wardour Street is one of Soho's better know streets. It became the centre of the British film industry, with the big production and distribution companies having their headquarters in the street. In the Fifties it drew in the jazzers who frequented the various clubs in the street and surrounding area. One such club, The Flamingo, was then drawing in the Mods in the Sixties. Pete Townshend even lived in a flat in Wardour Street. 90 Wardour Street was the site of the Marquee Club from 1964 to 1988, which is mentioned in the song 'The London Boys' by David Bowie.

The street was still a lively place to be in the Seventies, often with the sight of some punk making their way to The Roxy or the Vortex. It's the Vortex, a club owned by Andy Czezowski, that gets name-dropped in the song, although perhaps not in a favourable context: "not my scene at all". The song was

THE JAM

6

intent on reaching its final destination which it does ending with a ferocious 'apocalypse' screamed by Paul.

On the whole "A' Bomb In Wardour Street' is sharp and cuts through the drivel that the UK charts was filled with at the time. The summer of 1978 gave us No 1 hits from Boney M, John Travolta and Olivia Newton John, and The Commodores.

And to this day Rick still possesses the cowbell that was used in the recording of the song.

Rick Buckler:

I think "A' Bomb In Wardour Street' is one of my favourite Jam songs. I liked that it's one of those songs that's really in your face. It's a song that slams in from the off.

When we played 'A' Bomb In Wardour Street' live, at the end of the song we'd have all those explosives going off, which on many occasions scared the crap out of me, even though I knew it was coming. The road crew would position these explosives either side of the drum kit and on that last strike of the song someone would press the button and off they'd go with an enormous bang! I mean they had to have some fuel in them too because at the time we were playing at fairly big venues.

I think the song had this explosive element to it anyway. This was reflected in the history of the street in its Soho location. Since the Fifties it had been a hot spot for clubbers. There had been the jazzers with their clubs like the Flamingo, which later became a popular Mod hang out. Members of other major groups of the time such as The Beatles, The Rolling Stones and Jimi Hendrix would frequent the club to catch the likes of regular performers such as Georgie Fame and The Blue Flames (who released a LP titled *Rhythm*

and Blues at the Flamingo in 1964).

In its heyday great soul artists like Otis Redding and Wilson Pickett also performed at the club. There was also the Marquee Club, which had moved to premises in Wardour Street in the mid Sixties. The Marquee was the location of the first ever live performance by The Rolling Stones on 12 July 1962. The Manish Boys featuring David Bowie first played there in November 1964 and Peter Green's Fleetwood Mac gave their first performance there in 1967. The Who had a residency there for a while so it was only fitting when a blue plaque for Keith Moon was unveiled in 2009. Pete Townshend had a flat in Wardour Street in the Sixties and that pretty much overlooked Old Compton Street and the 2i's Coffee Bar - which was another club steeped in musical history. There are a few pubs in Wardour Street too and it's always been surrounded by coffee bars. It was a lively place twenty four seven - and still is.

There's always a way to look at the song and draw a comparison with the effects of a H bomb exploding, but in this case a musical one.

There's reference to the Vortex Club. This was a punk club that was run by Andy Czezowski. He'd had the Roxy Club. The Vortex nights ran on a Monday and Tuesday night in the premises of the disco club called Crackers, which was located in Wardour Street. The Vortex didn't last that long though and closed around the same time that *All Mod Cons* was released.

I don't really know what Paul was writing about when he referenced "being stranded on the Vortex floor". That punk scene was very cliquey. The Jam weren't accepted by everyone close to the punk thing. The punk fanzine *Sniffin' Glue* had no time for us at all, but Arian Thrills' *48 Thrills* did. I don't recall

6

Paul, Bruce or myself being that bothered by the lack of acceptance. We didn't really care that we weren't part of 'their' scene. The whole "if you're not like us you can't fit in" attitude seemed to me to be against what the punk ideal was all about anyway. The punk thing became very elitist very quickly. As a group we turned our backs on it and some of them didn't like that. We certainly weren't left feeling 'stranded'.

We just did what we wanted to do, wore what we wanted and wrote songs based on our influences. There was that moment when Joe Strummer turned up to one of our gigs wearing a t-shirt saying 'Chuck Berry Is Dead' and Paul told him that he didn't agree - Paul loved Chuck Berry. punk failed to evolve and in the end just didn't learn any lessons. They wanted to be different from everybody else and yet they all dressed the same. It was the same with the Mod ideal of striving to be an individual, but they dressed like all their Mod mates. It wasn't that individual at all, although to be fair to Paul, who took the ideals of Modernism very seriously always managed to stay one step ahead of everyone else. He's managed to keep that going for years really.

There' a violent aspect to the song throughout where Paul is writing about "streets paved in blood" and "fifteen geezers pinning down a girl". It's written in the first person too, so as if talking about a personal experience.

By 1978 punk was being replaced by new wave and The Jam had been labeled as a band based in both of these genres. It was a time when everything was being shaken up and what had gone before was being blown away. Kicking out and pushing to one side all that had gone before was what punk was aspiring to attain. It never really achieved that but what did come out of it was a lot more bands and some brilliant songs.

I think "A' Bomb In Wardour Street' was a great way of portraying what was and had been happening musically in that area of Soho and it always went down well when we played it live. I used a cow bell on the track. I think it was the first Jam song that did. It was The Rolling Stones' 'Honky Tonk Woman' that gave me the idea to use a cow bell. Interestingly, Charlie Watts didn't play the cow bell on that song. The way the pattern works it would be impossible to do so. It was Vic Smith who had worked with the Stones during those sessions and he told me that it was producer Jimmy Miller who played it in the drum booth at the same time as Charlie played the drums.

On "A' Bomb In Wardour Street' I played the cow bell pretty straight throughout of the whole of the song. It made a nice change from playing the hi-hat constantly all of the time. And it seemed to add to the attacking feel of the song. It's a strong feature in the song and it worked. I've still got that cowbell!

8. TOWN CALLED MALICE (PAUL WELLER)

Recorded December 1981, AIR Studios, London. Released in the UK on 29 January 1982.
Available on: *The Gift, Snap, Direction Reaction Creation* and *The Very Best Of The Jam: About The Young Idea.*

When Paul wrote 'Town Called Malice' Margaret Thatcher had been Prime Minister for almost two years. Britain had problems. During this period Paul was possibly at his most vocal when it came to politics. This period certainly set him up for his Style Council days, with

6

its political edge. Paul clearly wasn't a fan of Thatcher. On one occasion he didn't hold back when he said "I hope she rots in her own hell".

In the song Paul tells the listener that he could go on and on about the topic of how Thatcherism was ripping the heart out of the working class communities that Paul invested so much value and belief in. Paul is telling the listener that he understands that they struggle "year after year". He also implores them to "stop apologizing". After all, the British public shouldn't take the blame for things they've never done. Despite Paul's joke of voting for the Tories back in 1977 - of course, nothing could have been further from the truth.

'A Town Called Malice' entered the chart at No 1 and was The Jam's third No 1 UK hit, staying at the top for three weeks (preventing 'Golden Brown' by The Stranglers from reaching No 1). It's remained a hit amongst Jam fans ever since and, of all The Jam songs, it's the one that's most played by radio stations. It was also the band's sole chart entry onto any American chart. It's a head-nodder and foot-tapper for sure. Rick's Motown rhythm ensures this. Ray Davies said it was one of his favourite Jam songs - he especially liked the sound of the snare drum. The snare is at its most obvious when the song reaches the part about the steam train echoing down the track. Here Rick delivers a drum roll that he intended to represent the sound of that track. It does that!

'A Town Called Malice' was featured prominently in the 1985 comedy film National Lampoon's *European Vacation*, provided the soundtrack for a key scene in the 2000 drama *Billy Elliot*, and was the opening track to the 2005 film *The Matador*. It is also on the soundtrack to *FIFA Football 2004*, as well as

being featured in the video game *Rock Band*. The song also featured at the beginning of episode 3.5 of the popular 2006 British TV show *Ashes to Ashes*.

Also, where Chelsea FC walk out to Harry J. Allstars' 'Liquidator' and Charlton FC to The Clash's 'London Calling' before kick-off, Millwall FC play 'A Town Called Malice'.

Rick Buckler:

The promotional video for 'A Town Called Malice' was shot in AIR Studios. AIR which stood for Associate Independent Recordings was a company that George Martin founded in the mid-Sixties. He opened the AIR studios in 1970 on the fourth floor of 214 Oxford Street, London.

Just like we had done for the video for 'That's Entertainment', we wanted something simple and at the time of 'Malice' we were using AIR studios to record *The Gift*. There were several rooms in the studios, so we just cleared some space in one of the larger rooms and used that. The video had a simplicity to it that we liked. Like 'That's Entertainment' it was quite dark. The crew only used a few spotlights, which they pointed in the direction of Paul, Bruce and myself, and for the video we also included Keith Thomas and Steve Nichol. The coat stand featured in the video was just something that belonged to the studio. I don't know whose scarf it was that hung from it.

In the video Paul chose to not hold his guitar. Instead he grabbed the microphone and sung into that. The finger clicking worked well though, as did the slogans that someone wrote onto pieces of card. There was two 'anti complaney league baby!' cards, where whoever wrote them missed out the second C in what should have aid complacency. The second one said 'If we ain't getting through to you - you obviously ain't listening'. They just added something a little different to the video.

For 'Town Called Malice' I used a drum pattern that is very familiar to most people. It has that Motown-type feel that makes people want to dance. I used a tambourine too, which kind of enhances that snare. I heard that Ray Davies is particularly fond of that snare sound.

Across The Jam's recordings there's quite a frequent use of percussion. I would be playing it all, tambourines, cow bells, congas. I remember that Vic Smith was always very keen on getting percussive instruments onto songs.

9. PRETTY GREEN (PAUL WELLER)

Recorded June 1980, Townhouse Studios, London
Available on: *Sound Affects; Direction Reaction Creation; The Very Best Of The Jam: About The Young Idea.*

Five bass notes, repeated three times, introduce 'Pretty Green' as the opening track on The Jam's fifth studio album *Sound Affects*. Rick then joins in with a single snare drum strike and this is quickly followed by the hi-hats, which sound high in the mix due to the amount of reverb being used (and often used throughout the entirety of *Sound Affects*). The snare sounds sharp and clear, which contrast with the bass sound.

The Beatles had a song about the 'filthy lucre' called 'Money'. The Jam's song on the same topic was 'Pretty Green'. This was Paul referring to the green pound notes that were in circulation in 1980.

It was only by the time of 'Pretty Green' that Paul, Bruce and Rick were starting to see any real money. Up until this point so much

of their record label advances and what they had earned had been absorbed in other ways - like tours. But now they had money and Paul, being the main songwriter and therefore getting more money, also felt uncomfortable with this new-found wealth. He needed to make an adjustment and so did Bruce and Rick. After all this was the career they had chosen and like most bands they had no idea how long their careers might last.

Paul said that when he was touring North America he was watching TV and the host on a game show said "and here's a big barrel of pretty green for you, folks!" Paul liked the pretty green bit and used it for his song.

Throughout the verse there is minimal guitar and there is a slide down the strings that create a sort of cat being strangled sound. It's only when the chorus arrives that the guitar starts to drive the song along, whilst Paul's lyrics remind the listener that they can't do anything unless they have money in their pockets. True then and true today!

'Pretty Green' was a contender as the follow up single to 'Going Underground' but 'Start!' was decided upon instead. It's hard to imagine whether 'Pretty Green' would have reached No 1 - it's easier to understand how 'Start!' did.

The band drop down for the middle-eight, Rick keeping the momentum going using just his hi-hats and Bruce provides the backing vocals by repeating 'pretty green'. There's phase on Paul's guitar, but it's not overpowering and it reminds us that *Sound Affects* was the album where they experimented most with sounds and effects. 'Pretty Green' ends pretty much as it started with just Bruce's bass and Rick's hi-hats.

In 2009 Liam Gallagher launched his

THE JAM

6

clothing label Pretty Green. He was proud to name his clothing label after one of his heroes songs. In 2011 Liam collaborated with Paul on an autumn and winter range that drew its inspiration from Sixties style coats and knitwear.

> *"....it became a bit of a trend for fans to bring green pound notes to concerts. They'd then ask us to sign them"*

Rick Buckler:

I liked 'Pretty Green' as a track. It could have ended up as the single instead of 'Start!'. It's hard to say whether it would have got to No 1 though. But my biggest memories of 'Pretty Green' are about being on tour in Japan. It was soon after *Sound Affects* came out that we went to play some concerts there.

There was a guy called Alan Wick who was our out-front sound engineer at the time, and who for some reason was due to be leaving us to go and do something else. But whilst we were in Japan he bought Paul, Bruce and myself a Walkman each. Walkmans were a new invention at the time. They were amazing really. I mean a portable device that you could insert a cassette into, plug some earphones and listen to music!

They were top of the range too - really pukka! Those Walkmans became a favourite device to listen to the mixes of our songs on, and for some reason 'Pretty Green' was one song that I remember listening to a lot.

Another thing that started to happen once *Sound Affects* was released and people got to hear 'Pretty Green' was that it became a bit of a trend for fans to bring green pound notes to concerts. They'd then ask us to sign them. So we had this period where we would be signing singles, albums, posters and pound notes. When The Jam exhibition, *About The Young Idea*, was happening Nicky Weller had Paul, Bruce and myself sign a bunch of pound notes. We had to do it twice actually because the first batch got lost somewhere.

'Pretty Green' wasn't a term that Paul thought up. He picked it up whilst we were on tour in North America. I think it was from some game show they had on TV at the time and a reference to their green dollar. But it seemed to fit with the English onepound note too, so it found itself into a Jam record.

It was around the time of *Sound Affects* that the band first started to catch up financially. Up until this point we had been investing our money in buying equipment, spending time touring and in the studio. The way we started to realise we were doing well financially was the fact that the hotels that we stayed in got better and the transport got better, but as far as money in the pocket went, this didn't really seem to improve that much. But every now and again we'd have a little dish up of cash.

Paul was in a better place financially because he was the main songwriter so he was getting the publishing money, but I don't think Bruce and I felt any wealthier than we had setting off in 1977. I think Paul did feel uncomfortable with the way things were set up. But the way bands work is that they have members who are in a sense the secondclass citizens. In The Who, for example, Pete Townshend earned most of the money and Moon spent his share pretty much as he got it. He was always walking into Trinifold's offices asking for more money because he'd spent all of his.

6

The Jam had a partnership arrangement. It was split four ways to include me, Paul, Bruce and John Weller. When we needed some money, we dipped into that pot. There was a time when I needed a car but didn't have the money to buy one. I had been driving around in some second hand taxi. It was a Volvo 144 that I had bought off this guy who sometimes used to drive us around. I think I gave him a hundred pounds for it. It wasn't a great car. It was out of date and out of fashion and it broke down as I was leaving the studios where we'd been filming for *Top of the Pops*. I had only got about hundred yards down the road and it just stopped working. Just before it had broken down there'd been this horrible noise and when I got out of the car, there was oil and nuts and bolts everywhere.

I had to leg it back to the BBC studios in White City to catch John. I had absolutely no money on me whatsoever and I certainly didn't have anything as flash as a credit card back then. I wouldn't have even been able to get on a train and get home. Luckily I just caught him as he was about to leave, so I was at least able to get a lift home.

After this a decision was made that we'd all be given two grand each to spend as we liked. I used my money to buy a car. Even back in 1978 two grand didn't buy you much. I know that people think that rock stars and bands that are selling loads of records and touring the world are making lots of money, but this wasn't necessarily the case. The other thing was that all the time you were on the road - you're travelling and food and drink and accommodation is all being paid for, so you don't really need to spend any money. And also because you're travelling around so much and often up and out of hotels early the morning after a show and on the bus heading to the next town, you don't really have time to spend any

money anyway.

By the time of 'Pretty Green', The Jam had very much been caught up in this cycle. But we were happy with this situation because all we wanted to do was play decent venues and be able to go into decent recording studios to record our music.

Having more money in the band pot also meant that we got our own rooms. For the first couple of years we'd all had to share. I had always shared with Bruce, John with Kenny and Paul often with Gill, because she'd often travel with us. When I started seeing Lesley (my wife), she sometimes came along and so did Pat, who was Bruce's' girlfriend.

On one occasion we all went to Jersey and this included my mum and dad, Bruce's mum and dad and John brought his wife Ann along. We all stayed in the same luxury hotel for a couple of nights and it was really nice. Whilst we were there we did a show too. But this sort of thing was rare because we were always so busy all of the time.

The other thing that I liked about 'Pretty Green' was that the foundations of the song are based in the drum and bass parts. Bruce and I really drive that song along. It's Bruce's bass line that sets the song off. Bruce and I worked well on this track and I don't recall recording many different versions of it. We sort of fell into step pretty well with 'Pretty Green' and did what the song needed. It was a good song to open up *Sound Affects* with.

10. CARNATION (PAUL WELLER)

Recorded January 1982, AIR Studios, London.
Available on *The Gift; Direction Reaction Creation; The Very Best Of The Jam: About The Young Idea.*

6

'Carnation' is one of those Jam songs that rests easily on the ear, it's also one of those songs where the lyrics draw the listener in and leaves them feeling curious and asking "what is it that Paul has written about?" Rick's snare drum roll introduces the song and Paul's vocals. This is a Jam song based on the basic pop structure of verse, chorus, verse, chorus and then the middle eight. It's in the middle eight where Rick keeps the song's four/four beat going by dropping down to just a ride cymbal and a bass drum. The organ that has been present since the beginning of the song is joined by an electric piano, both of which are high in the mix. And then it's back into the song and contemplations about 'greed and fear'.

The song casually strolls towards its end with the full band in play. There's no need to rush and there's Paul providing a bunch of "la, la, las" and then the flowers petals close. In 1999 Simon Halfon (a designer who had worked on Jam album sleeves) organised a compilation album called *Fire And Skill: The Songs Of The Jam*. Various artists covered Jam songs including 'The Butterfly Collector' by Garbage, 'To Be Someone' by Noel Gallagher, 'English Rose' by Everything But The Girl and 'Start!' by The Beastie Boys.

There was also a double A-side single released - 'Going Underground' by Bill Janovitz and 'Carnation' by Liam Gallagher and Steve Cradock (and also on the recording were Damon Minchella and Steve White, with Paul Weller playing the keyboards).

A video was made of the band performing 'Carnation', with Liam dressed in a thick black coat and Lennon-esque hat and shades and Paul with his fingers taped up (he'd broken a couple). Simon Halfon filmed the performance and photographer Tony Briggs was also there on the day to capture the 'Mod super group' together. Also, Noel Gallagher is present in the video, even though he didn't actually play on the recording.

Rick Buckler:

This is not one of my favourite Jam songs but it was a good song to do that demonstrated how diverse The Jam could be. I think the song adds more colour to our repertoire. An important thing about the way that Paul, Bruce and I worked was that we never really said no or dismissed anything. We were always open to trying new things and giving something a go. Not everything worked out and there are songs that we made demos of with titles like 'Simon', 'Best Of Both Worlds,' 'Worlds Apart' and 'Sweeney', which have since found their way into the hands of some Jam fans. Some of the songs like 'Best Of Both Worlds' and 'Worlds Apart' turned up on *The Jam: Direction Reaction Creation* box set. Some songs just weren't considered good enough for being released to the public.

What a song like 'Carnation' did was to give The Jam much more breadth. And this is heard throughout *The Gift* and the end months of The Jam. The way we were working also contributed to this. We recorded 'Carnation' in AIR Studios, which at the time was a new studio for us to be working in.

I liked working at AIR Studios because there was something nice about being in the centre of London. The studios were located right by Oxford Street, so there was a lot of activity going on outside and inside too, because whilst working in AIR Studios we met both Paul McCartney and George Martin. Most people didn't even know that the studios were there. There was only a small door to enter the studio and you had to know what you were looking for. It wasn't like Townhouse Studios that had its name on the building. AIR was also a nice environment to work in. The studios were located right on the top floor of the building.

We also brought Pete Wilson back into the studio to work with us. He was a really good engineer and by the time of recording *The Gift* I think that we felt that we had a pretty good idea of how things worked in the studio and that we could produce the album by ourselves. We had a good idea of what we wanted to capture sound wise and we thought we could achieve this without the help or input of Vic Smith.

In some ways I think we approached recording *The Gift* with the same attitude that we had for *In The City*. Only back in the days of *In The City* we didn't know our way around a mixing desk and a studio so we needed producers and engineers. With *The Gift* we didn't have all of the same needs but we had the attitude that we felt would see us through.

On *The Gift* we did benefit from Pete's engineering ideas and experience. For example it wouldn't have occurred to us to mic up the snare drum at the shell of the drum. Usually the snare mic gets positioned on the top skin or underneath.

In 1999 someone did a cover of 'Carnation'. It was okay. It was released as a single backed with 'Going Underground' by Buffalo Tom. But like The Jam's attitude regards covering other people's songs, in that they need to be as good as or better, I took that view with the cover of 'Carnation' and any other Jam song that got covered. But also Paul, Bruce and myself are probably the worst people to ask when it comes to what do we think about our songs getting covered.

On the same album that the cover of 'Carnation' came out on the Beastie Boys did a cover of 'Start!' and when I heard that

they had done a cover of it I thought "right, this is going to sound good, this is going to have meat on it", but it turned out to be anything but, which I was disappointed about. Maybe they just missed the point of that aggressiveness that The Jam had.

11. DAVID WATTS (RAY DAVIES)
Recorded July 1978, Eden Studios, London. Released 18 August 1978. Available on *All Mod Cons, Snap, Direction Reaction Creation* and *The Very Best Of The Jam: About The Young Idea.*

'Fa, fa, fa, fa, fa, fa,fa, fa'.

'David Watts' was released in August 1978 as a double A-side with "A' 'Bomb In Wardour Street'. It reached No 25 on the UK singles chart.

Ray Davies wrote the song in 1967 and it was included on their *Something Else By The Kinks* album of the same year. It was also the American and European B-side to 'Autumn Almanac'. Davies said he wrote the lyrics about a gay and fancy-free man.

6

Paul Weller told *Mojo* magazine June 2008 that it was his idea to cover 'David Watts'. He explained: "The first time I went to America (October 1977), you could buy all these old Kinks records that you couldn't get here at the time. As a kid I'd only heard the singles. So it was our choice to record the track, with ''A' Bomb' on the B-side. We wanted 'Billy Hunt' as the single, but the record company turned it down. But 'David Watts' worked for us - it put us back on the map."

The real David Watts was a concert promoter from Rutland in the English Midlands. The Kinks band members were invited back to his house for a drink one night after a concert. Ray Davies recalled to Q magazine in a 2016 interview:

"My brother, Dave, was in a flamboyant mood and I could see David Watts had a crush on him. So I tried to do a deal and persuade Dave to marry David Watts cos he was connected with Rutland brewery. See, that's how stupid my brain was. I thought if I can get Dave fixed up with this Watts guy I'll be set up for life and get all the ale I want".

But the song's about complete envy. It was based on the head boy at my school. He was captain of the team, all those things, but I can't tell you his real name as I only spoke to him a few months ago."

Bruce Foxton took on the lead vocal duties on 'David Watts' with Paul joining in on the bridge. The lyrics are about a dull and simple lad observing a character called David. He wants to be like him, he wants (wishes) to be taking and passing all of his exams and be able to fight and lead the school team to victory - just like David.

The Jam made 'David Watts' their own. They lifted the tempo, giving it an edge that The Kinks hadn't - but then The Kinks hadn't been schooled in punk.

Paul met Davies in 1978. At the time Paul was wearing a pin badge that said 'who the fuck is David Watts?' In 2012 Paul and Davies performed one of Paul's all-time favourite songs, 'Waterloo Sunset', on the stage of the Royal Albert Hall.

The song gallops forward ending with some wild piano work alongside the fa, fa, fa's.

Rick Buckler:
I think for us we always told ourselves that if we couldn't do a better version of the original song then it wasn't worth trying. I always felt this was a good position to take. The Jam would never have released 'David Watts' if we didn't feel, not only that we'd done it justice and as good as the original, at the very least. For me, The Kinks' version of 'David Watts' never really stood out as one of the great Kinks songs. But it was a good track for The Jam to do and we played it in a particular way that gave it some edge and punch that the original version lacked. We made 'David Watts' a Jam song and we felt it was strong enough to release as a single and in November 1978 it got to No 6 on the UK chart. It introduced some Jam fans to a Kinks song that they hadn't perhaps heard before - or really taken any notice of.

12. DOWN IN THE TUBE STATION AT MIDNIGHT (PAUL WELLER)
Recorded August 1978, RAK Studios, London. Released 13 October 1978
Available on All Mod Cons, Snap, Direction Reaction Creation and The Very Best Of The Jam: About The Young Idea.

6

This is another of The Jam fans' favourite songs. From the off, the listener's attention is captured as the sounds of the London Underground help to usher in what becomes a story told in the first person narrative from a man, who is simply making his way home. Paul said his intention was always to write a short story and one which could fit into a three-minute song (it ended up closer to four).

Following the sounds of a train and a screaming child's voice, Rick enters using just his hi-hats to create an interesting affect, which along with Paul's guitar and one of Bruce's finest bass riffs helps to produce what can only be described as a brilliant song. The Jam had never written or recorded anything close to 'Tube Station' and if it wasn't for Vic Coppersmith-Heaven's intervention it may never have been recorded at all. It was only because Vic reclaimed Paul's lyrics from the wastepaper basket in RAK Studios that the song was pursued. Up until that point something was amiss, but Vic encouraged further attention and the song did indeed get recorded.

The main character in this short story shares his observations of people "boarding trains" and making their journeys "home to their loved ones". The lyrics paint a familiar picture of the Underground late at night. It's quieter at midnight, a different place to how it had been in rush hour. The steps are littered with "toffee wrappers" and "morning papers" with articles of "madman on the rampage" (a topic Paul would later re-visit in his song 'Savages').

And then the yobs appear. The character describes how they approach him demanding money. He replies that he has "a little" and "a takeaway curry" and that he intends to share it with his wife who is waiting at home.

The story next takes a nasty turn as the attack comes. First a "fist" then a "kick". The man can smell their beer breath. The lyrics mention Wormwood Scrubs. Affectionately known as "the Scrubs", this is a Victorian built prison with an impressive, if not daunting, front entrance. Located in west London, previous inmates include Keith Richards of The Rolling Stones and Pete Doherty of The Libertines. There's mention too of "right wing meetings" and "the smell of brown leather" which suggest the righter wing element of the skinhead movement, which in 1978 was very active.

Anyone who went to a football match in those days would have been familiar with gangs of right wing supporters and skinheads handing out right wing leaflets to fans as they made their way into their various football grounds.

Apart from the assault and the yobs committing it, perhaps the most worrying part of the story is when the character talks about how his house keys have been stolen by the yobs and how he fears for the safety of his wife who, when she hears the door being unlocked at home, will naturally think it's her husband returning home. The rest is left to the imagination of the listener, who alongside considering the lyrics is enjoying an amazing song.

'Down in the Tube Station at Midnight' was issued as a single on 13 October 1978 and reached No. 15. The singles front sleeve included a photograph of The Jam down in Bond Street tube station. In 2015 Rick Buckler returned to be photographed there again and that photo was used in promotional posters when he toured a series of Q&A events he was doing to support his autobiography *That's Entertainment: My Life In The Jam*.

6

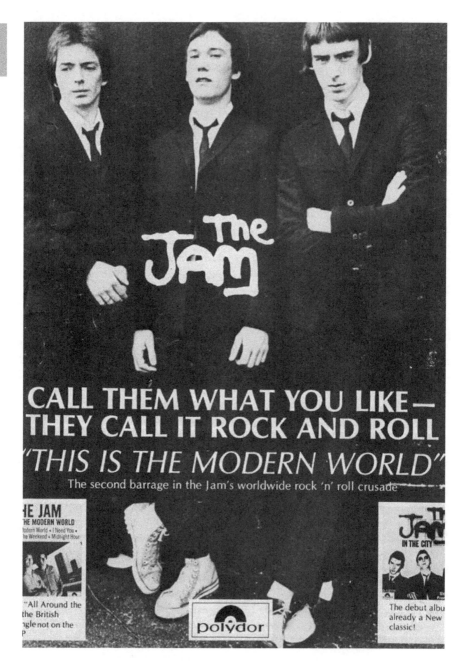

"Paul would hang back and refuse to re-join the song. He'd slip off to the side of the stage and light a fag or have a drink and he'd leave me to it. I had to just play until he was ready to dive back in."

Rick Buckler

Rick Buckler:

Down in the Tube Station At Midnight' was the first Jam song that we recorded in parts. We knitted together three sections to come up with the song, which at the time was a whole new experience for us.

The song may not have even happened if it hadn't have been for Vic Smith. I remember that in the studio we were approaching the recording of the song like we approached all our other songs. But we were working with these sections and changes and it just wasn't happening. We tried and tried but we just couldn't make it happen.

Many Jam songs got laid down in one or two takes. Usually that's all it took. I mean by the time we came to record a new track we had rehearsed it up enough to know what we were doing. But 'Down in the Tube Station at Midnight' wasn't coming together and we were all getting more and more frustrated with it. It reached a point where I think we just thought we'd bin it and move on.

The lyrics weren't coming together either and the story goes that in frustration Paul threw what he had into the bin. I don't

actually recall seeing him do that, but I believe Vic did and it was Vic who fished them out of the bin and read them. He liked what he read and saw the potential and encouraged Paul to persevere - which he did and so did we with trying to finish the song. There had been a moment of Paul saying "it's not working, I'm not liking it" and "let's just move on". But due to Vic's intervention we did push on with the song. It was also Vic who presented us with the idea of breaking the song down and recording it part by part. This was a whole new concept for us. We'd never tried recording any song in that way before.

So, agreeing to try Vic's suggestion, we did record the song in three sections and Vic stitched them together. We had to get over our own hang ups about using Vic's technique to record. We didn't like the idea of what we thought was manufacturing a song. Paul, Bruce and myself held the view that we were predominately a live band and we liked the honesty of being able to go out and play a song live that we'd recorded in the studio.

Once we played and recorded those three parts of the song and played them back to ourselves in the studio, we liked what we'd done. When you listen to the track you can make out the individual three parts. It all came together just fine in the final mix and there was a kind of "oh yeah, that's how we should have approached recording the song at the start".

After securing a recorded version of 'Down in the Tube Station at Midnight' it was then just a matter of being able to play it live, and this we did. This was a Jam song that was written and recorded in the studio and for The Jam this was unusual.

When I played the song live I enjoyed it.

THE JAM

6

There was also that part where it was just the drums. It wasn't really a drum solo, in the sense of a Keith Moon thrash about. It was really just a means of linking sections of the song together. But live it turned into something that that happened every time and this came about because initially Paul would hang back and refuse to re-join the song. He'd slip off to the side of the stage and light a cigarette or have a drink and he'd leave me to it. I had to just play until he was ready to dive back in.

Playing it live meant that we couldn't totally recreate the recording. For instance there's a bit on the record where the music fades out, and then Vic faded it back in, so it kind of built up again. That idea worked on a song like this. My memories of it are that it also just sort of happened. I think someone, probably Vic, just faded the song out and faded it back in. I don't remember us ever working out a proper end either, so that may have been the other reason why the fading in and out bit happened too.

Another bit on the recorded version was the sounds at the beginning. I don't think we used them from a BBC sound effects album - I have a feeling Vic or someone had to go down into the tube station to make those recordings. Alongside the sound of the train there's a few other sounds going on. There's the shout "the train is coming" but I've also heard people ask me if she's shouting "the skins are coming". I suppose people associate the skins bit with some of the lyrics about boots - meaning the Dr Marten's that the skinheads wore. Dr Marten boots were a very popular boot and sort of had that menacing element that some skinheads, particularly in the late Seventies, went for. And in the late Seventies it was very tribal. You had Mods, skinheads, Rude Boys, soul boys and so on

and they'd all be rivals and it wasn't uncommon to see the various tribes having a punch up. There'd be some trouble from such tribal groups at Jam gigs.

When we played live we'd also use that clip of the train station noises from the song and have it played through the PA as the introduction before we launched into the song. We'd let it build and then I would count us in and off we'd go. Although there was an occasion when the sound guys lost the tape, so someone suggested getting a copy of *All Mod Cons* out and putting that on instead. It didn't work out though because before the sound guys had time to stop the tape the actual song started. So there we were on stage listening to the beginning of 'Down in the Tube Station at Midnight'along with a few thousand Jam fans. It made us look stupid!

The hi-hat rhythm I used on the track was inspired from something I had heard Deep Purple drummer Ian Paice play on 'Smoke On Water'. The sound of the hi-hats was meant to represent the train noise rattling along the track. I wanted to try and capture this sound but avoid using a snare drum to do it. So I used the hi-hats and it seemed to work okay.

Thankfully Vic had stepped in by pulling those lyrics out of the bin and encouraging us to stick with the song: otherwise the track may have never happened. I'm pleased with the song. I think it's a strong song and it always seemed to go down well live. It was considered a good enough song to be released as a single in October 1978 and included as a live version on the B-side to 'That's Entertainment'.

We had a photograph taken of us down the Bond Street tube station in London. That was then used as the cover sleeve for the single. I don't remember who came up with the idea, but it was possibly Polydor's Bill Smith, after all he'd be the one who'd had to come up with something for the sleeve design. I think we went to Bond Street because it was the closest tube station to Polydor's offices in Stratford Place. My recollections of doing it was meeting up with the others, heading off to Bond Street, choosing the spot to be photographed at and waiting for the next train to come along.

I also remember getting some unwanted interest from the London Underground staff. They were suspicious about what we were doing and didn't like us being there. When I was doing a bunch of Q&A events around the time that my autobiography (*That's Entertainment: My Life In The Jam*) came out, I had a guy called Tony Briggs make a twenty minute video that was shown as part of the event. Tony was actually a photographer and had worked with Ocean Colour Scene throughout the Nineties. He'd also made some of the band's videos after Steve Cradock approached him.

I spent a day walking around Jam related locations with Tony. He filmed me outside places like the 100 Club and Ronnie Scott's and the spot where The Jam had set up and played one Saturday in Soho Market. We also went down to Bond Street Station and Tony filmed and photographed me there and the same thing happened again - a London Underground worker spotted us and came over to us to see what was going on.

At The Jam *About The Young Idea* exhibition in Liverpool, the team there built a tube station tunnel to represent the song. As people attended the exhibition they had to walk along it before entering the first room. They had covered the tunnel in posters of The Jam and it looked really good and worked well. Jam fans seemed to enjoy having their photographs taken inside.

13. THICK AS THIEVES (PAUL WELLER)

Recorded September 1979, Townhouse Studios, London.

Available on *Setting Sons, Snap, Direction Reaction Creation* and *The Very Best Of The Jam: About The Young Idea.*

'Thick As Thieves' is a phrase used to describe the closeness between friends - it's an endearing term. The song 'Thick As Thieves' is full of references about such friendliness. Paul sings about the time when times were not tough. Those times appear to be in the distant past - a past that is being missed. It's a song about growing up and having to accept that personal situations have changed - and maybe not for the best, but despite this what made those friendships so good, so right, so important, was that whatever the situation, those friends will, must, stick together for all time. The Jam provided a bond for many kids at the time. Forty years later, for many those bonds still exist and they still enjoy a night in a pub together, remembering and singing along, word for word, with a song like 'Thick As Thieves'.

Although some concluded that 'Thick As Thieves' was about the relationship between Paul, Rick and Bruce, it wasn't. In Paul's mind he was just writing about three friends who grow up and go in their different directions. In 2007 Paul revealed that the song was actually about Dave Waller, Steve Brookes and himself.

'Thick As Thieves' is a thumper of a song. Rick's drum roll (a favourite for an air-drummer) launches the song. Bruce provides that thumping bass. Paul walks the listener through the story whilst holding up the song with a great riff.

This song is timeless. It'll be an eternal

THE JAM

favourite amongst The Jam army and that's an army that will stick together for all time.

Rick Buckler:

I liked the use of the drums to introduce 'Thick As Thieves'. It's nice and concise and helps the song burst into life. We recorded the song in Townhouse Studios as part of the *Setting Sons* sessions. I look back on those sessions and recording those songs and think it was the most solid we had been as a recording band.

I think in some ways a song like 'Thick As Thieves' represents the fruition of what we were trying to do as a band. At the time of recording the song we were so at ease with who and what we were as a band that the songs just seemed to come together.

I think 'Thick As Thieves' also reflected the confidence that the band were feeling at the time. It was 1979 and we'd had three albums out, toured extensively and we had a good size fan base. The Jam felt established and by the time *Setting Sons* came out we were. Paul was also being regarded as an established musician too. It was during the *Setting Sons* sessions that Peter Gabriel approached him and asked him to play some of his 'intense style' guitar on a track called 'And Through The Wire' that he was recording for his next album. Paul accepted the invitation.

'Thick As Thieves' could have been a potential single. I don't recall any discussions about it being so, but it had all the components and qualities that a single requires. It certainly wasn't a song that just padded an album out. But then I don't believe we recorded any songs that were only meant to pad an album out.

I think 'Thick As Thieves' has gone down as a favourite amongst Jam fans. I think they can see themselves in the song. The Jam were a good band for being able to write songs that our fans could relate to.

14. SATURDAY'S KIDS (PAUL WELLER)

Recorded August 1979, Townhouse Studios, London.

Available on *Setting Sons, Direction Reaction Creation* and *The Very Best Of The Jam: About The Young Idea*.

Without doubt 'Saturday's Kids' is one of The Jam's most anthemic tunes, helped by the guitar riff, the cow bell strikes and the 'la, la, la' introduction. It's a song that a generation of kids can relate to. Images spring to mind of carefree Saturdays. This is for the younger kids in their "V-neck shirts" and "baggy trousers". For the older ones, the song paints a picture of work in Tesco and Woolworths and fumbles with the opposite sex in the back of the car - fun days indeed! It's all too familiar for the "everyday person" and, again, Paul captures the feel and presence of the working classes - ordinary people, ordinary lives, but no suggestion of unhappiness in those "council houses".

Maybe when Paul wrote the lyrics he harped back to the Saturdays when he and his Woking mates hung out in the locals like the Birch and Pines. He actually wrote the lyrics for 'Saturday's Kids' in a caravan in Selsey Bill whilst on a few days' break. As he scribbled down his thoughts, he peered at the rain outside.

But there is another side to their Saturday lives that Paul introduces into the lyrics and the point is made with the aggressive statement that there is a system that must be conformed to but it's okay to "hate the system", and Paul never shied away from expressing his feelings on the system.

Rick Buckler:
'Saturday's Kids' was another song that I used cowbell on. It was the same cowbell that was used on "'A' Bomb in Wardour Street'. It just seemed to work and stand out. I think the song touched Jam fans in a similar way to how 'Thick As Thieves' had - they could relate to it and they could see themselves portrayed in the lyrics.

I think there's something in the song that is very familiar to the fans. The song sort of mirrors aspects of their own childhoods with sights and sounds and smells that kids stumble across when they are just being kids and hanging around on dumps and street corners.

'Saturday's Kids' has a feel to me that conjures up being juvenile. It's a song that captures that juvenile view of the world and it's a very different view to the person who has grown up, left school, is out working, paying bills, driving a car, getting married and having kids and so on. There's a kind of innocence about 'Saturday's Kids' and I think The Jam fans appreciated this element. I also think that 'Saturday's Kids' represented a sort of optimism too and I think Jam fans sensed that.

I always felt that the track had a raw edge and raw sound about it. It's not a sophisticated song at all and I think this reflected the meaning contained in the lyrics. I think the overall sound of all the songs on *Setting Sons* was that they sounded very open.

Just like the fans I could also see my younger days mirrored in the song. I knew kids that wore baggy trousers and V-neck jumpers. I certainly remember having clothes that didn't quite fit. I had to make do with certain clothes. I was still too young to be going out and buying my own clothes, so this meant that I had to make do with whatever my parents bought for me.

My friends and I would hang around street

6

corners in Woking and loiter outside shops. When Paul, Bruce and myself were growing up in Woking, there wasn't a great deal to do on Saturdays. Like every other kid who lived in the town we had to find ways to keep ourselves entertained.

There was less of everything back in the days when I was growing up too. Less TV channels, less choice of shops, less choice for everything. This meant that people had more in common. More shared experiences. My friends and I had the same toys and we talked about the same shows that we'd watched on the television because there wasn't a great deal of variety. Things seemed a lot more simple back then and people worked with what they had. I think 'Saturday's Kids' captured how things were for people.

15. PRECIOUS (PAUL WELLER)

Recorded November 1981, AIR Studios, London

Available on *The Gift, Direction Reaction Creation* and *The Very Best Of The Jam: About The Young Idea.*

Rick says that this is his least favourite Jam song. He explains that 'Precious' is a style of music that just wasn't his bag - pig bag, even the listener can hear the similarity between the bassline in 'Precious' and the British dance-punk band Pigbag 1981 track 'Papa's Got A Brand New Pigbag' (the title is a play on The James Brown song 'Papa's Got a Brand New Bag').

Before 'Precious' was issued as the double A-side with 'Town Called Malice' Rick took a tape recording of the song to a disco. He handed the DJ the tape and

asked him to play it. He didn't tell the DJ what the song was or who it was by. The DJ did as he was asked and played the song and even though the crowd in the disco hadn't heard the song before or had any idea who they were listening to they got up and danced, as Rick describes it "as just another run-of-the-mill disco song".

It wasn't just Rick that struggled to fully embrace 'Precious' - many loyal Jam fans also questioned what was going on. Of all The Jam's songs, this is their 'marmite' song - you either love it or hate it.

Musically though, 'Precious' is a good song. Paul takes charge of his wah-wah pedal skillfully. It's not a sound that has featured a great deal in Paul's career, either at the time of The Jam or his Style Council or solo years - but it works perfectly on 'Precious'. And there is no trying to hide the fact that 'Precious' is a song to dance to. It is funky, it does have a soulfully disco feel and the beat, brass and percussion all gel well together. In its own way 'Precious' is brilliant.

As a double A-side single along with 'Town Called Malice', it reached No 1 in the UK singles chart, giving The Jam their third UK chart topper.

Rick Buckler:
Another example of a song that we tried out and worked on was 'Precious'. It wasn't really a Jam song, in the sense that it was so different from anything that we'd previously done. But we did it and it ended up as a track three on *The Gift*. It got mixed reviews and some Jam fans struggled with it but it is a song played by Paul Weller, Bruce Foxton and Rick Buckler.

16. RUNNING ON THE SPOT (PAUL WELLER)

Recorded January 1982 at AIR Studios, London

Available on *The Gift* and *Direction Reaction Creation.*

'Running On The Spot' was the sixth track on *The Gift* album. This is a song with Paul writing about the sense of disappointment he had at that time. He'd had high hopes for his generation, the optimism he'd felt for 'life and love' just wasn't bearing its fruit - if anything, what he observed was hordes of people that had become 'emotionally crippled'.

'Running On The Spot' begins with Paul counting the band in. It's another stomper of a song and one that when Paul started his solo career and included it some of his performances it always went down a storm.

Paul, Rick and Bruce sound tight and sharp: all feeding off each other's styles. The bridge includes Rick holding the song together with a nifty snare drum roll, whilst Paul and Bruce sing their 'ba ba bas' over the top and this builds before launching into the chorus.

The song continues until ending with the guitars, bass and drums fading out, leaving just the vocals and 'ba ba bas' overlapping each other before they fade and the last words the listener hears is Paul saying "running on the spot".

It's also easy to see the connection between the song's title and the photo, taken by Twink, on *The Gift*'s front cover.

Rick Buckler:

This track I really like. I think by the time we recorded the song we'd got to a certain stage where we felt confident when it came to recording our material. You have to remember that by the time of recording *The Gift* we'd really only been recording for a handful of years. It had only been five years since *In The City*, which in the bigger picture isn't that much time really. But then that's what bands did back then. Think about how many albums The Beatles or The Kinks recorded over five years.

The song's title then inspired the idea for *The Gift*'s front cover. It all happened on the spot really. Paul, Bruce and myself were already in AIR Studios and someone suggested that we go on to the roof of the Oxford Street building and take some photographs of us running on the spot. So that's what happened. We agreed with the idea and found ourselves being marched up some stairs to the roof. Twink was the photographer that we were using around that time. He'd been joining us on the road and had taken a lot of photographs of the band performing live.

If my memory serves me right the original idea for the album's front cover was to make it more cartoon-like. The suggestion being to take the photos then play around with the images to give them that cartoon edge. Designers had access to that kind of technology in the early Eighties. If you remember the video to that A-ha song, 'Take On Me', that's it. They messed around with the images of the band to create that cartoon/sketch type effect. It was something different and worked for the video but for some reason trying to do it with the photos of us on the roof didn't, so that idea got scrapped.

Instead the designer went with the idea of having the photos of Paul, Bruce and myself in different colours. I ended up in red, Bruce in yellow and Paul in green.

So once on the roof we were asked to run on the spot and whilst we did Twink

THE JAM

6

snapped away. I suppose this comes across on the album sleeve. Twink took lots of photos and later we all sat down and selected the ones that we wanted to use. I don't know if the other photos that didn't make the album cover have ever been made available for the public to see or not. I remember that the weather was nice on the day. That's why Paul's wearing sunglasses. I doubt that I really needed my MAl flight jacket on!

There was actually two different shoots done. This was because Bruce decided that he didn't like the trousers that he was wearing. This meant that the following day whilst we were back in AIR Studios, Bruce, with different trousers, went back up onto the roof and Twink took more photos of him. It didn't really make any difference in the end because of what the designer did with the colours.

I don't recall why 'Running On The Spot' was the track that we decided on to build the album's sleeve around. I mean it didn't connect directly with the album's title *The Gift* in any way at all. The Jam had never really wanted to use songs from our albums as the album's title every time. *Sound Affects* and *Setting Sons* were very much stand-alone titles.

I think some Jam fans attach a sense of mystery to *The Gift* album. I think some have wondered why people like Polydor's Bill Smith and producer Vic Smith weren't involved. Fans have possibly read too much into this sort of thing. I think things were just changing for the band at that time. And changes were coming, but at the time of making the album we had no idea what they'd be.

What I remember about that time, late 1981, was that we felt we wanted to shake

things up a bit. Going back to using Pete Wilson was just part of that idea. He was a good engineer and we knew we could trust him and we also felt more confident about producing the album ourselves. And we approached the recording of *The Gift* in a much more straight forward manner. We didn't fall into the trap of thinking we had to do more than the last album. *Sound Affects* had a lot of production and overdubs and percussion on it. Some of the arrangements were more complex and we didn't want to do that again.

I think we achieved our goals with *The Gift* and it sort of refreshed things for us at the time and also gave our next album a different sound to the previous ones. At least this was our point of view and it was our view that for *The Gift* we simplified things.

17. GHOSTS (PAUL WELLER)

Recorded October 1981, AIR Studios, London
Available on *The Gift, Direction Reaction Creation* and *The Very Best Of The Jam: About The Young Idea.*

'Ghosts' was included on *The Gift* album and is, as they say "short and sweet". Many years after Paul wrote 'Ghosts' he said "I was trying to call out to my generation, a rallying call in the name of inspiration and fulfillment". In some ways you can see the connection between what Paul was referring to in 'Running On The Spot' and the disappointment he felt because his generation was missing out on the fulfillment of life and love that they deserved.

6

A rim-shot strike from Rick starts the song off and sets a relaxed tempo that does indeed just shuffle along. Paul and Bruce's guitars enter as do some handclaps and then the vocals begin. Paul reflects back to the listener that they should take the time to look at themselves and see that there's more inside of them that they are not willing to show, but oh how things may be different if they did. In 'Ghosts' it's as if Paul is taking on the role of being a mirror and mirroring back to the listener who they are. Are they hiding things? Do they feel vulnerable? Are they using a ghost to disguise themselves?

The brass section work wonderfully with the backing vocals. And all the time Paul leads with his vocals, Rick holds down his hi-hat and rim-shot beat, Bruce guides the song along and the hand claps support.

Rick Buckler:
I felt that musically 'Ghosts' was like a ghost. It was a matter of how thin can we make a song so that its almost transparent. From the drums point of view there's very little in the way of kit used on the song - just hi-hats, rim shot and bass drum. Fewer drums just seemed to work and fit with the feel of the song. From the word go, the song felt completely fragile. The way Paul presented and portrayed the song called for a response from Bruce and myself that meant a less is more approach. It was a matter of how little can I get away with really and still retain that lighter, ghostly feel.

I think 'Ghosts' is one of The Jam's most atmospheric songs. Even live we

were able to recreate the song as it was meant to be. For us, as a live band, when it came to performing our songs live, we didn't change them much from how we recorded them in the studio. There were times when we had to, but most of the time the songs stayed the same.

The song literally does shuffle along. It wasn't a song that needed much dynamic, it quite happily just moved and shuffled along. Along with the occasional handclaps there's some brass that comes in later in the song. This was played by Keith Thomas and Steve Nichol, who we took on the road for the last tour as part of the live band.

I think Paul had seen Steve playing in his band and afterwards approached him about playing on some Jam songs in the studio. I think Steve then brought Keith along too. At the time it was just a matter of studio work but this then turned into inviting them to come on tour with us. The brass was then joined by Afrodiziak too and by the time we went on the road, The Jam became quite a big band.

I thought Afrodiziak were fabulous. Caron had started out in a three-piece called Brown Sugar but after this fell through she teamed up with Claudia Fontaine to form the duo that was Afrodiziak. They did session work which we heard and got our attention so we invited them to come on the road with us. Caron Wheeler later went on to join Soul II Soul, who were hugely successful in the later Eighties. In fact I still kick myself because in the last days of The Jam's last tour Caron approached me and asked if I wanted to be the drummer in a band she was forming. I declined!

THE JAM

AFRODIZIAK

Afrodiziak were a British vocal group composed of Caron Wheeler, Claudia Fontaine, and later Naomi Thompson. As a duo, Wheeler and Fontaine were best known for performing backing vocals on The Jam's final single 'Beat Surrender' in 1982 (with whom they also performed on their final tour). The duo also worked with Elvis Costello on his 1983 album *Punch the Clock*, including its single, the international hit 'Everyday I Write the Book'. After the addition of a third member, Naomi Thompson, they went on to sing for acts such as Heaven 17 and Howard Jones and performed backing vocals on the hit single 'Free Nelson Mandela', including the a cappella intro.

Caron Wheeler went on as a featured vocalist in Soul II Soul where she was the lead vocalist on the group's two biggest hits, 'Keep on Movin', and the UK No 1 and US No 4 hit 'Back to Life'.

Claudia Fontaine continued working as a backing vocalist on albums by EMF, Neneh Cherry and Hothouse Flowers, among others. She also appeared as a main vocalist with the British house music group The Beatmasters.

18. HAPPY TOGETHER (PAUL WELLER)

Recorded October 1981, AIR Studios, London

Available on *The Gift* and *Direction Reaction Creation*.

'Happy Together' is another song from *The Gift*. It's the opening track on the album which is introduced as "for all those watching in black and white – this one's in technicolour". The song begins with Paul's scream of "Babeeeeeeeeeeeeeeeeee." Bruce and Rick then fall into suit using just hi-hat and bass and the song is out of the traps and off, charging forward with vigour and vibrancy.

Rick holds down that punked - up Motown beat that he does so well and Bruce backs him up. A tambourine helps the rhythm dance along.

The fact that some Jam fans interpreted Paul's lyrics being about his relationship with Bruce and Rick was far from the truth. This is not the case, even though The Jam would be splitting up soon after the release of *The Gift*.

'Happy Together' is soulful - The Jam's way of being soulful - and it certainly set the tone for the rest of *The Gift* album.

The original release of *The Gift* was on 12" vinyl, and initial copies came with a paper bag stating 'The Jam... A Gift'. These copies are increasingly difficult to find, especially in good condition. Other issues included the regular vinyl issue, the Japanese vinyl issue (with a bonus lyric book), the CD issue, the re-mastered issue, and a recently issued Japanese version in a mini-LP style sleeve.

Rick Buckler:

'Happy Together' from *The Gift* is a song where people have liked to read something into the lyrics or the song and relate it to Paul, Bruce and I. However, this is not how I relate to the song. If it does have anything to do with relationships it probably has more to do with Paul's personal relationships outside of The Jam.

As a song it pounds away. I think it's an example of a Jam song that relies on the musicality of the song rather than the lyrics. There's energy and vibrancy and it shows where the band was at the time of recording it.

'Happy Together' and 'Running On The Spot' sit nicely together on the album. They have a similar feel. I think they may have even been recorded in the same session whilst we were in AIR Studios. There's a feel that runs throughout *The Gift* which does represent where we were at that moment.

I'm especially fond of that period in The Jam's recording history. When I hear the songs on *The Gift* I feel that there's a sort of relentlessness about them. Each song has something about it in the way that it moves along in a relentless fashion. It's an album that is consistent in that way and I think this marks it out as being different to our previous albums.

For me, the songs on *The Gift* have less stops and starts. This is what I'm getting at. I think by the time we were recording *The Gift* we had mastered that ability of being able to keep the momentum of a song going. We had done songs like that and 'Thick As Thieves' comes to mind.

The album's title *The Gift* came after the song. It wasn't the other way round. You have to remember that when we were recording *The Gift* we didn't know it was going to be

our final album together. We had started to record the songs in late 1981 and it would be another year before The Jam played their last concert. The understanding that we had been recording our final album didn't hit us until the summer. It was only after Paul told us that he wanted to leave the band that we realised *The Gift* was to be our last. So as far as the recording of the songs on *The Gift* they had all been written and played as a band that was still just doing their jobs as per usual.

When I went back to listen to some Jam songs the actual song 'The Gift' came across as being really strong and I felt it was a shame that as a band we never got the opportunity to perform it live on more occasions.

But I think 'The Gift' is a great song and the organ part worked really well on it. On the recording Pete Wilson played the organ but when we went on the road we used a different musician. By the time we went on tour the band had expanded. We had a brass section and backing vocalists in Afrodiziak. The Jam hadn't toured with a band as large as that. It was new to us and at times it felt like we had a bit of an entourage and being on the road like this felt busy, not quite circus-like, but certainly at times more hectic. For years The Jam had just been Paul, Bruce and me - it was us and a few others on the coach. Then there were more people on the coach and this changed the dynamic, but I don't mean in a negative way, just a different way.

I actually really enjoyed The Jam's final tour. The Trans-Global Express Tour was one of my favourite tours even though I knew it was to be the band's last. The band were playing really well, we were playing some great songs and in the back of Bruce and my minds we were thinking - hoping - that Paul might change his mind. We had a great album out, all the shows were selling out, the fans

THE JAM

were distraught regards the news of the band splitting up, we'd had another No 1 hit with 'Town Called Malice' and The Gift gave us our first UK No 1 album. There really were a lot of positives. Everything was going really well and it was like "Paul, what the fuck do you think you're doing?"

Over the years The Jam's albums had got better, our live performances had got better, everything had got progressively better. It never felt like we'd reached the zenith of what we had been doing. I hold the opinion that we could have gone on and done more and tried other things too. If Paul felt we were at risk of finding ourselves on a downhill slope, I don't believe we were anywhere close to that point. But Paul had made up his mind and so we played our last tour and we never got to record any more songs together.

19. JUST WHO IS THE FIVE O'CLOCK HERO? (PAUL WELLER)

Recorded January 1982, AIR Studios, London. Released 3 July 1982.
Available on The Gift, Direction Reaction Creation and The Very Best Of The Jam: About The Young Idea.

Paul had his dad John in mind when he wrote 'Just Who Is The Five O' Clock Hero'. Since the early days of The Jam, and before that even when Paul and Steve Brookes spent hours in Paul's bedroom at Stanley Road, trying to learn songs from The Beatles Songbook, John had been there, supporting his son every step of the way. In the years before The Jam signed to Polydor and had any kind of a regular and decent income, John was still a working man. He did all sorts of jobs, many

of which included laying bricks. He worked in the day and then spent many evenings driving The Jam around. John Weller was a grafter, working class and proud with it. It seems that Paul learned a great deal from his dad and the two were certainly very close. Growing up Paul was fully aware of the struggles and challenges that the working classes faced on a daily basis and living so close to Woking's train station he would have noticed the expressions on the faces of those 5 o' clock heroes as they returned home, following another day at work.

When 'Just Who Is The Five O'Clock Hero' was issued it hadn't been long since Prince Phillip had said something along the lines of the ordinary man needing to pull his socks up.

This sort of statement would have been like a red-rag to a bull for the young, working class and socially aware Paul Weller. What Paul could do was react in his way and his way was to write another fantastic song, with lyrics that his fans could relate to. The public bought the record too. It was not released as a single in the UK but was a Dutch import. Despite this it still made No 8 in the UK singles chart in July 1982.

The Jam regularly played the song live on their Trans-Global Unity Express world tour between March and June 1982, where it always segued into a brief cover of Sam Cooke's 1960 single 'Chain Gang'.

Rick Buckler:
The drums sound quite complicated and people have asked me if it was a hard song to play, but it wasn't and I enjoyed playing it live. I know people think it sounds a weird part but it worked for that particular song. The song that used to give me nightmares was 'Scrape Away'. That could be a

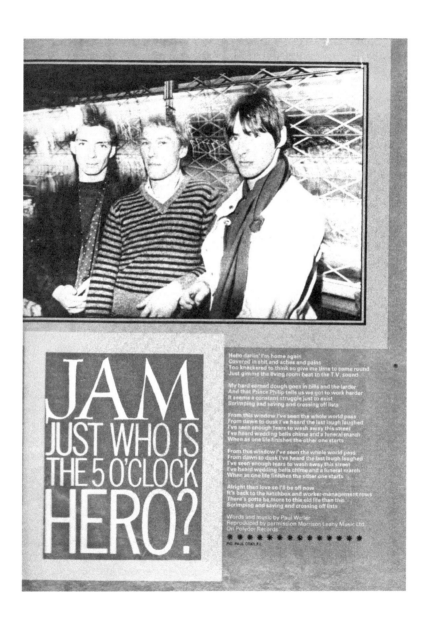

JAM
JUST WHO IS THE 5 O'CLOCK HERO?

Hello darlin' I'm home again
Covered in shit and aches and pains
Too knackered to think so give me time to come round
Just gimme the living room beat to the T.V. sound

My hard earned dough goes in bills and the larder
And that Prince Philip tells us we got to work harder
It seems a constant struggle just to exist
Scrimping and saving and crossing off lists

From this window I've seen the whole world pass
From dawn to dusk I've heard the last laugh laughed
I've seen enough tears to wash away this street
I've heard wedding bells chime and a funeral march
When as one life finishes the other one starts

From this window I've seen the whole world pass
From dawn to dusk I've heard the last laugh laughed
I've seen enough tears to wash away this street
I've heard wedding bells chime and a funeral march
When as one life finishes the other one starts

Alright then love so I'll be off now
It's back to the lunchbox and worker-management rows
There's gotta be more to this old life than this
Scrimping and saving and crossing off lists

Words and music by Paul Weller
Reproduced by permission Morrison Leahy Music Ltd.
On Polydor Records

* * * * * * * * * * * * * *

PIC: PAUL COXLF.I.

THE JAM

tough beat to hold down and you daren't screw it up because it would throw the song out and it'd be really hard to pick it up again.

The pattern for 'Five O'Clock Hero' was much more open. I'd just lock into the pattern and play it. I don't recall how the pattern came about - you tend not to think about such things too much at the time, you just do it. This was a song that was studio based and started off in there. Polydor decided to issue it as a single via their European department and it got shipped to the UK as a Dutch import. It sold enough copies to go top 10.

I thought the cover looked a bit cheap. The paper didn't seem to be of a great quality. It was a blue, white and black sleeve with an image of an old-fashioned microphone on it. I'm not quite sure if this was supposed to signify anything other than serve as some link to the style of record sleeves that came out of the Fifties and Sixties. It was a type of art form.

But I presume this is what Polydor liked and thought would work best to market the song. Not everything a record label like Polydor does works. But having said that I don't know that the record sleeve damaged the sales of the record at all. The thing about being contracted to a record label is that once you hand over the record that you've recorded, it's then in their hands and pretty much all over to them to get it out to the public using what means they think will work best. The band has very little say in that side of things.

The single sleeve was the first to include other musicians. The sleeve included a photograph of Paul, Bruce and myself as well as Keith Thomas and Steve Nichol. We didn't have an issue with that, after all they were part of the show on the road at that time.

The photograph was taken on the Snake Pass which is in Derbyshire. It's a stretch of road that snakes its way across the Pennines linking Manchester and Sheffield. There are some fabulous views to be seen as you drive along it.

We'd been on tour and en route decided to pull over and stretch our legs for a bit and take in some fresh air. It was whilst we were just sitting around on the side of a hill that the photograph got taken by Twink. Around that time Twink came on the road with us quite a lot. There are some other photographs taken from that same time. One shows Paul with his Dansette.

It was on the end of this road leading into Sheffield that Def Leppard drummer Rick Allen lost control of his Corvette C4, causing his left arm to be severed on 31 December 1984. Allen hit a dry stone wall and entered a field. He was thrown from the car because his seatbelt had been improperly fastened.

It was also on this record's sleeve that we used the Immediate style font as The Jam's logo. This was meant to be a direct link to that record label and a nod to the Small Faces who had been on Immediate.

The label had been set up in the mid Sixties by The Rolling Stones manager Andrew Loog Oldham and alongside The Small Faces he also signed PP Arnold and Chris Farlowe.

I think The Jam at that time just felt we needed a different logo and we settled on the Immediate font. It was kind of edgy, jagged, which worked for our sound and our fans got the Small Faces reference.

At the time there was no font available to copy so each letter had to be crafted by hand. We only needed six letters but that probably took some time to do.

I don't remember too much about the single's release. I think this is partly because we were just really busy at that time. The Jam wasn't a band that did a tour and then decided to take a few months out. Some bands operate like this. They release a record, a tour, and then withdraw their presence which then builds up a demand from their fans for the next thing. And then there's a big come back, another record and tour and so on. The Jam weren't like that. For us as soon as we got off the tour bus we pretty much went straight into the studio. This would lead to another song or songs being recorded and then single and album releases and we'd be back on the road again or flying out to Japan.

Our version of the Edwin Starr hit 'War' was included on the release. I thought it was a fabulous song to record. Rhythm wise I thought it was an unusual song to play. There wasn't much I could do to change the way the drums are played. The original version of 'War' is such a strong song and such a well known song, we had to stay close to it and do the best we could with it. It was a similar case with The Who's 'Disguises'. With songs like 'War' and 'Disguises' you just can't lose the identity of the original songs. If you change a song too much it just starts to sound wrong. When The Jam first set out we did loads of covers and we just stuck to playing them the way they should be played - the way that Chuck Berry or The Beatles had played them - and this worked for us. That doesn't mean to say we didn't put our own stamp on the covers we did, like 'War' - I think The Jam did the songs that we covered justice. I think for

The Jam covering songs like 'War' and 'Disguises' was just our way of giving those artists a nod.

20. MONDAY (PAUL WELLER)

Recorded July 1980, Townhouse Studios, London.

Available on *Sound Affects, Direction Reaction Creation* and *The Very Best Of The Jam: About The Young Idea.*

'Monday' is one of The Jam's most beautiful songs, and The Jam could create beautiful songs. Following 'Pretty Green' as track two on *Sound Affects*, 'Monday' gave teenage kids the permission to not feel "embarrassed about love". Whereas The Boomtown Rats sang about not liking Mondays, Paul encouraged the listener to be optimistic and look forward to Mondays - after all this was when lovers see each other again.

Paul's guitars introduce the song gently and then Rick and Bruce come to offer their support. Support is required as the listener is helped to navigate their way through 'rain clouds' and 'tortured winds'.

Paul plays piano over the verses and there's some organ featured on the track too, but the song isn't cramped. It's allowed to breathe and sigh right to its conclusion that lovers will always 'dream' of seeing each other again.

Rick Buckler:

I like 'Monday' as a song. I think it's a song that has a sense of looking inward. Many of Paul's songs were outward looking and observational, but occasionally Paul would write from the other point of view and I think 'Monday' was one of those. I don't know if this was Paul talking about any

THE JAM

6

particular personal relationship. I don't think it was as obvious as that.

There was something about the lyrics in 'Monday'. There's a kind of lament about waiting for Mondays. I think the lyrics mean one thing to one person and something different to another. I believe this was one of the brilliant things about Paul's lyrics. People can take different things from the words and it'll have different meanings to them.

It had only been a few months before *Sound Affects* came out that The Boomtown Rats had issued their hit 'I Don't Like Mondays', a song with a different meaning to The Jam's 'Monday'. Geldof wrote his song after hearing something on an American radio station about a sixteen-year old girl who'd gone on a shooting spree around some school. When she was asked why she did it she'd replied "I don't like Mondays".

Monday's are not the most favourite day for many people. It's not the most cheerful day of the week because it represents the first day back to work after a much needed weekend.

'Monday' was one of those Jam songs that wasn't an obvious Jam song, whatever that means. We were very conscious of trying new things and things that our fans wouldn't have expected from us. We could have easily stuck to doing the high-energy songs like 'In The City' but we didn't want to do that.

It was refreshing for us to do a song like 'Monday' and it still went down well with the fans. I think the fans appreciated that we did try new things too even though it often seemed to us to take them by surprise. I mean other songs like 'That's Entertainment' and 'English Rose' were not 'typical' Jam songs and 'English Rose' is a good example of a song that almost never got used at all.

What was nice about being in The Jam was that we didn't have to tie ourselves up with any rules. What was a typical Jam song anyway? As a band we played fast numbers, slow ones, more soulful ones, punkier ones. If anything The Jam were diverse.

I don't remember if 'Monday' was ever considered for a single release. There may have been conversations with the record label. The record label have their criteria for a single release and what should or shouldn't be used. The things that are important for the label are: can it played on the radio and can it get airplay first thing in the morning? Is it a catchy song that the public can latch onto and remember? Will the public buy it?

It was these things and more that determined whether a song was considered suitable for a single release or not. I don't know if 'Monday' met those needs. However, Paul, Bruce and myself didn't think like that and we had our thoughts regarding what we thought would work and what our fans would buy. 'Down in the Tube Station at Midnight' was one example. The label thought we were mad when we said we wanted that song as a single. It just wasn't a typical single and for many reasons. But it did get released and it did do well, which proved the label wrong.

Recording 'Monday' was pretty straight forward. For my part I don't recall trying any other patterns other than what ended up on the record. I didn't think it was a song that needed anything that was too clever. Some songs lend themselves to being a bit more clever and involved and some just call for simplicity. Monday had a simplicity about it and that contributed to the charm of the song. At the end of the day the song is the star.

21. BUT I'M DIFFERENT NOW (PAUL WELLER)

Recorded June 1980, Townhouse Studios, London
Available on *Sound Affects, The Jam Extras* and *Direction Reaction Creation*.

'But I'm Different Now' starts with a gritty sounding guitar riff and this is The Jam in full force and ready for a fight. The song drives along, helped by the tambourine, pushing its way nearer to a bridge where the band take their feet off the pedal and reflect on what they could have done differently. But they don't linger on such thoughts for long, because they are pretty much straight back into the verse.

This is a Jam song where the influence of The Who is easily noticeable. The middle eight proves this.

The structure of the song is straight forward, as are the lyrics - a man telling his girl that he is different now and he's glad that she's his girl. He's being convincing, he's owning up to his mistakes and he's optimistic for a better future.

Rick Buckler:

For me this was a song that is commenting on what it's like growing up and feeling confident enough to move on. But again, this is a song that will have different meanings to different people and that's a mark of a good set of lyrics.

I liked the energy of it and it was good to play live. I always liked the song's arrangement too. It was punchy and to the point. I really liked the middle sections too where the song stands back, takes a breath, then launches back in. 'But I'm Different Now' has a lot of colour in it.

I think people associate 'But I'm Different Now' and 'Set The House Ablaze' as being two of a kind and indeed they do represent where

The Jam was at that time. I think the song shows a three-piece band attacking a song and keeping it raw in that way. I suppose 'But I'm Different Now' would be considered a more typical Jam song because of the way we played it. It has that energy and aggressiveness about it.

A version of the song turned up on *The Jam Extras* but I don't think it portrays the song and some others on that collection in the best light. But Jam fans seemed to like it and that's fair enough. *The Jam: Extras* is a curio album and should be accepted in that way.

22. SET THE HOUSE ABLAZE (PAUL WELLER)

Recorded October 1980, Townhouse Studios, London
Available on *Sound Affects* and *Direction Reaction Creation*.

The Damned's 'New Rose' had a brilliant guitar intro. 'Set The House Ablaze' has one too and helps to literally set the song ablaze. 'Set The House Ablaze', which was track four on side one of *Sound Affects*, is Paul singing about "wishing he could do something" about the "hatred" that far right and neo-Nazi groups around in 1980 were promoting. Such groups pounced on angry young men, recruiting them in seedy pubs and outside football grounds in the late Seventies and early Eighties. They tried to instil a sense hope for a better England and promised such, but Paul saw through this. He saw those groups for what they were - misinformed.

The imagery of menacing looking men in black DMs comes to mind when Rick plays out the end of the song in that military snare way and then the song seems to exhaust itself, which isn't surprising because it's certainly one of The Jam's fastest songs.

THE JAM

6

Rick Buckler:
'Set The House Ablaze' was a great song to perform live. I always liked having that song in the live sets. The Jam played this song like there really was a house on fire. It just used to burn! It really did have something about it live. It was one of those Jam songs that seemed to go down well with our audiences too.

The title really did reflect the sound and energy of the song. I don't remember if the title came before the song, but I suspect it was taken from Paul's lyrics. I think Paul presented the lyrics and possibly a riff and we took it from there. Even with the lyrics it was still a matter of so how are we going to play it? Is it going to be another 'Mr Clean' or is to be something more upbeat? We played around with it and it just settled into what it became-packed full of fire and skill!

The song was built around those words 'set the house ablaze'. Bruce and I picked up on it. It was instinctive and we developed the rest of the song from there. The words demanded a fast-paced song and that's what we responded to. You just cannot imagine a song like 'Set The House Ablaze' being played slow. Some songs just do not work played slow! They sound wrong. It goes the other way if a song is too fast.

I think 'Set The House Ablaze' was a perfect song for *Sound Affects* and it represents where The Jam were at that time. As I've said we were a live band and what we attempted to do was reflect our live sound in our recordings.

23. MAN IN THE CORNERSHOP (PAUL WELLER)

Recorded October 1980, Townhouse Studios, London

Available on *Sound Affects, Direction Reaction Creation* and *The Very Best Of The Jam: About The Young Idea.*

If 'Dream Time' represented one street and 'Music For The Last Couple' the other, then sandwiched between them is 'Man In The Corner Shop'. There was a time when it felt like, growing up in England, there was a pub and a corner shop on virtually every street corner. Of course, it wasn't like that, but there were a lot more than there are today.

People that owned corner shops were respectable people, often pillars in the community. They were businessmen and they were different but they were still one of the locals. But despite what the loyal customers thought of them (before things changed and they were forced into the supermarkets), those men in the corner shops also had their own dreams and aspirations and this is what Paul's lyrics are about - the contrast between owning your business or working for someone else in some factory (Patti Smith's 'Piss Factory' springs to mind). But Paul is also pointing out the comparisons (of equality) and the contradictions (of divisions).

'Man In The Corner Shop' is also a song about being grateful for what you have and a reminder that when it comes down to it, everyone wants that something else.

Rick Buckler:
'Man In The Corner Shop' was another song with strong lyrics that people felt they could relate to. There's that envy

6

side and how great it would be to run your own business and be your own boss. 'Man In The Corner Shop' was a song that painted a great picture of a particular scenario.

I feel like this is one of the great Jam songs. Alongside the lyrics I also liked the melody and thought it helped make the song what it was trying to say. It was as if the song was sympathising with everyday life and what many everyday people would have been feeling.

The song builds up to highlighting the point that what it boils down to people are meant to be equal. This song was another example of trying to play or say something unusual or different. It was our way to not be confined to conformities or barriers. We wanted to break down those barriers and not feel restricted. It was always in the forefront of The Jam's mind to try and take a three-piece band into new areas. We always asked that question: "Where can we go next?"

One of our biggest fears was becoming boring. We didn't want to keep doing the same thing, write the same songs and play the same way. We embraced experimentation and for Paul, Bruce and myself this was exciting. There seemed to be so much for us to do and to try. After *The Gift* I believe The Jam could have made at least another two albums and they would still have been different to what had gone before. I really don't hold with the idea that *The Gift* was as much as we could have achieved. In 1982 there still felt like there was a lot of life in the band and we still had potential. But Paul had his point of view and his own thoughts and he acted upon them. I think it was unfair of Paul to break up The Jam when he did. And not

just unfair on Bruce and me but on himself too and what else he could have achieved with The Jam.

I understand that Paul wanted to try something else and he did go on and do that with The Style Council. I appreciate that music was changing too and, who knows, maybe I would have ended up experimenting with electronic drum kits. Whatever the case the approach would have been for us to see what we could do for the benefit of the song.

Looking back on that period that led up to The Jam breaking up we never really said to ourselves 'let's just take a break' or 'let's have some time off'. We never considered the benefits of taking the pressure off and recharging our batteries. We never really explored alternative options, instead we just allowed The Jam to split up. And it's a shame that we didn't have that re-think. That is the biggest shame of it all.

24. BOY ABOUT TOWN (PAUL WELLER)

Recorded September 1980, Townhouse Studios, London

Available on *Sound Affects, Direction Reaction Creation* and *The Very Best Of The Jam: About The Young Idea.*

It's never been an easy task trying to keep up with Paul Weller. By the time 'Boy About Town' came out on *Sound Affects* the Mod revival was in full swing. If anything, it was bigger than the Mod scene from fifteen years earlier. Paul was at the vanguard of it - he had been since 1977 anyway, it had just taken some Jam fan a while to ditch their punk garb and fall into line. In 1980 Paul was that boy

6

about town. Jam fans and young Mods looked to him for guidance. When they went to concerts or pored over the music rags, they focused on what he was wearing.

This month it's a Prince Charles check sta-prest, next month it's a red denim jacket, the next month white moccasins (as seen in the 'Absolute Beginners' photo shoot which Derek D'Souza took), the following day some monkey boots (as seen on the *All Mod Cons* album sleeve). Fans took note of what Paul wore (forty years later they still do) and went out and bought the same. Hairstyles were another subject that fans drew their attention too. They copied Paul. If he wore his hair Steve Marriot style so did they, if he cut it back into a crew-cut, so did they (and 40 years later, those that can are still copying Paul's hairstyles).

'Boy About Town' is one of The Jam's most pop like of songs. It's upbeat and carefree and full of life. The brass that kicks in during the middle eight sounds wonderful and vibrant and the mixture of drums and bass and tambourine serve to breath joy into the song.

Coming in at barely two minutes 'Boy About Town' is a firm favourite amongst Jam fans and it was certainly a great addition to *Sound Affects*. As Paul's guitar concludes the song with one last strum, the listener might even think that was Roger Daltrey helping out with the 'Oohs'.

Rick Buckler:

What I really liked about 'Boy About Town' was the way it just trucks along. There's absolutely no dilly-dallying whatsoever. We managed to avoid that with this song. I think the song just really goes for it. I liked the way the song gets going from the off. I enjoyed playing this song for that reason. Looking back it was a dream to play. I also think this

was the sort of song that really suited The Jam. It's a song that works for a three-piece band.

This was another one of our songs that started off in the studio - most of our songs did really. It would often be a case of all getting together to rehearse and whilst we were doing that something new, a riff, or a drum pattern would rise to the surface and we'd think "yeah that's good" and we'd try and do something with it. Not everything worked all of the time, but those that did might have ended up as a song. Some songs even had their beginnings from when we'd been on the road. Something we might jam on during soundcheck and we'd think there was something about it, so we'd hold onto it and maybe take it into a rehearsal. But The Jam formed most of our ideas in the studio.

All the time Paul would be in the background thinking about lyrics and the song's potential structure. He'd then bring these ideas to us and we'd work with them. Sometimes he'd bring just a couple of verses, but it was enough to get things started and we'd build on that. Then there'd be a moment where we'd agree that something was starting to work and come together and then we'd build on that and just keep going until we were happy with what we considered to be the final result. The Jam was very much a collaboration. Writing songs in The Jam always had a sense of fluidity about it. There was never any strict way of going about putting a song together.

I think 'Boy About Town' was another song that showed our fans who our influences were. The track has elements of The Who in it. Those early Who songs cut out all the rubbish and surplus to requirement stuff and this approach and attitude The Jam had too. It was only towards the end of the Sixties and going into the Seventies that bands started to produce self-indulgent songs. That period produced a lot of good songs but also a lot of nonsense too.

I think it would be hard for anyone to be bored by a song like 'Boy About Town'. It gets straight to the point both musically and lyrically. I've always felt the two to three minute song format works the best and we did that a lot in The Jam and still managed to keep the songs interesting. I think The Jam fans feel that our songs didn't tend to outstay their welcome, which is a good thing.

Sometimes we'd add extra things for the live performances. Adding an extension to a song might link to another song or just keep the audience engaged. But a band can do that live as a way to keep the show going. Live work and studio work are two different animals really.

25. GIRL ON THE PHONE (PAUL WELLER)

Recorded October 1979, Townhouse Studios, London
Available on *Setting Sons* and *Direction Reaction Creation*

Picture Paul, Bruce and Rick setting up their equipment in Townhouse Studios, they hear the phone ringing in the reception area, someone has an idea and the next thing you know, Vic Coppersmith-Heaven is recording it. And it's that phone ringing that ignites *Setting Sons* and opens the door to the first track on the album – 'Girl On The Phone'.

Although the song kicks off the album it was in actual fact one of the last songs from the *Setting Sons* sessions to be recorded.

Paul was familiar with Roy Fox Lichtenstein's work. Lichtenstein had been one of the prominent Pop Artists of the Sixties, along with the likes of Andy Warhol and Jasper Johns. How and when Paul got interested in Pop Art is hard to pinpoint. The interest first seemed apparent on the approach to making the *Modern World* album, as evidenced by the jumper that Paul wore on the day and stuck the arrows onto. And of course Paul would have been familiar with The Who's and The Beatles' love of Pop Art. Paul would certainly have been aware of Peter Blake too, and many years after The Jam had split, he commissioned Blake to do the *Stanley Road* album cover.

It was Lichtenstein that that came up with the Whaam idea that Paul borrowed for his Rickenbacker. It was those vibrant colours of yellows and blues that would feed into what The Jam were doing at the time and, it was also one of Lichtenstein's works, 'Oh Jeff...I love you, too...but...', that inspired The Jam song's title.

It was also when Paul was living in London with Gill that he did get unwelcome attention It must have unnerved him too because he had bars onto the windows of his London flat. Fortunately for Bruce and Rick they didn't have to put up with the same amount of unwanted attention. But 'Girl On The Phone' isn't about some stalker that Paul was having to deal with, despite the lyrics suggesting that there's some specific girls who knows everything, from weight to fate.

Once the ringing stops the drums, bass and guitar crashes in. This song is an example of the three band members working together. It's just them, no extras, and because of that, there is that raw Jam sound that only The Jam were able to create.

THE JAM

6

Rick Buckler:

'Girl On The Phone' starts with a telephone ringing and then ends with the voice of a woman. This was actually the receptionist at Town House Studios. The girl would always phone through to the studio when we had a visitor and they wanted to see us and she'd be checking if it was okay to send them through. I don't recall who came up with the idea of recording her but it worked really well for the song. Vic Smith simply recorded her from the studio saying "hello, are you there?" The telephone's ring wasn't the actual studio phone but a sound effect, probably lifted from one of those BBC sound effects albums. I liked the way the song top and tailed with the telephone and the receptionist's voice. I liked the way the song started and the way the band bursts in. It was a good album opener and the song felt compact and punchy. It was a really solid sound and demonstrated what we were sounding like in 1979.

I know there's been talk about the song being about some stalker that Paul was having problems with but I don't think this is completely accurate. There was indeed a time when Paul had just moved to London, it was in Pimlico. Paul had wanted to move to London because he wanted to be around the happenings in the city. He was in love with London. He wanted to be a bit of a boy about town. But I think the reality also hit him once he did start living in London. Fans found out where he lived and would hang around outside. It got that bad and unsafe that he had bars put up over the windows of his flat. For a while it did start to get a little bit out of control. I suspect living in London became a bit of a double-edged sword.

I didn't live in London. I could do what was needed in London, like going to the studio, doing press interviews, videos and so on but then go back to Woking. I could go home to family and friends and all the comforts and familiarities that that brings. Paul didn't have that as such. There was also a practical reason why I didn't live in London. I just couldn't afford to! Even back then London was an expensive place to live, well certainly more than in Woking. I remember that Paul was paying more rent on his flat in London than I was on my mortgage.

Paul had his way of doing things at that time. I remember he bought a black carpet for his flat and it was really expensive.

When we were all buying stack hi-fi systems he refused to and kept his Dansette Major because he wanted to keep it simple, even though the sound quality wasn't great. He held on to his AC30 amp for as long as he could because he wanted the simplicity of just a tone and volume button. He just didn't want anything too complicated. Only later did he experiment with other amps and devices.

I was also mobile. I drove so I had that freedom. Paul wasn't driving at that time, so he couldn't just jump in the motor and remove himself from what was going on and get out of London for a breather.

Bruce and I also had to deal with some unwanted fan attention, but it wasn't on the same level as Paul. I remember leaving a gig we did at the YMCA in Woking. I had parked my car in a bit of a wasteland area just opposite the YMCA. I had a TR6 at the time. I opened the door and slid inside and just as I put the key in the ignition and started the motor up I caught sight of someone popping their head up at the front of the car. They were trying to nick the car's number plate. If I hadn't have seen them I could have driven over them!

6

At times unwanted attention did get out of hand and a bit dangerous. I recall Paul, Bruce and I came out of a venue and we were getting onto the tour bus when someone grabbed one end of the scarf that Paul was wearing. He was into wearing some long scarves at that time. But then someone else managed to grab the other end of the scarf. This meant there were two fans pulling both ends of the scarf and it started to get tighter around Paul's neck. It got chaotic as more fans gathered around and the fans were trying to get Paul's scarf. They didn't really see what was happening, so they weren't trying to strangle Paul. But I remember Kenny had to step in and try to free Paul and get him onto the bus, which he managed to do and then we raced off into the night.

On the whole we were lucky though. I don't recall any incidents of people stealing off of the band, like from the changing rooms or from the tour buses. We pretty much looked after our stuff and we had good security too.

After gigs we'd throw out plectrums and drum sticks and we'd make ourselves available before and after gigs to meet fans and sign stuff. We had a good relationship and connection with our fans.

We never had any real bother back in the hotels either. The Jam were not like the Led Zeppelins or Whos of the rock and roll world. The kind of lifestyles and partying they got up to just wasn't the same for The Jam. I don't think Jam fans felt they needed to sneak into our rooms or whatever. We were open with them and made time for them and I think there was a kind of mutual respect between us.

I know Paul had fans turning up at his parents' house and Bruce and I a little bit of that, but it wasn't very often and was

never any real trouble. I've heard plenty of stories of Jam fans travelling to Woking and trying to see us. There's plenty of stories of Ann and John Weller letting fans into their home too and giving them cups of tea and sometimes even allowing them to have a look around Paul's bedroom. I don't know what Paul felt about this. I know when he moved to London it freaked him out that fans found out where he lived and he didn't know what to expect when he got up in the morning or returned home late at night.

There's a kind of line that some people do step over and that changes the game. It can be very weird and can leave you feeling uneasy. It's one thing seeing fans at a gig, or a record signing or something, but when there's fans showing up at your own home, your private and safe place, it's not always great.

It was only a few months after 'Girl On The Phone' came out on *Setting Sons* that John Lennon was shot dead on his door step. It was a huge thing, dreadful and tragic, and all because some bloke wanted to take on Lennon's fame and make a name for himself.

Thankfully in all my time with The Jam I found most people to be respectful and I didn't have any problems with girls on the phone.

26. LITTLE BOY SOLDIERS (PAUL WELLER)
Recorded August 1979, Townhouse Studios, London
Available on *Setting Sons* and *Direction Reaction Creation*

When 'Little Boy Soldiers' turned up on the *Setting Sons* album it struck Jam fans as being unusual. They'd never heard anything like it

THE JAM

before from The Jam - they had nothing to compare it with.

Only Paul will know what was in his mind when he wrote the song and the lyrics. Why soldiers? After all it had been over thirty years since World War II had ended and the Falklands War was still three years further down the line. But in just over three and half minutes 'Little Boy Soldiers' tells a story. A message from one person to another which mentions "being out of touch" and "can't be bothered", but the days are "fine": after all it's only war games. And then the song takes an unexpected turn. Paul and Bruce stop playing, which leaves just Rick playing a military style snare rhythm. Rick would play this live, much to the appreciation of the audience. Before the guitar re-enters there are sounds of exploding bombs and the song builds again and images are crated of little boy soldiers playing on a hill.

And then there is the mock lullaby section, a slow and gentle swing of a tale about killing and robbing the "fucking lot". But it's okay because it was done underneath the flag of democracy and from here on the song shifts a gear and charges forward like the Light Brigade. A piano is introduced to assist the song as it heads to its conclusion and final declaration of "we won".

Rick Buckler:

If memory serves me right I think we recorded 'Little Boy Soldiers' in a similar way to 'Down in the Tube Station at Midnight'. We did it in sections but not in a stitched sort of way. The structure of the song has different parts to it so as a band we would step in and step out as required. There's a section with just guitar. That would have been recorded and added as an over dub and this bridges two sections of the song. We knew what we were aiming for with this song, so I was just a matter of being able to record it using the various sounds that we wanted.

There's a part of the song where I played a military style snare drum. This was our attempt to draw on that military imagery. It added to the story of the song and helped to put the lyrics into some kind of context. As a song 'Little Boy Soldiers' probably was the closest The Jam got to a concept song. We included sound effects in it too which was meant to help create an atmosphere. There's the explosions and sense of a battle raging on. This was our first venture into using sound effects in our songs. *Setting Sons* was recorded before *Sound Affects*.

I enjoyed playing this live and when I did I used my Rota Toms. It was some of those drums that were found by one of the film crew from the ITV programme *After They Were Famous*. I was asked to be included in the show and they came down to my home to do the filming. At some point during the day one of the crew took a wander down to the end of my garden and stumbled across some of the Rota Tom set. They made a big thing of it in the show trying to make out that I had discarded the drums in some sort of protest or statement. That was not the case at all. The actual story was that when I got the set of Rota Toms I only ever wanted to use some of them. The ones I didn't want over time found themselves in the garden because my two kids would play with them. They then got left in the garden and I didn't even know that they were there. Over time they got covered in weeds and had started to rot away.

What that member of the film crew saw was those rotting drums and he came up with his own conclusions, which was far away from the truth of the matter.

In the studio I had used orchestral timpani

drums to record that part on 'Little Boy Soldiers'. Timpani drums are huge and certainly weren't practical to take on the road with us. The Rota Toms were a good alternative. I remember spending half the day in the studio trying to get the sound right on the timpani drum. They require skill because they have pedals and are tuned a certain way. We had to spend time getting the drum tuned right for the song.

27. SMITHERS-JONES (BRUCE FOXTON)

Recorded June 1979, Townhouse Studios, London
Available on *Setting Sons, Snap, Direction Reaction Creation* and *The Very Best Of The Jam: About The Young Idea.*

Rick's recollection of 'Smithers-Jones' is that Bruce wrote this based on some of his own experiences. Bruce's dad had been made redundant. This song is Bruce's best known and most loved contribution to The Jam's archive.

On *Setting Sons* a version was used with strings. Pete Solley was hired to do the arrangement. Paul takes a step back for this song, allowing Bruce to take the lead vocal, something which Bruce was more than capable of doing.

Bruce tells a story of a man, heading to work, the pressures of having to make that train into London again (he uses the Waterloo Line). The man in question is a city worker, pin-stripe suit, shirt and tie on of course. His daily travelling companion is a copy of *The Times* - you get the picture?

But loyal stands for nothing, years of service ignored. The man is just another in the 'production line'. The world doesn't owe him a living and on his arrival to his office one morning, he's told the boss wants

to see him. The man is hopeful, just maybe after all these years this is the promotion he's been waiting to be handed. But, no, the exact opposite, instead what Bruce tells us is that the man is told there's no longer a position for him - he has lost his job - he is made redundant and who cares?

The strings play on, Bruce sings the story of the man cast aside, Paul provides the backing vocals. Rick is absent on this version but would appear on other versions down the line. It's a wonderful song, chilling as it is.

Rick Buckler:
I think Jam fans regard this as being Bruce's best song that he contributed to The Jam. I can't recall whose idea it was (it may have been Vic Smith's) but someone suggested doing a version using just strings. It felt it would work so a version was recorded. We had to get some guy in to score the string arrangement. It was another opportunity for us to explore new areas.

'Smithers-Jones' was included on *Setting Sons* and an alternative version was used as the B-side to 'When You're Young'. I think both versions worked well. Bruce had to live with the unfair thing of having his own songwriting compared to Paul's. I certainly thought this was unfair. I think it's probably fair to say that Bruce wasn't a consistently great songwriter but he did contribute some good songs to The Jam.

Bruce wrote the lyrics based on some of his own experiences. I think his dad had been made redundant and this had left an impression on him. Bruce just presented the song to us one day whilst we were gathered in Townhouse Studios. We then spent time working on it and bashing around ideas until we felt ready to record it.

6

One recorded version made it onto *Extras*. Although Bruce was more used to singing backing vocals he did a good enough job signing on 'Smithers-Jones'. As a three-piece with only two members being responsible for vocal duties we had our limitations. I mean we didn't have a sole lead singer, someone like Roger Daltrey or Freddie Mercury. But this wasn't something that we ever got hung up about and we didn't need to because we stood together very strongly as a unit. This was one of the outstanding qualities in The Jam.

I remember that there was a problem with Bruce when it came to *Setting Sons*. We had been in the studio for weeks and the album needed to be finished on a certain day. The songs were all recorded and they had to be mastered and then be sent off to the factory to get pressed up and so on. When that day arrived we were sat in Townhouse Studios and Bruce decided that he didn't like the mix. He had some issue that the bass didn't sound right. Vic Smith was like "why didn't you say anything three days ago?" and "are you saying you want me to remix all the tracks just because of the bass sound?" so Vic ended up adding more EQ on the bass, on the two-track mixes that he had. So when you listen to *Setting Sons* there are some bass parts that sound a bit muddy. Even now when I listen to any songs from *Setting Sons* I'm reminded of how the bass had originally sounded really crisp but ended up not.

The sounds of our records were important to us. I remember something that Paul loved was that if our record sounded good on a Dansette Major record player, it would sound good on anything. In Townhouse there were some tiny speakers that the songs would get played back to us through and we were of the opinion that if the record sounded good

through that, then it would be just fine once it was committed to vinyl.

28. ETON RIFLES (PAUL WELLER)

Recorded August 1979, Townhouse Studios, London. Released 26 October 1979.

Available on Setting Sons, Direction Reaction Creation and The Very Best Of The Jam: About The Young Idea.

Paul said that he wrote 'Eton Rifles' on the same day as 'Saturday's Kids', whilst sitting in the West Sands Caravan Park in Selsey Bill. In the Sixties and Seventies the Wellers spent some of their holidays in caravan parks in Selsey Bill (they also liked to go to Bognor Regis).

With its explosive introduction, 'Eton Rifles' is rightfully placed as one of the greatest songs to have been born out of the punk and new wave scene - and as a revivalist Mod song is its king.

6

This is one of those songs that demonstrates the power and force of a three-piece band sounding like there are so many more of them. Paul is comfortable running his plectrum along the strings recreating that sound that Pete Townshend from The Who did so well and Rick rolls around the toms like Keith Moon.

'Eton Rifles' is an angry song. It's Paul being angry about something that he'd seen on the TV. He'd watched students from the prestigious Eton College make fun of those involved in an unemployment march. The march had begun in Liverpool and worked its way down to the South of England, passing by the Eton College in Windsor on route. What Paul observed both disgusted and angered him. The lyrics to 'Eton Rifles' are his response.

As a song 'Eton Rifles' is having a dig at the upper and more privileged classes. Paul, Rick and Bruce felt they had nothing in common with those people and what they represented.

All three Jam members had attended the Sheerwater Comprehensive in Woking, and that was a million miles from Eton (although Woking to Windsor is only twenty two miles away).

The chorus is one that a Jam fan enjoys singing along to and a reminder that it's good to be working class 'cheers then mate'.

'Eton Rifles' was released as a single in October 1979 and reached No 3 on the UK charts, their highest chart position to date.

Talking to *Sound on Sound* magazine in 2007 producer Vic Coppersmith-Heaven said they recorded 'Eton Rifles' three times. The first time he said it just didn't have the power or the excitement so they left it and worked on some other tracks before coming back to it. To capture that excitement is purely a question of performance, arrangement and sound all mixing together.

The second version of 'Eton Rifles' was pretty much the same story.

There were a lot of exciting tracks on *Setting Sons*, like 'Burning Sky', 'Thick as Thieves' and 'Private Hell' - they had loads of energy, and in the early stages of recording, the overall band sound developed during the course of recording *Setting Sons* - the drums improved, the bass sound would get better, and when that happened we'd often drop a new bass part, for instance, into a track that we'd been working on days before.

There was always a crowd of fans outside the studio, and occasionally the band would sneak them in. I'd be mixing at the desk and I'd feel this unusual presence behind me, and when I'd look round I'd see about 30 kids sitting on the settees. They'd probably been there for an hour while I was intensely mixing. In this case he just invited a bunch of them to sing on the chorus. It was a spur-of-the-moment decision.

6

Rick Buckler:

'Eton Rifles' was a good song to include on *Setting Sons*. It fitted with the theme of the album. I liked it as a song and it became our highest chart hit to date. I know Jam fans are fond of it and seemed to really engage with the song.

Bruce and I liked to play it and it was important for us to really get that rhythm section right. We saw this as our job. We did that part and Paul came up with the riffs and lyrics. We always tried to find the right thing to play for the song. Take for example the push behind when Paul sings 'Eton Rifles, Eton Rifles'. We made a point of this and emphasised it, which added extra weight to the way in which Paul sang it. Looking for ways to enhance hooks and accents and so on was an important part of what we did. I think this was one of the strengths of The Jam throughout our career.

The fans also got the 'Eton Rifles' lyrics. Paul had written it whilst being away for a few days on a holiday park on the South

6

Coast. That's how he got the riff. I think he then saw something on the TV about the Right To Work March that had set off from Liverpool and was making its way down the country. On its journey the march had passed Eton College and students of the college were filmed jeering at the marchers. This was like a red flag to Paul and from what he observed he wrote the lyrics.

The song's title related to something the college had called the Eton College Rifle Corps. I don't know how Paul discovered this. The idea that a college taught its students to shoot just seemed ridiculous and this alongside the college being full of the upper classes and wealthy and the type of people that get groomed to run the nation just added more fuel. 'Eton Rifles' was a song that picked up on all the irony of this.

Then of course there was that comment from David Cameron "I was one, in the corps. It meant a lot, some of those early Jam albums we used to listen to. I don't see why the left should be the only ones allowed to protest songs." Paul's response when he heard this was "which bit didn't you get?" Cameron was a student at the Eton College, so that says a lot. My response to Cameron's comment was one of bemusement. I thought it hard to accept that he was a Jam fan and I'm also certain that he hadn't listened to the lyrics properly. And full credit to Paul for many of his lyrics because he was able to put his observations into them and people could understand what he was getting at.

The military thing was further picked up on when we did that performance on *Top of the Pops*. We had four lads join us on the stage dressed in red army tunics dating back to the Victorian era. I don't recall how we knew them but they were members of an Essex Mod band called The Cards. It was all a bit

of a surprise really and it certainly wasn't like anything we'd done before. I mean Paul wearing the Heinz Baked Beans apron was yet to come. Maybe whoever came up with the idea was relating it to the Sixties.

From around 1966 - 67 it became quite trendy for people to wear tunics from past military campaigns. They'd go to boutiques like I Was Lord Kitchener's Valet, which was located in Foubert's Place, just off of fashionable Carnaby Street to buy up these tunics. The likes of Jimi Hendrix and Pete Townshend all wore them and of course they were made even more popular after The Beatles' *Sgt. Pepper* album came out. The brightness of the tunics kind of fitted with the whole psychedelic thing that London was swinging to. It was also very British and this sort of linked to what The Jam was about too. For that particular *Top of the Pops* performance I wore a boating hat and blazer and looked very much the university gent. Or so I thought!

We didn't set out to write a single. It was never a matter of telling ourselves that we need to come up with a single. It just didn't work like that. I think the only exception to this was 'David Watts'. Yes we had contracts and single and album obligations to meet but it was never a matter of booking a studio and telling ourselves that we need to come up with a single. It was only after 'Eton Rifles' was written and recorded that it was agreed it would make a good single issue. As a band we really detested the idea of having to write songs to order. Paul especially hated this because it put him under pressure and when there's pressure like that, it's hard to be creative and also simply enjoy what you're doing.

Besides when a record label says to you write a top ten song, how do you do that?

THE JAM

How is that even possible? So we side stepped the issue and ducked and dived around our record labels demands as much as possible. Dennis Munday wrote about the games and demands that record labels play in his book *Shout To The Top* and he was well placed to know what the labels thought and expected.

For The Jam it was a matter of write and record some songs and then choose a couple of single contenders and present them to Polydor. 'Eton Rifles' rose to the top on that occasion, Polydor agreed and off it went to the record pressing factory.

After recording 'Eton Rifles' I remember feeling pleased about it. I often did after recording sessions. I felt we'd written and recorded a really good song and that's a nice feeling to have. On other occasions I left recording sessions thinking we should have rehearsed a song more and maybe played it live first or more often. I believe that a song improves when you play it live and some Jam songs just didn't get that opportunity. I think this comes through on some of the songs on the *Modern World* album, which I think could have turned out so much better had they had time to be played live more. But pressures were put on us following the release of *In The City* and we accepted those pressures from the record label. We never repeated that again though.

We also found that taking songs on the road that people hadn't heard before also had a marked difference from songs that they had already heard and knew. The difference in the reaction from the audience from a song they know in contrast to one they didn't was very noticeable for us. Being on stage you could see it and you could feel it. For a new song you tended to find that people would only stand around and listen to it. This could be strange, especially if for the songs you'd

been playing before it, they'd been jumping around. I guess it was a matter of still liking what we played but enjoying it in a different way.

Reactions from the audiences also differed according to the new songs. Playing something like 'Fever/Pity Poor Alfie' for the first time live threw some people. We never performed those live that much, but that was partly because by 1982 we had built up quite a catalogue of songs and we had that option to choose what we wanted to play. I'm glad that we did and recorded songs like 'Fever/Pity Poor Alfie'. I thought songs like that were good to include at a point in the set when you wanted to take the tone down a little bit. I mean Jam performances were often intense and pretty full on.

29. MR CLEAN (PAUL WELLER)
Recorded August 1978, RAK Studios, London
Available on All Mod Cons and Direction Reaction Creation.

Paul playing D minor to A minor on repeat sets the song in motion. And then the band show up to pitch in - a crash of a cymbal and pluck on a bass string and the daylight has dawned.

It's another mid-week morning and 'Mr Clean' is readying himself for another day working for the man. The morning routine is well-rehearsed - a piece of toast from the one he loves most (the assumption here that it's his wife not a mistress) and then he's off to catch the train.

Before the song reaches a minute the listener has already been painted a picture of such a man and his life - which was probably not a reflection on most Jam fans lives. If anything the man in the story and what he represents would have been the type that Jam fans detested.

By the time the guitar solo arrives the listener has connected with the lyrics and the story and they're ready, willing and probably more than able to help stick Mr Clean's face in the grinder.

One night, in a hotel bar in the States, while The Jam were on tour, Paul and Gill were having a drink. Gill stumbled, knocking a man over in the process. The man helped Gill steady herself but in the process he groped one of Gill's breasts. Paul noticed this and it was the recollection of this afterwards that inspired the lyrics for 'Mr Clean'. He made the song very British too and his observations of the commuters boarding the train into London from Woking, was partially responsible for this.

Talking to *Uncut* Magazine Pete Townshend said that 'Mr Clean' gave him the 'willies' and it's easy to see why. There is a chill and a dark undercurrent. 'Mr Clean' is another Jam song that reminds us of the class divide and the 'them and us' world that faced everyone in the UK in 1978.

Rick Buckler:
'Mr Clean' was a song I really liked to play live. What I liked was that it was one of those high-energy songs that The Jam had a lot of. For me it was one of those 'take a breath' songs. Not being a high-energy song didn't detract from the song - I think it was still a very strong song. Being a song with a slower pace just meant we could do something different with it. This I liked because I think there was some expectation on The Jam to do everything at a hundred miles an hour. But

we didn't want to do that with every song. And our sets could get really quite frantic at times. 'Mr Clean' was a song we could throw into the set and really just sit with it and allow it to roll along. When we played that way we got the songs sounding right and steady and musically everything was correct. A song captures a certain feel that way.

I thought the lyrics on 'Mr Clean' were absolutely brilliant too. I heard that Pete Townshend said the song gives him the 'willies'. I suppose there is a feeling that the lyrics evoke. I think there's something quite threatening about the songs lyrics. It has that 'there's someone lurking in the shadows' feel. It's a song with a haunting energy about it and we'd capture that feel live too.

 **RICK BUCKLER** Polydor
on Polydor Records

By all accounts Paul wrote the lyrics after some incident in a hotel that included his girlfriend Gill, but I don't know about that and don't recall anything being said at the time. For me the lyrics in 'Mr Clean' are

6

THE JAM

pretty much self-explanatory, especially regarding the sort of person the song is aimed at. Conformist comes to mind.

The track came out of that period that led us into *All Mod Cons* and I have heard the stories and various thoughts about some supposed lost album. After the *Modern World* album there was a short period in The Jam's history that some songs were tried and even recorded but never used. We played around with songs and we played around with titles too. Some of those songs have made their way into the hands of Jam fan and some have been given song titles - which may or may not be accurate. All the way through The Jam's history we had working titles, titles that were just temporary. For example 'Tales From The Riverbank' started off with the title 'Not Far At All' and 'Absolute Beginners' had been called 'We've Only Started'.

Many of those songs from that 'lost third album' were never finished and were never really intended to be made public. And at that time the titles weren't really that important because they weren't finished products anyway. It's like having a sketchbook where all the ideas get written down and some develop further and some just don't get added to.

My recollections of that period between *The Modern World* and *All Mod Cons* was that there was an attitude from Paul wherein he just wanted to go into the studio and quickly knock out some demos based on the ideas in that Jam sketchbook. It was as simple as that. Some of those songs just didn't have any real musical input or time spent on the arrangements and what happened was that Chris Parry heard those demos in that form and came to his own

6

conclusions. What he heard he thought just wasn't good enough, which would be right because those demos were far from finished.

This period did change something though because it was from here on that Bruce and I started to put a lot more into the songs. From that point on we got more vocal when it came to the song's arrangements and putting forward our ideas. We also became more vocal when it came to speaking our minds and saying that we didn't think this or that wasn't working. And this approach from Bruce and me fed into the making of *All Mod Cons*. Take Bruce's style of bass playing. In many ways he made up for not having that other guitar. Bruce was never one for just sitting on a root note and in the same way it wasn't my style to just sit back and hold down a four/four rock beat. The Jam was a three-piece band that required each member to pull their weight. I think this is demonstrated well on the *All Mod Cons* album.

It wasn't that Paul had an arrogance and saw it as him coming up with songs and we were just a band that performed them. That was never how The Jam worked. But what Paul did have was the pressure on him to come up with an album's worth of songs.

Those demo songs from that period between *Modern World* and *All Mod Cons* were all written by Paul whilst under pressure. And that was unfair on him and the response from the record label was also unfair because they were judging from some unfinished songs.

What was great about having someone like Chris Parry around was that he would speak his mind and if he felt that something wasn't good enough, he'd say so and we needed that around us. The Jam were never a band who were content to rest on our

laurels and what Chris Parry's response did for us was to push us to come up with new songs and 'Mr Clean' was one of them.

It's quite common for bands to feel under pressure regarding their 'difficult' third album and having to have had 'made it' by that time. And that pressure comes from all angles: the record label, the fans, the press. We were aware of this and we wanted to get our third album right and come up with something that was the best that we could do.

The truth is that there was no lost third album and whatever songs we had been working on just got junked. It just wasn't like that and the thinking that The Jam were at some sort of crisis point just isn't correct either. The Jam were always learning and developing as a band. What was true was that the more successful The Jam became the more pressure we all found ourselves under. It was just something that came with the job.

30. BILLY HUNT (PAUL WELLER)

Recorded August 1978, RAK Studios, London
Available on *All Mod Cons, Snap, Direction Reaction Creation* and *The Very Best Of The Jam: About The Young Idea*

Paul wrote this song in the garden of Balmoral Drive on a spring day. Considered for The Jam's fifth single, it was only the intervention from Mickie Most that prevented this being the case. By all accounts Most advised them to issue 'David Watts' instead and the band, John Weller and Polydor took his advice. And why would they not take Most's advice? After all he'd been a producer working in the music business for over a

THE JAM

6

decade. Along with his business partner at the time, Peter Grant (who managed the Yardbirds and then Led Zeppelin), Most had founded RAK Records and RAK Music Publishing and later Most opened the RAK studios located in St John's Wood, London. He'd also worked with the likes of The Animals, Jeff Beck, The Nashville Teens, Lulu, Suzi Quatro and Herman's Hermits, so Rick, Bruce and Paul were already well acquainted with Most's history and with such a history, they were not going to dismiss his suggestion and David Watts' did get to No 25 in the UK charts.

So with 'Billy Hunt' not being chosen as the next Jam single, instead it found its place opening up side two of *All Mod Cons*. Weller opens the song up with an abrasive guitar, Rick quickly stepping up with a snare and tom roll and Bruce launches in, adding that extra support, that instantly delivers a song that's full of energy and vibrancy. It's also one of Paul's angriest vocals. If it was a glare it would cut you down.

Paul's lyric are of a character who amongst other things sings of a dog. A 'dog' was a derogative term for a female in the era when *All Mod Cons* was being made. It's possibly an extension of bitch. Characters were something that Paul had a talent for creating. He would continue doing this throughout his career, but during The Jam's day's a good playwright could produce something quite amazing using the likes of 'Billy Hunt', 'David Watts' or 'Liza Radley' and locate them in a town called Malice, along with an English rose love interest. That would be a worthwhile night out at the theatre.

'Billy Hunt' is someone that no one will 'push around', especially when he's backed by the laddish and terrace-esque chanting of 'Billy Hunt, Billy Hunt, Billy, Billy, Billy'. It's been chanted countless times since The Jam

unleashed the song and is a favourite amongst Jam fans and at a live performance was always one of the most engaging songs.

'Billy Hunt' is also a song about dreaming and having aspirations - again a recurring theme in Paul's songwriting career ('To Be Someone') and it is making a statement that no one is entitled to make another person's life a misery - those are the people the world wishes hadn't "been born".

Paul's guitar solo one and half minutes into the song injects a sense of The Who, with feedback and a slide down the guitar neck and Rick confirms this with some Moon-esque drumming and then its all three members back into a signature well-crafted Jam song.

The song builds to a chaotic ending, more handclaps adding an extra something to Rick's attacking drumming, and then Paul's guitar rings out a chord to fade.

Rick Buckler:

This was one of those Jam songs that the audience liked to chant along to. It was always good being on stage and looking out into the crowd and seeing them getting into the song. I think Jam fans got the title too and understood that it could be used as a bit of slang for another word. I have a memory of a conversation about the lyrics and how they related to some of the other pupils from Sheerwater School. I don't think Paul had a certain individual in mind, it was more about some of the characters that we encountered whilst we were there. I suppose most people experience school in similar ways. You connect with some people and others you don't.

When we were at Sheerwater we had our crowd and many of those were of the music room school lunch time sessions. One guy for example was Roger Pilling. He was one of our mates and like many others stuck with us as The Jam got more successful. I remember seeing him in some hotel. Paul, Bruce, Roger and me were sitting down in the reception area. Whilst we were chatting and catching up some guy recognised us and approached us asking if we'd sign a bit of paper. I signed it, then Bruce, then Paul and then one of us handed it to Roger who also signed it. The guy thanked us then ambled off. I watched him as he looked at his signed piece of paper and how it dawned on him that there were four signatures but only three members in The Jam. He then tore off the bit of paper with Roger's autograph and tossed it to one side. We all thought that was very funny. It was just a bit of fun.

I liked playing 'Billy Hunt' live. It was a lively song. I think it was a song with attitude too. This was a song that came out of a period in The Jam's history where I think we were still like rough diamonds. After *All Mod Cons* I think some of our songs started to get a bit slicker. But I think 'Billy Hunt' represents that time when we still running around with our shirts hanging out of our trousers.

I think 'Billy Hunt' also captured that live Jam sound too. It often gets included on live albums. I think it's a song that could have worked as a single and believe that it was considered for a single too.

6

31. THE PLACE I LOVE (PAUL WELLER)

Recorded August 1978, RAK Studios, London

Available on *All Mod Cons*, *Direction Reaction Creation*

'The Place I Love' is a song that strikes a chord with probably every Jam fan. After all who doesn't have a special place, some retreat and maybe somewhere that also may be a little "overgrown" and have "colourful flower".

When Paul wrote this song The Jam were on the brink of becoming one of the busiest bands in the music industry. Their diaries were full up with tour dates, studio dates, interview dates - their feet hardly touched the ground. Rick described these periods like "riding the crest of a wave" and having the feeling of being so caught up in what was going on that at times they felt like all they could do was "hang on".

The song fits perfectly on *All Mod Cons*, beginning with Paul's guitar riff before Rick and Bruce slide in alongside him. There's a driving guitar riff that pushes the song towards the chorus. All the time Paul sings about the place he loves - wherever that may be, Paul has never confirmed a certain place.

Throughout the song there are flurries of activity from Paul and one of these includes a burst from a Hammond organ - the first time the instrument was used on a Jam recording. And then, two and half minutes later, the song halts and virtually falls into the lap of the next song on *All Mod Cons* – "'A' Bomb In Wardour Street'.

Rick Buckler:

This was another song where it's difficult to comment on Paul's lyrics in any real depth.

I don't know for certain what the meaning of the lyrics were for Paul. But I think this song has a meaning for everyone. I like to think the idea behind the song is something that everyone feels. I think most people have a fondness for somewhere. A place doesn't necessarily need to be a building, or forest, city or town. Being on the road in a band can be that place too. As tough as it can be for some musicians, being on the road is that place for them. For another musician being in the studio could be their place. But for some their place may just be the place where they grew up, or used to play, or hang out with friends.

I think 'The Place I Love' as a song can mean various things. To widen the idea even further a person can be just happy with themselves and who and what they are and have become. They are that place and perfectly okay to think and feel that.

'The Place I Love' is one of those songs that a Jam fan wants to tell you about. Countless times fans have told me what that place is for them and no two are the same. What's important about this song is that everyone can relate to it in some way and in their own personal way.

And a person doesn't have to have just one place either, there could be several places. One of mine was playing live. Playing live was a place that I loved. I also liked being on the road. I thought being on the road was fabulous. But as much as I loved that, there was that other side when you have had your fill of that and then you just want to be home. And being at home with my family was another place that I loved.

For The Jam the place that we loved was being successful. We had worked towards it and we achieved it. It was a really good place to be knowing that people liked our songs,

6

went out and bought our records and came to our concerts. I certainly loved being in that place that I felt the band had worked for. Being in that place also meant that certain things could happen - the venues we played in got bigger, the hotels better, the studios improved in quality.

I think the meaning behind 'The Place I Love' is varied and it just doesn't just need to be restricted to a physical place like Woking.

32. STANDARDS (PAUL WELLER)

Recorded at Basing Street Studios, August 1977
Available on *This Is The Modern World*, *Direction Reaction Creation* and *Dig The New Breed*

'Standards' is undoubtedly one of the stand-out tracks on *This Is The Modern World*. From the moment the song opens up with a Who-esque guitar riff the song captures the listener. Although Bruce joins in with some backing vocals towards the end of the song, the only thing missing are some 'oohs' from Roger Daltrey.

The lyrics are of self-worth, respect, taking control, taking power and being proud to be a member of the working classes. The Jam kept the song in their sets up until the end of 1979 so 'Standards' really did rule OK.

Rick Buckler:

'Standards' was one of our songs that came out of that punk period that The Jam was around. It was included on the *This Is The Modern World* album but unlike most of the songs on that album, which were written for that album, my memory

is that 'Standards' was already a song that we'd been 'mucking' around with, like in soundchecks or when we had a few minutes in rehearsals.

I think 'Standards' is similar to 'Billy Hunt'. It's straight forward and we are playing exactly what the song needs. It was another intuitive song and what was in the forefront of Bruce's and my mind was to bring our parts to the song. The content and the meaning of the lyrics was Paul's business. Again it's a song that has lyrics that people will interpret as they see fit. But it may well be political, it may well be a reflection on society in 1977 - as Paul saw it.

With all The Jam songs what was important for us was to be able to produce something that would work live and this more so than what would just work in the studio. We never wanted to limit ourselves like that because we were a live band and loved to perform our songs live. We wanted to put together songs that we thought were exciting to listen to. The stops and starts and bridges and so on was our attempt to achieve that. How our songs were arranged was an important factor for Paul, Bruce and myself and when we were recording 'Standards' we were still in that phase of not experimenting too much in the studio.

I have heard fans liken the track to Who songs and I can see how it relates to the riff and approach of, say, 'I Can't Explain'. Bands like The Who in their earlier days didn't hang around studios for too long. Studios were expensive to use so it was a matter for bands to get in, record the song and get out quick. This approach can be heard in Who songs and indeed on The Jam's early albums. And 'Standards' was a product of that.

33. BURNING SKY (PAUL WELLER)

Recorded at Townhouse Studios, London, September 1979.

Available on Setting Sons, The Jam Extras, The Very Best Of The Jam: About The Young Idea, Direction Reaction Creation

'Burning Sky' opens side two of *Setting Sons* and begins with some guitar noise from Paul, some gong from Rick and a thumping bass line from Bruce. The song builds up nicely as it rolls into a three and half minute track that has strength in its dynamic. There are pushes and pulls all over the song. The middle eight slots in well and this even includes a brief burst of a guitar solo and that's all it needs. Overall 'Burning Sky' is a song that is brilliantly crafted and it was perfect for *Setting Sons*. And in the end let us all hope we will be happy and wise and The Jam's gong will echo through eternity under burning skies.

Rick Buckler:

When I think of 'Burning Sky' I think of the song's complicated arrangement. Drum wise at least there were specific changes that I needed to play on every verse and throughout the song. Someone also came up with the suggestion that a gong would work on the song too and I liked the idea. I thought doing things like that were great fun to add into our songs. Throughout The Jam's recording career we used a lot of percussion, increasingly so from *Setting Sons* onwards. Something like a gong was fabulous to use because they have such a great sound. I didn't own things like gongs or timpani drums so we had to hire them in for studio purposes. Most studios don't have these sort of things just hanging around because they are expensive to buy, take up space and don't get used that often. There were companies all over London

that hired instruments out and it was quite big business back then.

I really enjoyed banging that gong at the end of 'Burning Sky'. I liked the way it rang out too. Gongs are great for that.

34. DREAMS OF CHILDREN (PAUL WELLER)

Recorded at Townhouse Studios, London, January 1980

Available on The Very Best Of The Jam: About The Young Idea, The Jam Extras and Snap!

Issued as a double A-side with 'Going Underground', 'Dreams Of Children' begins with a fading in of a reverse guitar. The sound builds before taking an abrupt U-turn and diving into the main body of the song. Throughout the song the guitar is high on the mix. The scratching sound of the sixstring is inescapable.

The bridge softens the blow and takes the listener on an inward journey where they can contemplate their own dreams, dreams that "crack up" under threat. Foxton's bass takes the lead here supported by a synth played by Paul and this section serves as a bridge as the song slides back into the verse. The drums pick up again and off the song goes.

There's a middle eight where the band sit back. Foxton's bass takes the lead again. There's more reverse guitar and bursts of snare drum. There is a sense of being alone in a dream or a nightmare. There is a sense of 'choking' or being 'suffocated'. It's no wonder the song didn't receive much air play despite it being an A-side in its own right.

This is another example of The Jam experimenting in the studio. The

THE JAM

6

production credits were shared between Vic Coppersmith-Heaven and The Jam.

Rick Buckler:

What fascinated me about this track was the use of the backward guitar effect. It gave it that psychedelic edge and gave us the opportunity to experiment with new ideas and sounds.

We were trying to evoke an atmosphere with this song that was not expected from us. I think we managed to come up with something with its own feel and sound, which stood it apart from other Jam songs. I liked recording the song because it liberated us from the confines of what a three-piece was supposed to be capable of. 'Dreams Of Children' provided us with an opportunity to stay creative.

We recorded the song in Townhouse as a band and only afterwards played around with the backwards guitar effect. The Beatles helped to make the sound of that backwards/reverse guitar popular in the mid Sixties when they used it on songs like 'I'm Only Sleeping' and 'Tomorrow Never Knows' and of course it's very evident on 'Strawberry Fields Forever'. Paul, Bruce and I were very familiar with those songs so I imagine we had been waiting for the opportunity to employ it on a Jam song.

I don't remember how many times we performed the song live because it would have been hard to recreate the guitar sound at the start of the song. We just got around that by excluding that part and instead using some other effect on Paul's guitar. I know we included it in the Rockpalast set when we did that show in Germany in 1980.

The thing with songs is that people generally hear the songs more on record than they do live. This means their ears are

conditioned to hearing what was included on the recorded version and that's what they expect to hear. Thankfully most Jam songs sounded the same live as they had done in the studio, apart from a song like 'Dreams Of Children', but they were in the minority. By the time we had recorded the track we had a pretty hefty back catalogue of songs to choose from, so a song like 'Dreams Of Children' probably wasn't a priority song to have to play live.

Having Vic Smith producing the band was great when it came to experimenting with sound effects. He had the imagination that could conjure up visions from the recordings. Having him in the studio helped us keep things interesting. Vic's role, his job, his purpose for being with The Jam was to get the best possible recording for a song. What we did live didn't matter to him. If we did something in the studio but that something couldn't be replicated on stage, it was of no matter to him.

I don't remember any discussions around why 'Dreams Of Children' should be kept off an album and instead be used a double A-side with 'Going Underground'. I don't know if it got overshadowed by 'Going Underground', especially because 'Going Underground' got the air play because it reached No 1.

35. HERE COMES THE WEEKEND (PAUL WELLER)

Recorded at Basing Street Studios, London, August 1977

Available on *This Is The Modern World* and *Direction Reaction Creation*

'Here Comes The Weekend' was produced by Chris Parry and Vic Smith in Basing Street Studios, also known as Sarm West Studios. The studio was established by Chris Blackwell

6

who founded Island Records. Located within the walls of a former church the recording room was used by the likes of Steve Winwood, Jimmy Cliff, Led Zeppelin and The Rolling Stones.

A Who-esque intro consisting of all three band members kicks off the track and this and Weller's 'OK' 'Alright' Here it comes' eases in the verse. The song is typical of many of the others on the *This Is The Modern World* album in that it doesn't carry that attack or vibrant energy. And yet the song still retains moments of aggression. This is demonstrated in the way Weller shouts out "the weekend starts here".

This is another song that Jam fans could connect with and see themselves in. It's a story shared by the working people. It's a song of counting down the days and looking forward to the weekend. 'Here Comes The Weekend' is a song about celebrating the weekend which is something we can all relate to.

Rick Buckler:
When I hear 'Here Comes The Weekend' it does remind me that the song came from what I consider to be The Jam's first foray into making a studio album. Unlike *In The City*, *This Is The Modern World* was pretty much written in the studio. It had to be.

We were still very new to studio work and we hadn't discovered the differences between us as a live band and us as a studio band. But there were differences that in time we did indeed discover. With *In The City* all the songs on that album we'd been playing live for some time, years in some cases. But a song like 'Here Comes The Weekend' was new and hadn't had the time to be played at gigs before taking it into the studio.

Paul came up with the majority of the

songs on *This Is The Modern World* pretty quickly. He needed to because of the pressure from Polydor. It had only been something like five months since our debut album that we found ourselves back in the studio recording our follow up and during those five months we'd still be out playing live and promoting *In The City*. Things moved and happened very quickly for The Jam in 1977.

As a band we were used to working quickly. In the studio we usually worked very quickly. We didn't really spend a great deal of time laying down version upon version of the same song. We did find time for this later on, but in 1977, we worked quickly, usually just one or two takes and we'd be happy with the result.

The pressure in 1977 was also just something we went along with. I suppose from the record label's point of view they wanted another album out as quickly as possible and to ride on the 'going is good' vibe and Paul, Bruce and myself just didn't know if we'd even be a band or making records or have a record label the next year.

The thing with being in a band, and this is often heard, is that you don't know if your success is going to last. It's a strange job to have. You never know when you're going to be out of work. You don't know for certain that if the people who bought your record the last time will do it for the next one and a band needs people to buy their records or else the record labels won't get you a deal. In 1977 The Jam was no different.

The general feeling in The Jam was that we felt we needed to prove ourselves on two fronts. On the first front we had to prove ourselves to the fans so that

THE JAM

they continued to support us and we'd continue to build a decent fan base. We understood that without fans a band was nothing. The second front concerned the record company. We knew and accepted that we had to prove ourselves to them, because without them we couldn't have records released. We also understood that the fans and record label saw things from different points of view. The fans wanted to hear good songs and the record label wanted good record sales. Both agendas needed to be met if you as the band are going to make it and survive. With this in our minds Paul, Bruce and myself pushed ourselves to be the best band we could be and make the best records that we could.

By the time we recorded 'Here Comes The Weekend' Paul, Bruce and I had made up our minds that being in a band and making records and going on tour was what we wanted to do. Maybe 'Here Comes The Weekend' did hark back to a time before we were in a successful band. In the period before we had a weekend but once The Jam started to take off we'd be playing gigs every weekend. For at least a couple of years before In The City was released we'd not had free weekends any more. We were working our jobs in the week and then we were out working at the weekends.

I think there was a little bit of nostalgia in 'Here Comes The Weekend'. Not that we complained because even before we went professional, and that meant working pretty much seven days a week, we loved doing what we were doing. We looked forward to the weekends because it meant we could go out to the clubs and working men's clubs and play our songs.

We were still young men and I suppose

there were times when we felt we may have been missing out on some things. But then I suppose our mates looked at us and maybe felt they were missing out. The grass is always greener, isn't it? But there was times when I'd be invited to a party or some other event, which I would have loved to have done but had to decline because I had a gig to play. I think Paul, Bruce and I had an attitude that nothing would get in the way of the band and nothing was going to stop us. We had that dedication and I think bands that don't have just don't make it in the industry.

I stayed alert to any potential threats because I didn't not want to be in a band like The Jam. I had seen how things came along like jobs, girlfriends, holidays, whatever and had stopped bands or band members progressing. In the early days I dealt with things as they came up. In the years leading up to getting signed by Polydor I changed jobs a lot. I almost expected my employer to sack me because I'd leave early on Friday afternoons because I was playing a gig that night or I show up late on Monday mornings because I had been out late on Sunday night. But I never saw it as a problem because there was plenty of work around and I just told myself that if I got sacked I'd just go and get another job - which I did, a lot.

There was one job I had at a place called Walkers that I left because I told the boss I was going to be going on tour in Germany. John Weller had told Paul, Bruce and myself he had a month's work for The Jam playing at American Air force bases in Germany. I was very excited and immediately told my boss I was handing in my notice. I left the job and

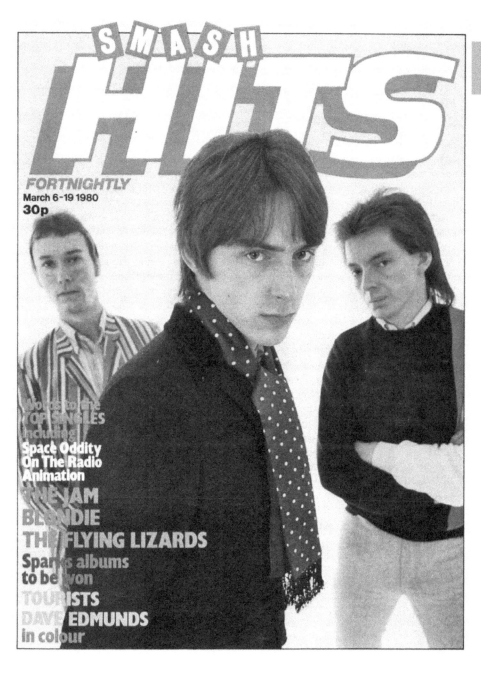

6

then the German thing fell through. So I found myself with no job and no trip to Germany. I couldn't bring myself to go and tell the boss and ask for my job back, so I just went and found something else.

The Jam ended up as a three-piece because the other members we had like Dave Waller and Steve Brookes wanted something else and that was their choice. I suppose also being in a band like The Jam was risky. We were on a bit of a treadmill and going round and round playing the same clubs and pubs and I guess it was hard to see a future. I think Paul, Bruce and myself just had a hope and a different dream. The early days of being in The Jam certainly didn't come without their fair share of frustrations and dashed dreams but we hung in there.

As a song I think 'Here Comes The Weekend' also represents something so important to working people. The Jam had grown up in that era when shops closed on Wednesday afternoons. Nothing opened on Sundays or public holidays. It wasn't anything like nowadays where shops can be open 24/7 and on pretty much any day of the year. In our era everyone got paid on Fridays, Saturday was your own day and on Sundays nothing happened, unless you went to church. In that era families spent more time with one another and then on Monday it was back to work and around it all went again. This was what my parents knew, this is what Paul, Bruce and I knew. This was how the world worked for us. 'Here Comes The Weekend' represented how the world used to be.

36. THE GREAT DEPRESSION (PAUL WELLER)

Recorded at Maison Rouge Studios, London, February 1982.
Available on *The Jam Extras* and *Direction Reaction Creation*.

'The Great Depression' was released as the B-side to 'Just Who Is The Five O'clock Hero' in July 1982. It reached No 8 in the UK charts. The production credits went to The Jam and Tony Taverner. Taverner was the in-house engineer at Maison Rouge at the time.

On this song Weller, Buckler and Foxton were joined by Keith Thomas on tenor sax and Steve Nichol on trumpet. They both helped out with some handclaps too which also sound like they could have been a drum machine.

As a song 'The Great Depression' relies on the percussive element. The drums, the handclaps, the brass, even the piano played by Weller are all played in a way that gives the song a unique percussive feel. There is some use of a phased snare drum too, enough to insert some variety and a direct link to the effect used on some Small Faces tracks, which wouldn't have gone unnoticed by the Mods in The Jam army.

'The Great Depression' hung around The Jam's live sets during their final year and it was last performed by the band at their Guildford concert on 9 December 1982.

Rick Buckler:
Again the meaning of the song is open to interpretation. For my part I could see how it related to that being stuck in a tower block type of thing, where there is no escape, where your life is mapped out for you and there's not much you can do about it. I think

the song is pointing out just how depressing that could be. There's that attitude of 'eat, sleep, die' and there's nothing that you can do about it - which of course is not true and other Jam songs talked about breaking away from those ways of thinking.

Paul, Bruce and I grew up in a time when class distinction was much more obvious and there was an element that if you grew up in a certain class or a certain part of society, then that's where you stayed. 'The Great Depression' was the flip side to 'Five O'Clock Hero' and that related to working class people, grafters and people stuck in the rut of the nine to five or the daily grind.
I found the song to be a little bit lumpy and I never felt especially chuffed with my drumming part on the song. I'm not sure why. Most things we did came out great but 'The Great Depression' for me just didn't. We worked quickly on the song but I felt some parts of it just didn't click together. But this is only my opinion and perhaps Bruce and Paul feel differently and, as far I know, it went down okay with Jam fans.

The song had a certain rhythm and I played what I thought was needed, but looking back I feel I could have come up with something better. I don't think I had time though. The other thing was because we worked quickly as soon as something started to feel like hard work and it wasn't coming together we'd more often than not just abandon it and moved on.

But having said it feels lumpy to me, maybe that's what gave it that jarring-type feel and that's what maybe did work. We must have felt it was good enough though because we decided to commit it to vinyl and it did demonstrate how The Jam could come up with a variety of songs. 'The Great Depression' was one of our most quirky.

37. STRANGE TOWN (PAUL WELLER)

Recorded at RAK Studios, London, January 1979.
Available on *Snap!*, *The Very Best Of The Jam About The Young Idea* and *Direction Reaction Creation*

In late 1978 Paul was working with a song titled 'Worlds Apart'. The song never really progressed but part of the tune was developed into what became 'Strange Town', which The Jam recorded soon after the Christmas break.

The story goes that Paul had got the idea for the song after reading some newspaper article about a UFO landing. There had been some sightings across the UK on New Year's Eve and this had caught Paul's attention.

'Strange Town' has one of the best Jam song intros. From the off it caught the listener. This is then followed by that Motown style beat. It stomps. Buckler wouldn't use this beat often but when he did he put his own stamp on it, which removed it from the style in which the Funk Brothers drummers played it.

The song has a strong chorus, which like all sections of the song has no messing. And with an outstanding B-side like 'The Butterfly Collector' this was a 'go to' single for the die-hard Jam fan... every time.

It would be three months after recording the song that 'Strange Town' was released as a single and when it did it got to No 15 in the UK charts. This was to be their second highest chart success to date.

In a 2015 interview with *The Guardian*, Paul Weller stated that 'Strange Town' was one of thee perfect songs he'd written in his life. (The other two being 'Wings of Speed' from *Stanley Road* and 'Going My Way' on *Saturn's Patterns*).

6

THE JAM

THE JAM—No. 1 in your hearts

PAUL, BRUCE & RICK CLEAN UP NME READERS POLL — FULL RESULTS CENTRE PAGES

Rick Buckler:
I liked the picture sleeve that the single was issued in. It showed a blurry image of a man at some crossroads. That was actually Bill Smith from Polydor. He had driven out to Norfolk with photographer Martyn Goddard and it was Martyn who asked Bill to stand in the road and he'd take his photo. I think the photo was meant to represent someone who doesn't know which way to go, which road to take.

'Strange Town' was popular amongst the laddish element of The Jam army, especially the football goers. When the song came out in

1979 football was still a very popular pastime in Britain and each Saturday would see hordes of young men travelling the length and breadth of the nation, following their football team into all kinds of strange towns.

For The Jam's part because we were on the road a lot, we found ourselves in many strange towns. This often meant we didn't know the place at all, had no idea of the customs and do's and don'ts and when we were abroad the different languages and so on. I think this was also experienced by the fans that followed us to those places. I suspect many Jam fans found themselves in situations which they didn't understand because they didn't know about the place.

One of the strangest towns and concerts I ever did with The Jam was in Sweden. The stage we had to play on was situated in the middle of a fun fair. This meant that whilst we played there were people whizzing around on fairground rides all around us. It was weird to say the least smashing out Jam songs as people had fun on the rides. It was like being in the middle of Billy Smart's Circus, with all the chaos and noise and activity. We sort of played to an audience that was hardly paying us any attention at all. I don't know how John got us that booking but apparently the venue had bands perform on that stage on a regular basis.

Going to Japan was great but again they had their ways of doing things and these couldn't have been further away from what we knew in the UK. As an example our concerts had to end at 9pm. This meant we'd play out sets and leave the venues and it would still be light outside. We just weren't used to it.

We also found the Japanese to be very polite. They'd sit down in the concerts and wouldn't make any noise at all. They would just listen. This was a complete contrast to what it was like playing to UK audiences, who'd be jumping around and shouting and sometimes even fighting.

There were times in Japan when I just didn't know if they liked us at all or if our music was going down well with them. But it seemed to because we went back and toured Japan a few times.

What I initially found odd about the music fans in Japan was how they carried around their autograph books with absolutely any musician in it from any genre of music. You'd autograph your name on one page and it would be sandwiched between Deep Purple and the Bay City Rollers.

There'd be a very strange mix of bands. But the Japanese just loved live bands from the UK and the USA. They weren't a blinkered nation like the UK could be when it came to music.

In the UK if you were a Mod you could only be seen to like 'Mod' music, if you was a punk it had to be 'punk' music and a Soul Boy 'Soul' music and so on. Britain was much more tribal and this was something quite unique to the UK back in The Jam days.

Going to the States was also very strange. It differed so much from state to state too. Some states just didn't get The Jam at all and some were still very sceptical of British music. The tour we did opening for Blue Öyster Cult was odd – their fans just didn't connect with us at all and those concerts were tough. But touring the States was still good to do even though it did take The Jam out of our comfort zones. What we also found was that the more industrial type towns took to us better than the not so industrial. I think we had more in common in those places and we recognised something in each other. New York took to us but towns in the Southern States didn't.

Also we found it strange whenever we played outside concerts in the daytime. For years we'd played gigs in clubs and pubs at night and when we left it was near midnight or later. It's what we had got used to.

I found some places to be more accommodating than others. For instance I really liked playing to the people in Holland, France, Sweden and Japan.

In the UK I felt we had more of affinity with places like London, Newcastle, Liverpool and Glasgow rather than places like Brighton. Jam audiences were always enthusiastic but some were more so than others. In the UK during the years when The Jam were going there were some very tough places and I guess they connected with the tougher edge of The Jam sound.

THE JAM

THE CHARTS IN THE EIGHTIES

To give a flavour of music in the UK charts and other artists who were having No I hits at the same time as The Jam here are the songs that sat either side of The Jams four No I hits.

15 March 1980, Together We Are Beautiful - Fern Kinney

22 March 1980, Going Underground/Dreams of Children - The Jam

12 April 1980, Working My Way Back To You - The Detroit Spinners

23 Aug 1980, Ashes To Ashes - David Bowie

6 Sept 1980, Start - The Jam

13 Sept 1980, Feels Like I'm In Love - Kelly Marie

6 Feb 1982, Computer Love/The Model - Kraftwerk

13 Feb 1982, A Town Called Malice/Precious - The Jam

6 March 1982, The Lion Sleeps Tonight - Tight Fit

13 Nov 1982, I Don't Want To Dance - Eddy Grant

4 Dec 1982, Beat Surrender - The Jam

18 Dec 1982, Save Your Love - Renée and Renato

CHART HISTORY

The first British singles chart was published in the 14 November 1952 edition of the New Musical Express. It was at first little more than a gimmick in the circulation war against NME's much older (and more popular) rival weekly music paper Melody Maker. The chart, at first a top 12, was the creation of the paper's advertising manager, Percy Dickins, who compiled it by telephoning around 20 major record stores in the UK and aggregating their sales reports. He would continue to personally oversee the compilation of the chart well into the Sixties.

The forerunner of today's official chart first appeared in the music trade publication Record Retailer (now Music Week) in 1960 as a Top 50, but was not immediately recognised as the definitive chart in the country. Arguably, the NME chart was still the most recognised chart, and had the advantage of widespread exposure due to its use by Radio Luxembourg. Throughout the Sixties, the various different charts battled for public recognition, leading to some historical anomalies - for example, The Beatles' second single 'Please Please Me' which was released on the 11 January 1963 reached No I on the New Musical Express and Melody Maker charts. However, it only reached No 2 on the Record Retailer chart. To add to the confusion, the chart used by the BBC on Pick of the Pops and Top of the Pops was actually calculated by averaging out all the others, and so didn't agree with any of them, and was prone to tied positions.

It wasn't until 1969 that an official chart emerged from an alliance between the BBC and Record Retailer. For the first time a professional polling organisation, BMRB, was commissioned to oversee the chart, and a pool of 500 record shops was used - more than twice as many as had been used for any previous chart. The new Official Top 50 was inaugurated in the week ending 12 February 1969.

For the first three years of the Eighties the UK Singles Chart was compiled by the *British Market Research Bureau* who had been compiling the charts throughout the Seventies. On 8 January 1983 *Gallup* took over the compilation of the UK music charts and continued to provide the chart data for the next eleven years. The charts were produced from the sales data of a representative panel of around 500 record shops across the country.

The panel sales data from each shop were sent to the chart compilers where week and a multiplication factor was then applied to obtain an estimate of total sales across the country.

Under the *BMRB* this sales data was posted to the chart compilers, but when *Gallup* took over they automated the system by installing computer terminals in the shops that registered each sale and sent the information to *Gallup* immediately.

Singles sales remained very healthy during the Eighties. Dexy's Midnight Runners' 'Come on Eileen', sold 1.31 million copies, Culture Club's 'Karma Chameleon' 1.47 million copies and Frankie Goes to Hollywood's massive hit 'Relax' two million copies, making it the seventh best-selling single in UK singles chart history.

Arranged with their record companies many artists were encouraged to make 'appearances' in major record stores like HMV Records around the UK to promote a new single or album. By doing this sales were boosted in stores as the acts would sign newly purchased records on the day which would all add to the shops chart return figures.

THE JAM

6

38. BEAT SURRENDER (PAUL WELLER)

Recorded at Phonogram Studios, London, October 1982.

Available on *Snap, The Very Best Of The Jam: About The Young Idea* and *Direction Reaction Creation*

'Beat Surrender' was to be The Jam's last song that they would record together. Weller, Foxton and Buckler knew this when they went into the Phonogram Studios on an October's day. The following month it was released as the band's final single. It got to No 1 on the UK charts where it stayed for two weeks, giving The Jam their fourth chart topper.

In the studio on that October day Pete Wilson was on hand to produce the song. He was The Jam's producer in those final days. Alongside Buckler, Weller and Foxton, Tracie Young and Afrodiziak were invited in to provide extra backing vocals and Martin Drover and Luke Tunney provided the trumpets.

'Beat Surrender' begins with Weller's piano part and vocals, which are subtly supported by the backing vocalists. And then The Jam burst into life, just like they had on so many records before. "Come on boys, come on girls" pleads Weller as the song soulfully pushes along, the piano part very much a driving force. The song is full of life and energy and it was certainly a brilliant choice for The Jam to choose as their farewell record. For The Jam fan it had everything in it that they had come to love about the band - energy, vibrancy, attack, passion and heart!

Rick Buckler:

I honestly don't know whether Paul wrote 'Beat Surrender' because he thought it was to be the last Jam song and said something about the demise of the band. I can't really comment on the song's title either because I don't know what Paul had going on his head.

As a song I think it's really good. If you just allow it to wash over you and don't get too hung up on the lyrics, it works very well. I liked the middle eight section in the song and the way it takes the song in a different direction. I thought this other direction had a darker side to it. There was something about the way the vocals drop down. There's almost something Jekyll and Hyde like about it.

'Beat Surrender' was released when things were a bit weird for us in the band. It was a bit like 'we're going to commit suicide but let's release a song anyway'. We did release a song and we were still trying to keep things going and on the 'up'. The song was far from gloomy. We couldn't go out on a gloomy song. Despite the fact that we had to fulfil our contract with Polydor we didn't take an attitude of 'sod it, let's just bung out a single'. I think Paul, Bruce and I were proud that we didn't take that attitude and instead put out a quality song.

Our last single could have been something different to 'Beat Surrender'. At the end we still had a raft of material that had been rehearsed and some even recorded. Some were match fit and could have easily been used for singles. A couple of songs ended up in The Style Council like 'Solid Bond In Your Heart.' That song would have made a good Jam single.

But 'Beat Surrender' was decided on as the track to serve as The Jam's swan song and it did get to No 1, which gave us our fourth chart-topping single. Who knows if it would still have got to No 1 if the fans didn't know the band was splitting up and that it would be the last single? It was great that the song did get to the top. It cheered us up knowing that The Jam was going out with a bang.

We had Tracie Young sing vocals on 'Beat Surrender'. Paul had got her involved with Respond, which was the record label that he'd started up. He had other artists like The Questions on the label and singles were starting to be released. We liked her voice and it was felt that it would suit 'Beat Surrender', so we got her into the studio.

I found Tracie to be really nice. I got on with her well. She had her own mind and own ideas and I think these sometimes clashed with Paul. She was also quite young and still discovering things for herself - especially how the music industry worked. When she was with The Jam for that short period she was very excited and seemed to enjoy what was happening.

I remember Tracie joined us for the *Top of the Pops* appearance when we performed 'Beat Surrender'. That was all a bit unusual. The drums were set up at the front of the stage and Paul danced and sang but didn't hold a guitar and Tracie danced and sang beside him. I'm not sure what Jam fans made of it really.

After The Jam split up Paul kept her around to sing on some Style Council tracks and I think she released a few records of her own too. I didn't see her for a while but then bumped into her one night when I was with Time UK. She was very friendly and we had a good chat.

I thought the singles gatefold sleeve worked really well. The photo of the band actually ended up as part of the collection in the National Gallery: it was the photograph that they chose to portray The Jam.

The photo of us sitting on those spiral steps, the fire escape, was located in the Phonogram Studios in Stanhope Place. Before The Jam started to use the studios they had been used by the likes of Dusty Springfield, Roy Wood and Status Quo. After The Jam, Paul took over the studios and re-named it Solid Bond and he recorded with The Style Council and his Respond artists there. I think he held onto the studios for most of the Eighties.

We needed a photo for the next single release and whilst we were in the Phonogram studios one day we just went outside and we did the shoot. My strongest memory of the shoot was of the little lawn that was just by the fire escape. It was on that lawn that I learnt to play congas that I then used on 'Funeral Pyre'. I had never played congas before so I had little or no idea what to do. We got some conga player in to teach me a few things and he did so on that lawn.

The sleeve also had a photo of Paul's then girlfriend Gill Price on it, credited as girl model G.P. For some reason she's holding a flag - I have no idea why or what that was meant to symbolise. I think people have read into it all sorts of meanings. The white flag of surrender meaning one and what that may mean as regards the end of The Jam. I just liked the simplicity of the sleeve really and didn't read too much into the images on it.

THE JAM

6

TRACIE

Tracie Young was discovered by Paul Weller through an advertisement in *Smash Hits* magazine for his Respond Records label. The advert solicited demo tapes from female singers between the ages of 18 and 24. Although just 17 years old, Young replied and sent a cassette of a Phoebe Snow-inspired version of the Betty Wright hit 'Shoorah Shoorah'. Young's tape was singled out from among the hundreds received, and shortly thereafter she was invited to London for an audition where she sang old soul numbers 'Band of Gold' and 'Reach Out (I'll Be There)' at the audition. Weller was impressed enough

for her to become his priority signing for the Respond label.

Young was featured on the cover of the 9 April 1983 issue of *New Musical Express* with the banner 'Tracie: The girl star Paul Weller would build'. She was also voted 'Most Fanciable Female' in *Smash Hits* 1983 readers poll and had UK hit singles 'The House That Jack Built' and 'Give it Some Emotion' (both credited simply to 'Tracie').

Since the late 1990s Young has enjoyed a second career as a radio presenter, working at Radio Essex and also Connect FM in Peterborough and Northamptonshire.

39. WHEN YOU'RE YOUNG (PAUL WELLER)

Recorded at Townhouse Studios, London, July 1979.

Available on *Snap!, The Very Best Of The Jam: About The Young Idea* and *Direction Reaction Creation.*

Four notes from Foxton and some 'who hoos' from Weller and Foxton and The Jam's eighth single release is out of the blocks.

The verse begins having been helped on by some handclaps. The handclaps serve as a distinctive part to the song. Handclaps were something The Jam would use on several of their tracks and each time they did they added that something extra.

In many ways the structure of the song is simple and straightforward. It's a strong enough song anyway so it doesn't need to have too much going on. But there is the middle eight where the band drops off. Again the handclaps come to the fore which clear the way for an almost reggae-style section.

And then there's a guitar solo, one of Weller's longest whilst in The Jam and then the 'who hoos' bring the song back in and this takes the song out.

Released on 17 August 1979, it charted at No 17 in the UK Singles Chart. The B-side, 'Smithers-Jones', is widely considered to be Jam bassist Bruce Foxton's finest song-writing moment and also appears – with an orchestral arrangement – on the band's 1979 album, *Setting Sons.*

Rick Buckler:

This was another song that we felt we just wanted to be released as a single and not one that had been lifted from an album. I remember doing the video. I don't know why or how but we ended up on the bandstand in Queens Park, London. The bandstand had been there since the late 19th Century and had been given to the people of London for "free use and enjoyment of the public", so we took advantage of it and filmed some of the video on it. There were a bunch of kids hanging around and having a laugh and somehow they managed to be included in the video.

Of course we just mimed along as the song got played. The video would then cut to footage of kids and young people going about their everyday business. It was a good depiction of working class folk just being themselves in 1979.

Although we were miming we actually look like we are having a laugh. At one point we sat in amongst a bunch of kids who had gathered on some wooden chairs by the bandstand to watch us. I think Bruce even tried to get them involved with some singing.

It's only my opinion but I never felt 'When You're Young' was one of the live favourites amongst Jam fans. But I think it is a favourite record for many people. Maybe this is because it's a song about being young and celebrating youth. I thought the song captured a young fresh feel, which people could relate to. I really liked the tempo and the melody of the song and I think it did reflect being young.

This was also one of those Jam songs that just seemed to work well in the studio. As we were putting it together it felt right and the parts worked and fitted well together.

The song came together naturally, which isn't always the case. The parts made sense, which I think gave the song a sort of seamless feel.

THE JAM

40. NEWS OF THE WORLD (FOXTON)

Recorded at Morgan Studios, London,
February 1978.
Available on *Snap!, The Very Best Of The
Jam: About The Young Idea* and *Direction
Reaction Creation*

'News Of The World' was recorded in some
modest studios in Willesden called Morgan
Studios. Both Chris Parry and Vic Smith were on
hand to produce Bruce Foxton's composition.
When it was issued as a single in February it
reached No 27 in the UK charts.

Beginning with Weller's distinctive riff and
bass drum thumps and a bass guitar 'News Of
The World' presents itself to the record-buying
public. And the public get what the public want
as this Jam song delivers everything that the
band was about in 1978. The song has a good
melody that mixes with the aggression that the
band pulled off like no other band at the time.

It's Foxton who steps up to take on the lead
vocal duties. This came as a surprise to The Jam
fans at the time. But there's nothing to worry
about because Foxton does a fantastic job as he
serves his song well. But the song would have
been nothing if it hadn't had been for Weller
and Buckler adding their talents.

'News Of The World' was released at a time
when changes were afoot again. Punk had come
and gone. Only a few weeks before 'News Of
The World' was released The Sex Pistols had
split up. New wave music was what the music
journalists were interested in and The Jam, for
a brief period, got lumped in with those bands.
But 1978 would also be the year that *All Mod Cons*
was released and the first signs of the new Mods
were seen surging onto the London scene and
hanging around Carnaby Street. The following
year the Mods had swelled in numbers across the
UK and Sid Vicious was dead.

Rick Buckler:
'News Of The World' was one of Bruce's
songs and one of his better-known songs.
The song has been used as the theme tune to
the BBC2 programme *Mock The Week*. This is
a show that has been going since 2005 with
Dara O'Briain and Hugh Dennis.

For me, the vocals just never seemed to fit
the tune. I think that lets the song down. It
was a song that did go down well live though
and it gave Paul an opportunity to have a
brief break from taking centre stage. I don't
think Paul was ever really at home with the
guitar lead break. But the song was recorded
at a time when he was quite against the lead
guitar ethic. I don't know why because he did
some really good lead parts. Vic Smith often
had to help him but this was a good thing.
Jam recordings have quite a few lead guitar
bursts but they couldn't be done live.

We shot the video at Battersea Power
Station. The chimneys could be seen for
miles away, they were huge. Before The Jam
went there the power station had been used
in other musical projects. Pink Floyd had
used the imagery on their 1977 *Animals* album
sleeve and The Who also used it on their
Quadrophenia inner sleeve.

I remember Paul, Bruce and I being told
that there'd be a helicopter shooting part of
the video but for whatever reason that never
showed up. The idea was that whilst we were
miming the song on the roof of the power
station the helicopter would swoop over and
capture us playing our instruments.

We were perched on the edge of the
roof area. It was quite high up. The whole
Battersea Power Station is a massive complex.
It's currently being turned into homes and
offices. What I do remember is that it
was very windy being up there. It was that
windy my cymbal stands kept blowing over

and I had to keep standing them up again. Thankfully none of my cymbals got damaged.

I was using a fibreglass kit at the time too and that was really light so that too kept moving due to the strength of the wind. The kit was made by Dallas Arbiter, which was made by Hayman. It was actually a piece of rubbish, it failed on every front and I didn't keep it around for much longer after the 'News Of The World' video shoot.

> *"Unlike a lot of bands The Jam went from strength to strength and when they split they were on top of their game. I thought that was very cool."*
> **Johnny Marr**

PETER WILSON

Producer Peter Wilson worked with The Jam on their final studio album *The Gift* and *Dig the New Breed*, which was the final album by The Jam - a collection of live performances recorded between 1977 and 1982. His role as producer also saw him working on the singles 'Funeral Pyre', 'Absolute Beginners', 'Town Called Malice' and 'Beat Surrender'.

After leaving Surrey University he started to work as an engineer at Polydor Studios, working with Brian Eno, Neil Sedaka and Peggy Lee.

The first work that established his career was his production of 'Angels With Dirty Faces' by Sham 69. He went on to produce further singles for Sham 69 including 'Hurry Up Harry' and 'If the Kids Are United' as well as four albums by Sham 69. Wilson also produced The Passions and four albums with The Comsat Angels.

It was at Polydor that Wilson first worked with Paul Weller (then still with The Jam) on some demos which in turn led to Wilson producing the last Jam studio. He continued to work with Weller with The Style Council, co-producing three studio albums and hits such as 'Speak Like A Child', 'Long Hot Summer' and 'My Ever Changing Moods'.

6

41. THE MODERN WORLD (PAUL WELLER)

Recorded at Basing Street Studios, London, September 1977

Available on *Snap, The Very Best Of The Jam: About The Young Idea* and *Direction Reaction Creation*

Almost getting inside the UK top twenty but stalling at No 22, this was still a massive achievement and a boost for The Jam as their third single. 'The Modern World' was released on 28 October 1977 as the first and only single from the band's second album *This Is the Modern World*. With a word like 'modern' in the title this didn't go unnoticed by the few Mods that were just starting to appear on the streets of East London. It had been more than a decade since youths in parkas, three button suits and Ben Shermans had been seen on the streets of the capital. And it wouldn't be too long before they found themselves searching garages and sheds for discarded and disused Vespas and Lambrettas to bring back to life.

For many youths in 1977 going into 1978, the 'modern world' was going to be their Mod world and The Jam was leading the way.

Rick Buckler:

'The Modern World' was recorded at a time when we were still finding our feet in the studio, but for this song, we stripped it right back and punched our way through it, and this worked for this song. There were accents in the song that gave it the edge. It wasn't the most subtle of Jam songs and in many ways it was quite 'in your face'.

For the single issue we decided to include live versions of some of the songs that we'd been playing in our set. There were two cover songs 'Sweet Soul Music' and 'Back In My Arms Again', and one of our own, 'Bricks And Mortar'. We felt proud of those particular cover versions. They had been recorded at a gig we did at the 100 Club in London and had come out well. Throughout The Jam years we recorded a lot of our concerts.

I don't remember who came up with the suggestion to put out some live recordings as the B-side for 'The Modern World'. The record label may have been putting some pressure on, but Paul, Bruce and I always stuck to our guns and refused to put out stuff just to fill gaps. Regarding those songs on the B-side if we hadn't agreed it was a good idea, they wouldn't have been used.

Record labels really only liked A-sides. They know that it was the A-sides that were only going to get the attention, get the air play and it was only the A-sides that sold. The Jam felt differently to this and to us the B-sides were just as important as the A-sides.

We'd been playing songs like 'Sweet Soul Music' for years and we felt we played those songs well and put our own stamp on them. Many did get carried through to the sets we played in the early days of being signed to Polydor and they seemed to go down well with the audiences. In 1977 there weren't many bands playing songs like 'Sweet Soul Music' and 'Back In Your Arms Again' and they worked as an interesting contrast to a song like 'The Modern World'. Those cover songs also represent what The Jam was about at that particular time, in the same way the live cover songs we used on the B-side to 'Beat Surrender' showed what we were about at that time, some five years on.

42. THE BUTTERFLY COLLECTOR (PAUL WELLER)

Recorded at RAK Studios, London, January 1979.
Available on *Snap, The Very Best Of The Jam: About The Young Idea, The Jam Extras* and *Direction Reaction Creation*.

An acetate documents the song as having the title 'Collecting Butterflies', which was either a mistake by whoever wrote it down or it was just the working title before The Jam settled on 'The Butterfly Collector'.

A firm favourite amongst Jam fans and for many the band's finest B-side, 'The Butterfly Collector' stands proud and upright.

The song begins with just Weller playing an effected guitar and introducing the lyrics where he sings about someone finally getting what they wanted. The lyrics were about the groupies that Weller observed hanging around some of the more successful bands at the time. These groupies were like collectors and the person he had in mind was 'Soo Catwoman'. She was one of the Bromley Contingent who hung around with the Pistols and the Banshees. She was also one of the main faces who frequented clubs like The Vortex and the Roxy.

Weller has already painted a picture of the butterfly collector before Buckler and Foxton burst in to help out. They help elevate the song to another level before taking a back seat again and allowing the tune with its organ, played by Weller to continue with the next verse.

Weller continues to tell the story and share his observations of the 'collector' and how things are changing for them. The lyrics are a bit scathing as they talk about falling status and being a second-rate person, like their perfume. But the lyrics also point out that the person fails to see this because they are still wrapped up in their own dream world and they still see themselves as the queen of the butterfly collectors, at which point Buckler and Foxton return and the song takes off again, eventually reaching its climax where it ends pretty much as it began with Weller's voice and effected guitar.

Rick Buckler:

'The Butterfly Collector' is one of my favourite Jam songs. I thought it was a bit off the beaten track for a Jam song and I liked that. The song had subtle elements too which I thought worked well. These were contained in the lyrics, which were about the women that were collecting pop stars.

Pop and rock music is notorious for attracting such 'butterfly collectors' and we started to notice it in the punk scene. There were people like 'Soo Catwoman' popping up and being part of the 'scene'. There was a kind of badge collecting amongst them.

During the punk period we were all young and still finding our way and I suppose we were like butterflies. I think the lyrics can represent the parallel between being crusty old moths/bands who develop into sharp and brilliant looking butterflies/bands. There was also a sense that we weren't going to last the summer and before long the next new shiny thing would come along. I think the butterfly collectors/groupies were hanging around capturing the flavour of the month, but then they'd discard you.

The Jam was actually quite lucky when it came to liggers or hangers on. It was never really much of an issue for us. Of course there were some people that tried to get close because they had fallen in love with the band's fame or success and wanted to

6

have a piece of it. It's inevitable, being a part of the music industry. On the other hand there are also people around the band because they are just fans of what you are doing and their interest is more genuine and honest. The Jam had lots of fans like this and we appreciated them. They were no trouble.

Rock and roll history is also littered with bands who fell apart because the wrong people and the liggers infiltrated the set up. And this has been really unfortunate and some bands just never recovered. Sex, drugs and rock and roll has its dark side.

The butterflies and liggers can become quite dangerous people. They become 'yes' people. Whatever the band does, whether it be rubbish or too far out, those people still say 'yes' and the band believes them and it can be a big mistake.

In The Jam we had our manager John Weller and if something didn't seem right or he could see where it might be heading he'd say so and we'd at least listen. We knew that John had the band's best interests at heart and so we could trust him. I don't think all rock bands can say the same about their managers.

Another thing that The Jam was good at was keeping in touch with the fans. We weren't like the Led Zeppelins and big stadium bands that came up in the Seventies who were like rock gods and lived on a different plane and the fans couldn't get near. I believe The Jam had a good relationship with the fans and we could communicate. They'd tell us what they liked and what they didn't. They felt they could speak their minds. There just wasn't much of an "us and them" situation going on. I think Paul, Bruce and I were

conscious of not cutting ourselves off from our fans. It just wasn't us.

Regards the structure of 'The Butterfly Collector' I recall having 'Because The Night' by Patti Smith in my mind. That song and her style was a bit of an influence at the time for me. There was this sort of stop start thing going on with the drums. 'Because The Night' starts with just piano and then vocals and then the drums burst in and the song unfolds. On 'The Butterfly Collector' the song starts with guitar and then vocals and then the drums come in. I liked this idea and it totally worked on 'The Butterfly Collector'.

There was something about Vic Smith's production on this song too that worked well. He was able to capture something with the mixture of sounds coming from the guitars, organ, bass and drums whilst retaining a very clean sound. I liked the sound of the drums on the song too. The toms sounded great.

43. IN THE CITY (PAUL WELLER)
Recorded at Polydor Studios, London, March 1977
Available on *Snap, The Very Best Of The Jam: About The Young Idea,* and *Direction Reaction Creation*

'In The City' was released as The Jam's debut single on 29 April 1977. It reached No 40 in the UK charts and saw the beginning of their streak of 18 consecutive Top 40 singles. With a brilliant guitar riff and energetic drums and bass, this is a song that shows a band on fire.

The songs lyrics refer to an incident of

police brutality that caught the attention of the public. On 16 January 1976 thirty nine year old Liddle Towers was arrested outside a club in Birtley in County Durham. Six police officers bundled him into a police van. He was taken to Gateshead police station. Early the following morning Towers was rushed to hospital. He was demanding treatment and complaining he had injuries sustained at the hands of his arresting police officers.

Towers went to the hospital but was discharged. He later told a friend about his ordeal in the police cells and said "they gave us a bloody good kicking outside the Key Club, but that was nothing compared to what I got when I went inside".

Towers died a few days later on 9 February 1976. On 8 October 1976 an inquest returned a verdict of justifiable homicide.

Paul heard about the Towers case and the incident left that much of an impression on him that he wrote the lyrics in response. The lyrics were also having a dig at the punks who weren't embracing The Jam. Weller and The Jam would soon leave them behind.

On May 2002, Polydor Records decided to commemorate the 25th anniversary of The Jam by re-releasing their debut single in its original packaging, in its original 7 vinyl record format and at its original price of 75 pence. The limited pressing sold out immediately, and the song made the Top 40 one more time, peaking at No 36: higher than it did in its original release and two subsequent reissues. It became the first single to chart in the UK Top 40 based solely on limited edition 7" sales since the late Seventies.

Rick Buckler:
In The City was The Jam's debut single. This was the song that introduced us to the record buying public. It got into the top forty too, which we thought was a good start!

I think it was Chris Parry who identified 'In The City' as being the best song we had at that time that would work as a single. He pushed for it and we agreed. We knew it was going down well in our live sets so it did appear to be the right and most suitable choice. Looking back I think 'In The City' was probably the only song we had that would have worked as a single. As an unknown band we knew we had to get it right. An opportunity to have a single released was a big deal.

'In The City' had its own meaning for The Jam. We'd had the desire to play in London. We knew that was where we needed to be and we'd put the work in to establish ourselves in the city. We played all the main venues where bands needed to play like the Hope and Anchor, Red Cow and 100 Club, and we had built a decent London fan base. In the city was where it was all happening. There'd been the pub rock scene and this had given way to the punk scene and not that long after 'In The City' came out the first signs of the next Mod wave was also starting to come through.

During 1977 we'd often play 'In The City' at least a couple of times in our sets. We felt it was a strong song and it was very much a song of that time. The song had lots of energy and attack and it was good to play.

Having our first single released was a very exciting time. I still have a fresh memory of the initial contact from Chris Parry telling

6

THE JAM

us that he liked us and then him coming back and telling us he wanted to record some demos and then us going into the studios and recording some songs. I can vividly remember getting the call at home - I was still living at my parents' - from John Weller telling me that Polydor wanted to sign the band and release a single. It all happened really fast - bang, bang, bang - but it was really exciting.

Throughout 1977 The Jam seemed to get elevated very quickly through all sorts of levels. We got signed, we had a contract, we had our debut single out, then an album, then another single and another album and then there was *Top of the Pops* and interviews and reviews and it just kept going on and on. And then I'd go to a pub and someone would put 'In The City' on the juke box and then you'd have someone telling you that they'd heard 'In The City' on the radio. It really was an amazing time, an incredible buzz. Everything was new and we had nothing to compare our new experiences with.

Once 'In The City' was released we hit the ground running and it was everything that we'd wanted, everything we'd been working towards and there we had it, it was real and it was happening. And from 'In The City' onwards we fought really hard to make sure we kept it. Paul, Bruce and myself worked hard. We fought our corner, always did things to prove ourselves and we sustained that until the end in 1982.

"**In** those days, I used to buy the *NME* every week and I remember there were about six or seven editions in a row where there was a new punk band on the front cover each week, and The Jam were on it just as 'In The City' was coming out. I'd never heard The Jam, but when I saw their photos – with their black and white bowling shoes and their suits – there was something I really liked about them.

My friend Vinnie O'Neil bought this single – without hearing it first – and the first time I heard it was when Vinnie put it on the record player back at the house and I just loved it. Looking back on it now, compared to some of The Jam stuff it sounds slightly simplistic – and I'm in The Undertones, we can hardly call out anything as simplistic! – but it has an energy and a real pure spirit. "In the city there's a thousand things I want to say to you…" what a great line. I still love this record after all these years, and what they went on to do with *All Mod Cons* and *Setting Sons* was just brilliant."

Michael Bradley
The Undertones

44. LIFE FROM A WINDOW (PAUL WELLER)
Recorded at Basing Street Studios, London, August 1977
Available on *This Is The Modern World* and *Direction Reaction Creation*

'Life From A Window' was produced by Chris Parry and Vic Smith. It would be one of the last songs that Parry would have any production influence over.

6

The song begins as if the three band members have just strolled into the studio and are just picking up their guitars and sitting on the drum stool. Next Weller is heard counting the band in and off they go, throwing themselves into the song. It's a brilliant intro the way the band build the song up, ease off, then build up again. Weller's vocals sound great too. Instantly the listener also finds themselves taking in the view and becoming part of the song.

'Life From A Window' was one of the more outstanding songs on *This Is The Modern World*. This was an album that The Jam pretty much needed to come up with quickly. They wrote the majority of the songs in the studio.

It was then a matter of getting the Polydor team behind the album and getting it released. Album sleeve designer Bill Smith was just one of the team. He worked on the sleeve with the photographer Gered Mankowitz, who had previously photographed the likes of Jimi Hendrix and The Rolling Stones. Smith suggested the photo shoot happen under a section of the Westway in London.

On the day of the shoot Paul was wearing a white jumper. He told Smith that he wanted something to wear with a Sixties Pop Art feel. It was very pop art. So Smith found some gaffa tape and stuck the two black arrows onto Paul's jumper.

Rick Buckler:
I think it's fair to say that 'Life From A Window' is one of the best songs on *This Is The Modern World*. It was well crafted and had a good tune to it. It's also one of my earliest memories of the band looking at the lyrics and thinking that it was an interesting aspect, ie. watching the world from within something. There was this sense of watching the world pass by but from the viewpoint of a window. The lyrics

were reflective and had depth and you have to remember that Paul was still only eighteen or something when he wrote the lyrics. 'Life From A Window' was an interesting song.

I think the track was written at a time when The Jam were starting to reap the fruits of all our previous labours. For years we'd been playing other people's songs. We had learnt from other artists how to structure songs and breathe life into a song and drew upon all this sort of stuff on a song like 'Life From A Window'.

45. TONIGHT AT NOON (PAUL WELLER)
Recorded at Basing Street Studios, London, August 1977
Available on *This Is The Modern World* and *Direction Reaction Creation*

The title of 'Tonight At Noon' was borrowed from British poet Adrian Henri, who in turn had borrowed it from Charlie Mingus, who had had an album released in 1965 called *Tonight At Noon*.

By the time of *This Is The Modern World* Weller had discovered Adrian Henri's works. Henri, born 10 April 1932 in Birkenhead, Cheshire, had been one of the founding members of the Liverpool Scene, so for Weller there was already some connection to The Beatles.

When Weller was asked about Henri's poetry he replied "I really admire his work". Admiring Henri's work had led Weller to find his own inspiration in the title and write the song, which he named 'Tonight At Noon'. (Weller also used another Henri title 'I Want To Paint' for a song that to date has never been officially released).

6

There are noises - sound effects dropped in between some tracks on the *This Is The Modern World* album. Before 'Tonight At Noon' someone is heard blowing a raspberry. The idea had been used by The Beatles on their albums and Weller was fully aware of this.

Rick Buckler:

I had some difficulty with 'Tonight At Noon'. For me it missed something. It never featured much in the sets we played live. For some reason this song and some others on *This Is The Modern World* got skipped over. I think this was partly because when the album came out it wasn't totally embraced by the media and there were a number of unfavourable reviews. Our response at the time was to quickly move on and, by doing so, songs from the album were simply left behind.

'Tonight At Noon' was also a studio track. The song had been written in the studio because we needed to record our second album. Time was an issue and we just hadn't time to run 'Tonight At Noon' out live. Songs get better when you play them live and this means that by the time you go into the studio to record they are well rehearsed and much more ready to get recorded. 'Tonight At Noon' never had that opportunity. Sadly, I just don't think the track got much of a chance and that was unfair for the song.

It was one of the gentler Jam songs. I think there was a dark edge to it too. This may have something to do with the way it and the rest of the album was recorded.

I think Jam fans liked the track. I think they listened to the lyrics too. It was a song that was very different to most of what else was going on around that time. I don't remember what the voice saying stuff about 'eggs' and stuff and the fart noises was all about, but someone in the studio must have thought it was a good idea.

46. AWAY FROM THE NUMBERS (PAUL WELLER)

Recorded at Polydor Studios, London, March 1977.

Available on *The Very Best Of The Jam: About The Young Idea*, *In The City*, *Snap* and *Direction Reaction Creation*.

'Away From The Numbers' was recorded at Polydor's studios and really captures the feel of The Jam at that early stage in their recording career. It's a brilliant song with its punchy start. If you close your eyes you can almost imagine Weller striking his Rickenbacker and windmilling his arm just like Pete Townshend from The Who. Buckler bashes his cymbals and rolls around his toms (very Keith Moon like) and Foxton pumps the bass (very John Entwistle like) and the song sets off.

The influence of The Who on The Jam is clearly evident on a song like 'Away From The Numbers' and this is something to be enjoyed. Their classic song 'Pictures Of Lily' springs to mind.

It wouldn't be until 1979 that Richard Barnes had his book published called *Mods*. This book is still regarded as the Mods' bible. In his book he wrote about the various names that Mods were known by: Modernists, Faces, Stylists, Individualists, Tickets, Mids, Mockers, Seven and Sixes, States, Moddy Boys and Scooter Boys and Numbers were amongst them. Barnes goes on to explain that the Numbers were mostly the 'kids' and got their name because they wore numbers on their t-shirts. But it's doubtful whether Weller had this knowledge when he penned the lyrics to 'Away From The Numbers'.

Rick Buckler:

At the time of coming up with the song and then recording it I remember thinking "this

THE JAM

is a classy number". I think there was a lot of our influences in it, bands like The Who. I think there was especially a lot of Who-esque influence going on.

People have read too much into the connection between The High Numbers/The Who and it having some meaning to 'Away From The Numbers'. I don't recall there being any conversations about trying to get away from something like being pigeon-holed into a certain tribe or genre.

The Jam were able to have connections in many scenes or camps but whilst doing so maintain a position of not getting sucked in. The Mod scene had bands like The Chords, Secret Affair and Purple Hearts and these were boxed up in the Mod scene. Other bands were boxed up in the punk scene and other bands in the Rude Boy scene. The Jam managed to sit outside all of these. When the punks were spitting on Chuck Berry records we were saying we loved Chuck Berry. When bands were moaning about Motown groups we were covering Motown songs. We did what we wanted and didn't need to make any compromises so that we fitted in with the Mods or punks or whatever. The Jam wanted to create our own sound and visual identity and we did this and this set us apart. I think The Clash did the same too and this contributed to their success.

If anything I think the song had more to do with people just being a number and another person in a crowd. The theme of being an individual and standing out popped up several times in Jam songs. It was a topic that The Jam revisited a lot. Paul's lyrics were often social commentaries and he'd have a way of pointing out how people can be faceless or nameless and all that you are is just a number. But this was related to politics and attitudes from certain people or quarters in society.

Maybe 'Away From The Numbers' was telling people it's alright to step outside the norm and the conformities. Like all Jam songs people can read into it what they want. 'Away From The Numbers' was a big sounding song for The Jam and we played it a lot in our live shows throughout the time that we were together. It always went down well live and with The Jam fans.

47. ABSOLUTE BEGINNERS (PAUL WELLER)
Recorded at AIR Studios, London, August 1981. Released as a single 16 October 1981.
Available on *Snap, The Very Best Of The Jam: About The Young Idea,* and *Direction Reaction Creation*

The production for 'Absolute Beginners' was credited to Pete Wilson and The Jam and it was recorded at AIR Studios in August 1981 and issued as a single in October. It reached No 4 in the charts.

A video was filmed in the vicinity of Nomis Studios, Shepherd's Bush to promote the single. In old movie style writing the video begins with the words "And now... the absolute beginning". The video then cuts to Buckler, Foxton and Weller standing back to back. They each then run off in different directions. They are filmed sprinting down streets outside the studios. There's additional footage of The Jam miming along to the song in a room in Nomis too. There's a clock behind Buckler's white drum kit. It says six minutes past seven. Not that this has anything to do with the lyrics in the song but at some point in the video Buckler smashes the clock's face with his drum stick. Weller played piano as well as guitar and

6

singing on the song, with Buckler and Foxton on usual duties and Martin Drover, Michael Laird and Luke Tunney drafted in to play their trumpets, which add a really good dynamic to the song.

The video ended with the words "And that was the absolute beginners". The song also appeared on the soundtrack for the 1997 film *Grosse Pointe Blank*.

Rick Buckler:

A good song with a good energy about it. I thought the song was another diversion into another area. I don't know if you can call it funk as such but it had an edge to it. Maybe the brass stabs helped to give it that funk feel.

Musically I thought 'Absolute Beginners' was a strong song but I wouldn't even take a stab at guessing what the lyrics were about. The song did okay though and got to No 4 on the UK charts in late 1981. It came out of that period between *Sound Affects* and *The Gift* and as usual we were experimenting with new ideas. I think we recorded it not to be used as single or for an album as such, it was just one of those songs that we recorded because we thought it was good and we wanted to spend some time in the studio.

I took the photograph that was used for the single sleeve. We were on the road at the time and this was the view from my hotel room. I think we were in Leicester.

I remember looking out of the window and being struck by the rows upon rows of rooftops. Those terraced houses caught my eye so I grabbed my camera and took the shot. It was also early evening and the lighting left an impression on me. You can just get that sense of the day and the way the sun is cutting across the chimneys. That haze just gets captured in the photograph. I think the view reminded me of a hundred other towns. The Jam travelled a lot and we'd go to working class towns and cities that all had similarities. Those rows of terraced houses on the photograph could have been in Liverpool, Manchester, Newcastle or London.

I was interested in photography and I took loads and loads of photos whilst being on the road. It was a nice hobby to have and which helped keep at bay the boredom when being on the road.

The 'Absolute Beginners' single sleeve used a different font. I don't think another Jam single used this again. The single sleeve was unique in this way. I don't recall how my photograph got used for the sleeve. I guess I must have just been showing Paul and Bruce some of my photos and one of them suggested it might work as a single sleeve.

I'm not sure what 'Absolute Beginners' was about. I don't know how my photograph related to the song either. Perhaps it didn't need to. I know of the book by Colin MacInnes and maybe Paul had read it and borrowed the title for the song.

The back cover included a photograph taken by Jam fan Derek D'Souza. He'd been invited to take photographs of The Jam down in Chiswick Park. On the day it was a matter of getting picked up by Kenny and getting driven to the location. It may well have been Paul's idea to go to Chiswick House because of The Beatles connection. They had filmed promo videos there for a couple of their songs. I remember that Paul had also seen pictures of Steve Marriott in a certain stance and with a certain haircut and he copied this in that photo shoot. The whole band look good in the pictures and

THE JAM

6

the setting was amazing. There were all sorts of statues we could lean against. And of course there's the shot of the big gates that Derek photographed us standing behind, which was the one chosen to be used on the singles sleeve.

Derek's photographs from that shoot were very good and they captured something special. There was an atmosphere and a presence about them. There were many from the day. In Some of them we are posing and looking serious and some had us pranking about. I remember Bruce tore his trousers due to leap frogging but you can't see the tear and his arse hanging out in the photos.

There was another photo where Paul is looking quite grumpy but in the background Bruce and me are messing around. My recollections of the day are that it was a fun day and I think it meant a lot to Derek too.

48. TALES FROM THE RIVERBANK (PAUL WELLER)

Recorded at AIR Studios, London, August 1981.
Available on *The Very Best Of The Jam: About The Young Idea, Snap, The Jam Extras* and *Direction Reaction Creation*

'Tales From The Riverbank' is right up there with 'The Butterfly Collector' when it comes to Jam B-sides. The song actually started off with the working title 'Not Far At All' which was a song that Weller had had knocking about since the summer of 1981. The song didn't stand still though and a speeded-up version was recorded. This was included on *The Jam Extras* and with the title 'We've Only Started'. But it is the final version that got included as the

B-side to 'Absolute Beginners' that is the most favoured.

Weller played guitar (electric and acoustic), organ and piano on the song and Steve Nichol and Keith Thomas were brought in to add the brass. It was recorded in AIR Studios and the production credited to Pete Wilson and The Jam.

A different version of the song was recorded and used as a fan club flexidisc release in December 1981.

Rick Buckler:

'Tales From The Riverbank' is credited as being one of The Jam's most atmospheric tracks and it is. I remember us laying down the backbone of the track and then rubbing our hands thinking "now we can have some fun with this". It was things like the fade in at the start and so on that we just played around with in the studio.

There was something about 'Tales From The Riverbank' that loaned itself to being creative with. We also achieved that final result by stripping the song back to a bare minimum. The song just sits back and rolls along. Whenever I listen to it I do think of still waters. Images of mist enveloping riverbanks also come to mind and there's a quietness about the scene. I think the song managed to capture a feeling of timelessness feeling that the listener can connect with.

The lyrics also add to the song's atmosphere. I have no idea what they are about but I can see how they can be a bit like 'Life From A Window' where someone is watching life, only this time from the viewpoint of a riverbank.

When the single was released it came with an insert. This was a good idea and I liked the way that it included the lyrics to 'Absolute

Beginners'. The photograph was taken inside the conservatory, which was where The Beatles had been filmed for part of their 'Paperback Writer' and 'Rain' videos during the Sixties.

I enjoyed playing 'Tales From The Riverbank' live. I don't think we played it that much but this was because of the way we structured our sets. The Jam would usually kick off with a bang and keep building the set up, then take it down a notch and then it would go up again and 'Tales From The Riverbank' didn't always have a place in that set up.

49. FUNERAL PYRE (WORDS PAUL WELLER – MUSIC THE JAM)

Recorded at Phonogram Studios, London, April 1981.
Available on *Snap, The Very Best Of The Jam: About The Young Idea,* and *Direction Reaction Creation*

Words Paul Weller and music The Jam, such are the songwriting credits. This was because 'Funeral Pyre' was a song that was born in the studio and which Buckler instigated. It was Buckler's drum pattern that caught the attention of Weller and Foxton and it was from this foundation that the song was built upon.

'Funeral Pyre' starts with a thumping bass line from Foxton and this is supported by Buckler playing his bass drum. He then introduces the snare drum and it would be the snare pattern that the song is best remembered for and which many a Jam fan has air drummed along with.

The song's strength is also in the fact that its just Weller, Buckler and Foxton doing what they do best, playing their songs as a three-piece band, just like they

had been doing since getting signed to Polydor in 1977. 'Funeral Pyre' captures the raw side of The Jam and the sound that only they could create.

The track, which was the thirteenth single release by The Jam, does not appear on any of the band's studio albums. Backed by the B-side 'Disguises', a cover of a Who track, 'Funeral Pyre' is the only single co-written by the band, and only the second song which has writing credits for all three members, the other being 'Music for the Last Couple' which features on the *Sound Affects* album. 'Funeral Pyre' was released in May 1981 and reached No 4 in the UK charts.

Rick Buckler:
I suppose Jam fans remember the drumming on 'Funeral Pyre'. The drums had quite a lead part in the song. The song was born in the studio. I was messing around with a drum part and Bruce joined in and then Paul and we thought there was something we could develop. This was how the credits became recorded as words to Paul and the music to The Jam.

Most right-handed drummers tend to end up with better and stronger right hands than their left. This is because in modern drumming the right hand plays the hi-hats and rides and the left just dips in and out really. So I used to have an exercise that I hoped would make my left hand better. I would play it on the snare drum and mess around by speeding it up and slowing it down. The rhythm on 'Funeral Pyre' really just became an extension of that. Bruce came up with a good driving bass line and Paul found his guitar part and the song started to form with the rhythm

section really pushing the song along.

Once we were happy with what we'd come up with we recorded the song. We actually recorded 'Funeral Pyre' three times in three different studio sessions. I think after the first session we just didn't feel we had the right version. But we persisted and after the sessions agreed on the version that was selected to be used as a single and, I think this was the first version we'd recorded.

When I'm asked if I enjoyed playing it live I usually reply "yes and no". It was a relentless song to play and I just had to get it right each and every time. There was no room for mistakes because it would throw out the whole song and if that happened it would be very noticeable. It was more a matter of drawing in a breath and saying "right here I go" and launch into the song. We tended to put 'Funeral Pyre' in towards the end of the set and that helped. It also felt like a natural place to add a song like 'Funeral Pyre'.

We shot the video in the sandpits at Horsell Common, which is an area just outside of Woking. It was the same sandpits where Orson Wells wrote about when he described the aliens landing in *War Of The Worlds*. It's not a huge area so I can only presume that the UFO they arrived in wasn't that big!

We shot the video throughout the day and into the night. I remember it felt like it was a very long day. We needed to go into the night because we needed the footage of the bonfire roaring away.

The actual bonfire was massive. Wood was stacked up pretty high. We even needed to have the Fire Brigade on standby in case the fire got out of control. As the night drew in the wind picked up and it kept changing direction which caused us problems. The wind also swept up hot ash and several times they landed on the drum skins and burnt straight through them.

Some of the ashes also landed on the drum shells too and damaged the white laminate. They were ruined and I had to send the white kit back to Premier so they could replace the laminate covering.

During the shoot we moved the drums and equipment around a few times. This meant we could capture different angles of the band playing. We also invited friends and local people along to be in the video. They were filmed carrying wood and torches ablaze. Nicky Weller and the Carver brothers were amongst them. It was a word of mouth thing and word certainly got around.

I returned to the sandpits when I was in Time UK. We were there to do a photo shoot. Whilst we were there the warden who looks after the place came over and asked us what we were doing. We explained to him that we were in a band and were just taking some photos, to which he turned to Time UK's bass player Nick South and started telling him about some band that had been there a few years back that had nearly set the woods on fire. I just lowered my head as Nick pointed to me saying "yeah, it was him".

'Funeral Pyre' was another stand alone single. It wasn't included on an album and it did well getting to No 4. And it was certainly an example of another very different sounding Jam song.

50. THE BITTEREST PILL (I EVER HAD TO SWALLOW) (PAUL WELLER)

Recorded at AIR Studios, London, July 1982.

Available on *Snap, The Very Best Of The Jam: About The Young Idea, Snap* and *Direction Reaction Creation*

'The Bitterest Pill (I Ever Had To Swallow)' was recorded in July and released as a single two months later.

By the time the song was released as a single a twenty four year old Weller had told Rick Buckler and Bruce Foxton that he was leaving The Jam, therefore splitting the band up. It was a time of mixed emotions and discussions and there was still a contract with Polydor to fulfil. It had only been a few months since The Jam had a No 1 single with 'Town Called Malice' and a No 1 album with *The Gift*. It must have been hard for Buckler and Foxton and indeed their manager John Weller and the record label to stomach. But Weller's mind was made up and despite pleas and suggestions such as "how about The Jam just take a break?" or "why doesn't Paul make a solo album?" The Jam would play their last concert in December.

'The Bitterest Pill' was a song that came out of those last months and yet it's still a great song. The public thought so too because it peaked at No 2 in the UK charts.

Rick Buckler:

There was a lot going on with the 'The Bitterest Pill (I Ever Had To Swallow)' single sleeve's front cover. There's a story behind the imagery. It was Vaughn Toulouse on the front cover. I think he was meant to be dressed as some sort of French revolutionary in what appears to be a prison cell. Vaughn was a nice fella, very genuine, who we knew

6

THE JAM

since he played with Department S. They'd had a hit with a song called 'Is Vic There?' in 1980. After Department S he went under the name Main T and had a single out on Paul's Respond label called 'Fickle Public Speaking'. He sadly died in 1991.

We had Jennie McKeown come and do some backing vocals on track. She was having success with her own band The Belle Stars and had been doing stuff with Madness. She was going out with Chris Foreman from Madness at the time. Her voice was a nice addition to the record.

People have read various things into the song's lyrics but it was actually to do with something very personal to Paul. Basically he'd picked up a dose of the clap and he'd decided to come clean about it to his then girlfriend. The bitterest pill kind of had a double barrel meaning - coming clean and the medication needed to shift it. It was certainly a strength of Paul to be able to turn that experience into a song. It was done very cleverly. He was brave and honest to do so, so full credit to him on that one.

Some people linked the lyrics to whatever they thought was going on in The Jam's camp and how they presumed things may have been falling apart. I don't believe the lyrics related to what was going on with Paul, Bruce and me at the time at all. The song had nothing to do with the ending of The Jam and how we may have been feeling.

I don't think 'The Bitterest Pill (I Ever Had To Swallow)' was one of the better Jam songs. I didn't find it an uplifting song. There's definitely a moody side to it and I think this got captured in the video, which has moments of being a bit dark, haunting and gloomy. But it does evoke its own atmosphere and from that point of view it's okay.

'The Eye Of The Tiger' by Survivor kept The Bitterest Pill from getting to No 1 and that was frustrating. The Survivor song was popular because it had been used in the *Rocky* film and people were all over that.

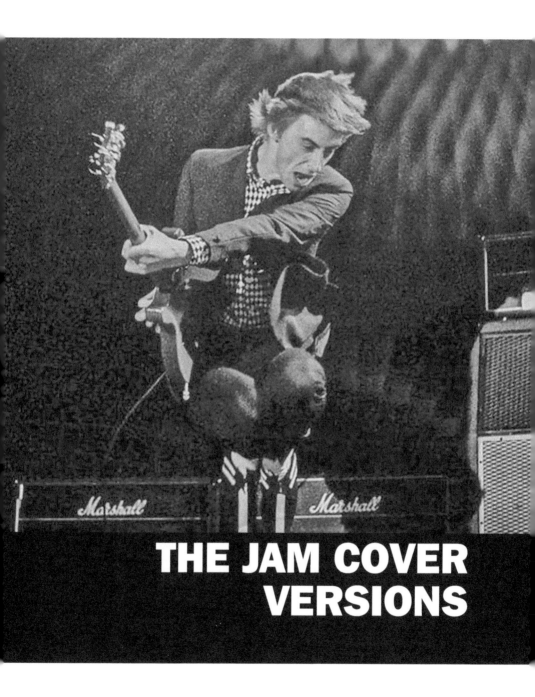

THE JAM COVER VERSIONS

7

"*When we first got signed we thought, 'oh this is great, we're here – this is us!', but then you really find out that that's not quite the truth. People at Polydor would whisper in your ears things like, 'if you haven't made it by your third album, you never will.'*"

Rick Buckler

THE JAM COVER VERSIONS

As they were always a band with a sense of where they had come from covers were an important reference point for Weller, Buckler and Foxton. From John's Children, Small Faces, The Kinks and Prince Buster through to Wilson Pickett and Stevie Wonder The Jam's studio work and live performances included many classic tracks. Here are all of those amazing covers…

There are a number of songs that were recorded by The Jam or just Paul working in the studio with whoever was on hand that day. It could be Pete Wilson or Dave Liddle.

Nowadays most have found their way into the hands of Jam fans. Some have been officially released, some haven't. There are several early Jam recordings available too, like 'Left, Right And Centre', 'I Will Be There', 'Korina' and 'One Hundred Ways'.

There has been mention of recordings by The Jam of songs like 'Desdemona' by John's Children and 'Rough Rider' by Prince Buster. Maybe one day in the future all the recordings will be compiled and officially released. Below is a selection of some of the known recordings and the stories behind them and what they represent are the bands and artists that influenced both Paul's songwriting and The Jam's sound.

'In The Midnight Hour' by Wilson Pickett was a No 1 hit in the US R&B charts in 1965. The song also appeared on

Pickett's album, also called *In The Midnight Hour*. Pickett co-wrote this great soul song with the great session guitarist Steve Cropper. They met at the Lorraine Motel, Memphis, where Martin Luther King Jnr was murdered two years later. Cropper also played on the song, along with two of Sixties soul's best-known names, Al Jackson (drums) and Donald 'Duck' Dunn (bass), who between them helped create numerous soul hits that Paul, Bruce and Rick would have been extremely familiar with. One was the Mod anthem 'Green Onions', which Cropper, Jackson and Dunn all played on. The Jam's version appeared on their 1977 album *This Is The Modern World*.

'Get Yourself Together' by the Small Faces was a song that graced side two of their Small Faces album, which was released by Immediate Records. The label's logo font would also find its way into Jam history. The song, written by Steve Marriott and Ronnie Lane, was recorded in the spring

of 1967 at Olympic Studios. In 1992 Paul said that the *Small Faces* album was in his top ten of all time and the Small Faces influence can be seen throughout Paul's songwriting career.

The Jam included the song in their set from 1981 onwards and when *Snap!* was released a limited edition EP came with it. A live recording from Wembley Arena of 'Get Yourself Together' was included on it.

'Stoned Out Of My Mind' by The Chi-Lites was the final track that appeared on the group's 1973 album, *Chi-Lites*. The origins of the group dated back to the Fifties when Eugene Record formed The Chanteurs along with Robert 'Squirrel' Lester, in their home city Chicago, Illinois. They then teamed up with Creadel 'Red' Jones and Marshall Thompson who had their own group called The Hi-Lites. It was the merging of Chi of Chicago and the Lites of the Hi-Lites that resulted in the group's name, The Chi-Lites.

Although 'Stoned Out Of My Mind' did well in the US R&B charts, it failed to make an impact in the UK, but The Chi-Lites did have a massive hit with 'Have You Seen Her' in 1971, which helped to introduce the group to the UK soul scene.

The Jam's version was released as part of the 'Beat Surrender' pack and included Keith Thomas on saxophone and Steve Nichol on trumpet. The song was recorded at Marcus Studios in Fulham and produced by Pete Wilson, who had been recruited for *The Gift* album. Wilson also laid down some Hammond Organ on the song and there's even some drum machine - a very new inclusion in The Jam camp.

'David Watts' by The Kinks was included on The Kinks fifth studio album, *Something*

Else By Kinks, released in 1967. 'David Watts' was released as a double A-side with "A Bomb In Wardour Street'. Penned by Ray Davies, 'David Watts' was a song about someone who had a crush on one of the members of The Kinks.

When Ray first met Paul, at a festival in 1978, Paul was wearing a pin badge that said "Who the fuck is David Watts?" The Jam's version had more drive and momentum than The Kinks, and there's some nice piano work on the track as well.

'Dead End Street' by The Kinks was written by Ray Davies and released in 1966. It was a top ten hit for the band. A promotional video, one of the earliest in pop history, was made to help promote the song, which was embraced by the BBC. The black and white video showed The Kinks dressed up like Victorian undertakers carrying a coffin along Little Green Street in Kentish Town, North London. This was a familiar stomping ground for the North London group. The lyrics refer to life as experienced by the lower classes and the video supports this by flashing up photographs of working class Londoners going about their day-to-day business. The sights and sounds would have also been familiar to The Kinks, who themselves were also working class lads.

It wasn't so much a Jam cover but rather a Paul Weller/Pete Wilson collaboration, which they cut as a demo towards the end of the *Sound Affects* recording sessions. The Weller/Wilson version was included on the *Direction Reaction Creation* album released in 1997.

'Waterloo Sunset' by The Kinks was released as a single in May 1967 and was also included on their *Something Else From The Kinks* album of the same year (it can be

THE JAM

assumed that Weller had this album). As a single it reached No 2 in the UK charts. Written by Ray Davies, the lyrics depict the tale of two lovers crossing a bridge over the Thames (dirty old river) with Waterloo Station in sight. The two lovers, Terry and Julie, were thought to have been Terence Stamp and Julie Christie at the time, but Davies has since quashed this saying that when he wrote the song he had his sister and her then boyfriend in mind. Davies also said that the song's original title was 'Liverpool Sunset', but this was changed in favour of celebrating Davies' familiar London setting.

Like 'Dead End Street', this was also a Paul Weller/Pete Wilson collaboration and also recorded during the *Sound Affects* recording sessions and it was made available for public consumption on the deluxe edition of *Sound Affects* in 2010.

'Move On Up' was a song written by Curtis Mayfield and included on his debut album *Curtis* in 1970. It was also issued as a single but failed to chart in the UK. The song was released on Curtom Records, which was a label formed in 1968 by Curtis Mayfield and Eddie Thomas. The label's name incorporated letters from both of their names. Thomas managed The Impressions, the R&B/Soul group that Mayfield had been in since the late Fifties.

Mayfield was a prolific songwriter and The Impressions a prolific recording group. They recorded 11 albums in six years and one of their most interesting was the album they released the year before 'Move On Up' was recorded, called *The Young Mods' Forgotten Story*.

The Jam released a version of 'Move On Up' in 1982 on the *Beat Surrender* pack. Soulful to a note it also included Steve

Nichol's trumpet and Keith Thomas' sax and Paul blew a whistle, something he was often spotted wearing around his neck during those last months of The Jam. A live version from one of the 1982 Wembley concerts was also issued on the limited edition EP that came with *Snap!*

In 1988, whilst Paul Weller was still in The Style Council, he interviewed Curtis Mayfield at Ronnie Scott's in Soho, London. Paul asked Curtis the questions and Curtis provided responses that touched on the topics of church/gospel music, writing lyrics that contained inspirational messages relating to love and what he was observing at the time, black exploitation, and scoring the soundtrack to *Superfly*. Paul appeared to be enjoying every second of the interview.

'So Sad About Us' by The Who was recorded at IBC Studios in October 1966 and was included on the groups album of the same year *A Quick One*. It was sandwiched on side two between 'See My Way' and 'A Quick One While He's Away'.

Issued by Reaction Records and with production credits assigned to one of The Who's managers at the time Kit Lambert, this is one song that has been covered by other artists numerous times.

Primal Scream recorded the song in 1987, just over a decade after The Jam had done. The Jam included their version as the B-side to 'Down in the Tube Station at Midnight' in honour of the passing of Keith Moon. Moon had died in his bed at Curzon Square on 7 September 1978, (American singer Cass Elliot had died at the same flat four years earlier, at the age of 32).

The Jam's single was released the following month. A picture of a Sixties

Mod-days Moon was featured on the single's sleeve.

By the time The Jam recorded 'So Sad About Us' they had already been playing it in their set and it had been in the hands of Jam fans on various bootlegs. At one recorded concert at the 100 Club in 1977 Paul had dedicated the song to "all the Who fans out there", adding that he was one too. The Jam also played it at their second-to-last concert at Guildford on 9 December and then it wasn't heard again until a version was included on the *Direction Reaction Creation* album a further decade on.

'Disguises' by The Who opened up side one of their 1966 EP, *Ready Steady Who*. The title was borrowed from the popular television show *Ready Steady Go!*, on which they'd had their own episode in October 1966, which was titled Ready Steady Who. The Who were the most featured group on the programme, appearing 18 times in total: their last appearance was just a month before the show ended.

Ready Steady Go! was broadcast on Friday evenings at 6pm between 1963 and 1966. The show opened with the phrase "the weekend starts here", something that may have inspired The Jam's 'Here Come The Weekend'. *Ready Steady Go!* was presented by Cathy McGowan and Keith Fordyce, and was a show that embraced Mods. Mods would make a point of tuning in to listen to their favourite acts that during the shows life included the Small Faces, The Who, The Yardbirds, Rolling Stones, Otis Redding and Dusty Springfield. It was Dusty who hosted the special edition show *The Sound of Motown*. *Ready Steady Go!* was also the show for music fans to check out the latest hairstyles and fashions that the London Mods were wearing. And then there were the latest dances.

Producers from the show would drop into the hippest Mod clubs in London like the Scene Club and the Flamingo and invite dancers to appear on the show. Ready Steady Go! was essential viewing for an aspiring Mod, because if you couldn't frequent the hottest Mod spots on a weekly basis then you'd be left behind, and being left behind on the Mod scene was to be avoided at all costs. *Ready Steady Go!* was the source and during the three years that it was broadcast served the nation's youth well.

Ready Steady Go! and The Who's popularity amongst the Mods was further reinforced when it was featured in the 1979 film *Quadrophenia*. The scene shows the main character, a young Mod named Jimmy, sitting on the settee in his soaking wet Levis, watching The Who perform 'My Generation' on the show. This is much to the annoyance of his father, especially as Jimmy keeps turning up the volume and playing air drums along to

7

Moon's explosive performance. It's one of *Quadrophenia's* most endearing scenes and clearly demonstrates the importance of *Ready Steady Go!*

Ready Steady Who also included 'Circles', a song which Paul Weller would record a version of for a Who tribute album in 2001, the 'Batman Theme', which The Jam had recorded a version of for *In The City*, 'Bucket T' (Jan and Dean) and 'Barbara Ann' (The Regents/Beach Boys).

The Jam's version of 'Disguises' was used as the B-side for 'Funeral Pyre'. The Jam's cover doesn't quite follow the psychedelic feel that The Who captured, but then this is understandable because when The Who recorded it they were caught up in London's psychedelic scene, especially Pete Townshend who frequented clubs like the UFO, and then reflected what he was around, taking and doing into his songs during that period. The cultural landscape for The Jam in 1981 was very different and The Jam's London resembled nothing of London's swinging Sixties. However, in The Jam's version they held onto the delayed guitar effect to keep that psychedelic feel and Rick pretty much mirrored Moon's drumming, especially the use of the tom toms.

The Jam's 'Disguises' was included on *Direction Reaction Creation* and *Extras*.

'Every Little Bit Hurts' by Brenda Holloway was a hit for the American singer/songwriter in 1964. She also recorded an album of the same title in the same year. The song was written by Ed Cobb and Holloway had actually recorded a version of it for Del-Fi Records before she recorded it for Motown. 'Every Little Bit Hurts' launched her career as a soul artist, something which sustained her

through several more albums and singles and led to her becoming a legend on the UK Northern Soul scene, especially with a soulful stomper like 'Reconsider', which would always pull the crowds to the dance floor.

A year after Holloway's 1964 release, the Spencer Davis Group recorded a version, Steve Winwood providing an excellent vocal, and then in 1968 the Small Faces recorded a version, with Steve Marriott also delivering a superb performance.

Paul Weller recorded 'Every Little Bit Hurts' during August 1981. At the time The Jam were booked into AIR Studios. Pete Wilson was on hand to man the desk whilst Paul laid down the guitar and piano and vocals. You can hear Paul's love for the song because of the way he sings it. Paul's version found its way onto *Direction Reaction Creation*.

'War' by Edwin Starr had originally been recorded by The Temptations in 1969 and had been included on their album *Psychedelic Shack*. It was considered as a single release by the groups label Motown, but the idea was quashed after concerns were raised that the song may damage the group's reputation. 'War' was a protest song written by Norman Whitfield and Barrett Strong. At the time the Vietnam War was raging and American society was asking the government some direct questions. But not getting the direct answers, 'War' was written to deliver a direct message to the masses. The masses did indeed hear the message and when Edwin Starr was chosen as the act to record the song in 1970 and have it released as a single, it reached No 1 in the US *Billboard* Hot 100 Chart.

Before Starr became a Motown act he'd

been a recording artist for the Ric-Tic label. It was when Ric-Tic was taken over by Berry Gordy's Motown that Starr started recording for the label. He recorded his version of 'War' in the Hitsville studios, the very 'snake pit' studios where so many great songs had previously been recorded.

Norman Whitfield oversaw the production of Starr's version and brought in a new act he was working with for the backing vocals, called The Undisputed Truth.

Although 'War' is probably Edwin Starr's best known song he has recorded many other much liked and much danced to tracks. In the Sixties the Mods embraced his 1965 release 'Double-O-Soul' and in the Seventies the various Northern Soul scene deejays frequently include '25 Miles and Time' in their sets. In 1973 Starr relocated to the UK where he continued to live up until his death in 2003. In the Eighties Starr entertained many a scooter boy at various scootering weekenders up and down the UK and he is remembered as one of the legends from that time in the Mods and Scooterists' history.

The Jam initially recorded their version in the Maison Rouge Studios in Fulham in February 1982 before attempting a second version at Marcus Studios, also in Fulham, in October 1982. Tony Taverner was credited as producer on the first recording and Pete Wilson the second.

Backing vocalists Caron Wheeler and Claudia Fontaine (Afrodiziak) and brass

THE JAM

7

section Keith Thomas and Steve Nichol were drafted in to help out on the recording and they certainly helped to bring out the raw soul in the song.

When 'War' was first released the world was being challenged by the agendas linked to the Vietnam War. When The Jam released their version, it was the Falklands War that had been dominating the news throughout the spring and summer.

Whatever The Jam's stance about war and conflict in 1982, the song was considered strong enough to be included on two Jam releases. The first as the B-side to 'Just Who Is The Five O Clock Hero' and the second as part of the Beat Surrender pack, which got to No 1 in the charts.

'Sweet Soul Music' by Arthur Conley is one of the great soul songs from the Sixties. It was first recorded by Conley in 1967 for the ATCO label (a division of Atlantic Records). Although Conley had been releasing songs with Arthur and The Corvets since the late Fifties, it wasn't until he befriended Otis Redding in the mid Sixties that his career got that much deserved boost. It was Redding's suggestion to re-work Sam Cooke's song 'Yeah Man'. So Conley and Redding did just that and came up with 'Sweet Soul Music'. The song was recorded in Muscle Shoals Sound Studio in Alabama. The lyrics provide a nod to several great soul singers of the time. Redding himself gets a mention along with Lou Rawls, Sam and Dave, Wilson Pickett and James Brown. When 'Sweet Soul Music' was released it reached No 2 in the US charts and No 7 in the British charts and sold over a million copies.

The Jam always performed a much faster version of the song, but then they were not trying to recreate a soul song. But when The Jam played it live it was always well received by the fans. After all, they knew the Conley version from being played in their discos and clubs, just as the Mods had known it when it had been played in places like The Scene Club or The Flamingo. Conley's version has the memorable brass section that provides its edge - The Jam had the fire and skill of the day.

Arthur Conley was gay. This was a secret he managed to keep for many years. But it was a struggle and one way he attempted to deal with it was by moving to Amsterdam and changing his name to Lee Roberts in the mid Seventies. Conley died in 2003 at the age of 57 from intestinal cancer.

'Slow Down' was a song originally written and performed by New Orleans born Lawrence Eugene Williams, better known as Larry Williams. The song featured as the B-Side to 'Dizzy Miss Lizzy' when it was released in 1958. The Beatles covered both songs in the earlier part of their career and it may well have been The Beatles' version that The Jam heard before the Larry Williams version. The Jam recorded their version at Polydor's studios in March 1977, Chris Parry and Vic Smith serving as producers.

Once recorded the song claimed third place on the In The City album. It was often performed live. In fact the song had been included in The Jam's set since 1975.

Like all the songs that The Jam covered, they made it their own and there are few comparisons between the sweeter, smoother Williams version with its rock 'n' roll piano and 24 bar rocking guitar riff and The Jam's rougher, fired up version with that punk energy that was fuelling the band's furnace during that period.

Paul may have also heard another of Larry Williams' better known songs and it's a certain classic, especially within the Northern Soul scene. 'Too Late', by Williams and Johnny 'Guitar' Watson, is a wonderful song and served as a much needed return to music for Williams following a three year prison sentence for drug dealing in 1960. 'Slow Down' has also been covered by Elvis Costello, The Young Rascals and Brian May.

'And Your Bird Can Sing' by The Beatles. On an April day in 1980, whilst working towards completing *Sound Affects*, Paul and Pete Wilson pulled their resources and laid down a version of this Beatles song.

The track had originally been released on the *Revolver* album in 1966. Although credited to Lennon and McCartney it was, by the majority, a Lennon composition with McCartney contributing some lyrics. Lennon had been using the working title of 'You Don't Get Me' before settling on 'And Your Bird Can Sing', which some reports claim to have been about Mick Jagger's girlfriend and Sixties darling Marianne Faithfull. Others say it was inspired by a press release for a US TV programme called the *Sinatra TV Special*.

Whatever the song's original inspiration, some fourteen years down the line the song was committed to tape in Polydor's Stratford Place Studios. It then emerged for the first time on *The Jam Extras* in 1992.

A marked difference between The Beatles version and Paul's is the tempo, the cover being quicker. The original also had the Fabs adding handclaps but this is missing in Paul's version. Paul's version also includes an organ that was most probably played by himself. The drums are more than likely to be the handiwork of Pete Wilson.

'Rain' by The Beatles was released as the B-side to 'Paperback Writer'. Recorded at EMI Studios in April 1966 many people share the view that the song is The Beatles' first great psychedelic rock song. Although credited to Lennon and McCartney the song was a John Lennon composition. 'Rain' could have been included on *Revolver* because it has all the ingredients of the songs that appeared on the album.

The song's inspiration was the intense downpour that the band were greeted with on their arrival at Sydney Airport, something which left enough of an impression on Lennon to write a song about.

Three promotional videos were filmed, two of which had The Beatles performing the song as a band, but the third - and the one which Beatle fans get drawn to - is the one that Michael Lindsay-Hogg directed at Chiswick House on 20th May 1966. In this colour video the group are filmed wandering around the grounds at Chiswick

THE JAM

House. And here is the second Jam connection, because although Paul Weller and Pete Wilson and Jam crew member Dave Liddle recorded a version at Polydor's Studios in April 1980, it wasn't until 1981 that Paul, Bruce and Rick based themselves at Chiswick House for a photoshoot. On 31 August 1981 amateur photographer and Jam fan Derek D'Souza took the photos on the invitation from Paul Weller. Paul had suggested the location and also that Rick, Bruce and himself should wear dark suits because they would work well in contrast with the great natural backgrounds that surrounded the main house. One of the photographs from that day that showed The Jam peering through some gates was selected to be used on the single sleeve for 'Absolute Beginners'.

'The Batman Theme' was written by Neal Hefti. Hefti was a jazz trumpeter who turned his hand to composing and arranging and throughout the Sixties he worked in the Hollywood movie industry. During this period he wrote music for several films, one of which was *Barefoot In The Park*, starring Jane Fonda and Robert Redford.

Hefti was asked to write the theme music for the *Batman* TV series in 1966. He composed a tune with a distinctive surf sound - something that was being made popular by the likes of The Beach Boys and Jan and Dean. In fact Jan and Dean covered the song, which they included on their album *Jan and Dean Meet Batman*. Both The Who and The Kinks also covered the 'Batman Theme'. A further Jam connection exists with the Liverpool poet Adrian Henri, who along with his band Liverpool Scene linked the tune to one of Henri's poems called *Bat Poem*. Weller credited

the lyrics for 'Tonight At Noon' as being inspired by a Henri poem.

The Jam were fully aware of the 'Batman Theme' having sat through numerous episodes as teenagers. Paul even had a poster of Batman up on his wall in his bedroom in Stanley Road. It would have been there whilst the early incarnation of The Jam strummed their way through rock and roll classics.

The Jam had been including the 'Batman Theme' in their set for some years by the time they went into the Polydor Studios and cut it for the *In The City* album.

'Heat Wave' by Martha and the Vandellas. In the late Fifties Martha Reeves had been in a girl group called The Fascinations. They'd been recording for Checker and then Chess Records. The Fascinations rivaled another girl group called The Del-Phis, who included Annette Beard, Rosalind Ashford and Gloria Williams, but by the early Sixties the two groups had merged and after Williams left, Reeves stepped up to take on the lead vocal role. Next calling themselves The Vels they found work recording backing vocals for Motown acts. One of these was the new Motown signing Marvin Gaye. Within months Berry Gordy signed the girls to his growing label and The Vels became the Vandellas.

The Vandella's first Motown release was 'Come and Get These Memories', which did well in the *Billboard* Hot 100 Charts, reaching No 29. This was good enough for Gordy to invest further in the group, which led to their follow up record 'Heat Wave'.

'Heat Wave' was a song written by the hit Motown songwriting team Holland-Dozier-Holland. The group released it

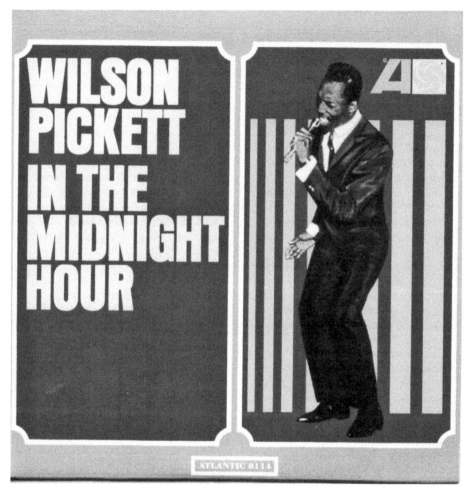

in 1964 and it sold over a million copies. This launched Martha and the Vandellas career and hit after hit followed, including 'Nowhere To Run', 'Jimmy Mack' and 'Dancing In The Street'. (The Jam also covered this song and a recording of it taken from a rehearsal in 1976 at Michael's Club exists, but has never been made available to the public).

When *Ready Steady Go!* broadcast the *Sound of Motown* show, Martha and the Vandellas performed four songs. 'Heat Wave' was one of them, along with 'Nowehere To Run', 'Wishin And Hopin' and 'Can't Hear You No More', which Dusty Springfield joined them for.

Dusty Springfield recorded her own cover of 'Heat Wave' as did The Who, which they recorded for their *A Quick One* album.

THE JAM

The Jam's version of 'Heat Wave' was naturally the meatiest of them all and when they recorded it in Townhouse Studios in October 1979 they asked Mick Talbot of The Merton Parkas to lay down the electric piano part and X-Ray Spex member Steve 'Rudi' Thompson to play the saxophone. Mick Talbot would later join The Jam on stage a few times and of course would become a big part of Paul Weller's life once The Style Council was formed. The Jam's version of 'Heat Wave' signed off Side 2 of *Setting Sons*.

'I Got You (I Feel Good)' by James Brown. Brown was born in Barnwell, South Carolina in 1933. As a child he loved to sing and like so many found himself singing in gospel choirs. By the early Fifties he was singing with the Gospel Starlighters and was also learning to be a performer.

When Brown was 16 he spent some time in a juvenile prison for robbery but after this and with support from Bobby Byrd and his family Brown took singing more seriously. He joined The Famous Flames, who in time would become James Brown and the Famous Flames. The track 'Please Please Please' was released in 1965 and became a hit, selling over a million copies. The inspiration for this song came after Little Richard scribbled the three words onto a napkin and handed it to Brown.

James Brown went on to record other songs that made him a household name and it was one song called 'Night Train' that really caught the attention of the Mods back in the UK. 'Night Train' was released in 1962 just as the first Mods were starting to be defined in London. By 1964 'Night Train' was a Mod anthem, often getting played at Mod strongholds like The Scene and The Flamingo.

In March 1966 James Brown and the Famous Flames performed 'I Got You (I Feel Good)' on *Ready Steady Go!* A year later he was introducing the world to a new form of music, which was called funk. Brown was already known as the Godfather of Soul and Brown's brand of funk would serve him well for the next few years.

During his career Brown recorded many brilliant songs, 'Papa's Got A Brand New Bag' and 'It's A Man's Man's Man's World' amongst them. The Jam recorded their version of 'I Got You (I Feel Good)' in February 1982 at the Phonogram Studios in London. With Pete Wilson producing the song and Steve Nichol and Keith Thomas to hand, The Jam played through the song, but it was decided to not commit it to vinyl. The Jam attempted to perform it live once at a concert in Portsmouth, England but it was never tried a second time, although it sometimes got played in sound checks. It was released on *The Jam's Extras* album.

'Pity Poor Alfie/Fever' by Paul Weller and Eddie Cooley/Otis Blackwell.

Cooley was an American R&B singer/songwriter who'd had a mid-Fifties hit with a song called 'Priscilla'. Blackwell, also a singer/songwriter, preferred to use the names Jack Hammer or John Davenport. Cooley and Blackwell wrote Fever for rock and roll and R&B artist Little Willie John. John's version was released in 1956 and did well, but it was Peggy Lee's 1958 version that the song is best associated with. The Lee version included some different lyrics. However, The Jam's version neglected to use these, preferring to stay truer to the original.

Fever has a mixture of influences in

7

it. There's jazz, soul and R&B and these influences hint at where Paul's musical interests were heading. It's as if the writing was on the wall. The Jam's walls were tumbling down.

'Pity Poor Alfie' contained the influences that inspired 'Fever' and although it has the edge of 'Just Who Is The Five O' Clock Hero' it still works.

When The Jam performed it live, they would begin with 'Pity Poor Alfie' before a bridge of 'Hit The Road Jack' eased it into 'Fever'. It was experimental to say the least, but it was also felt good enough to commit to vinyl and The Jam recorded it at AIR Studios in 1982, using their brass section Nichol and Thomas but also a second trumpet played by Steve Dawson. Pete Wilson produced the track and it was used for the B-side to 'The Bitterest Pill'. A version of 'Pity Poor Alfie/Fever' was also included on the *Extras* album.

'Back In My Arms Again' by The Supremes was a song written by Motown's songwriting team Holland/Dozier/Holland. When the song was released in June 1965 it became The Supremes fifth consecutive No 1 hit, following 'Where Did Our Love Go', 'Baby Love', 'Come See About Me' and 'Stop! In The Name Of Love'.

The Supremes were Motown's most successful act clocking up a total of twelve No 1 records. Berry Gordy had three major talents on his artist roster in Diana Ross, Florence Ballard and Mary Wilson.

Back in 1959 the Detroit group were originally called The Primettes and included a fourth member, Betty McGlown. The Primettes were a sister act to another Detroit act called The Primes. Two of The Primes members, Eddie Kendricks and Paul Williams also went

onto become Motown signings as The Temptations.

Berry Gordy signed The Primettes to Motown in 1960 and renamed them The Supremes. McGlown left the group and was replaced by Barbara Martin, who stayed for just two years, which left The Supremes in their trio formation that they'd best remembered for.

Although The Jam had recorded 'Back In My Arms Again' at a session in Bob Potters Studio in 1976 it was a version of the song recorded live at the 100 Club on 11 September 1977 that was included as part of their soul covers collection on the B-side to 'The Modern World'. The song also found its way onto the *Fire And Skill* box set that was released in 2015.

'Big Bird' by Eddie Floyd was a song that he released on the Stax label in 1967. Previous to the release of 'Big Bird' Floyd had been an R&B singer in a group called The Falcons. One of the groups other members was Wilson Pickett. The Falcons split up after Pickett left to pursue a solo career with Atlantic Records. At this point Floyd found employment as a songwriter for Stax Records and teamed up with guitarist and songwriter Steve Cropper. The duo would go on to write songs for Wilson Pickett.

Alongside Floyd's songwriting career he also recorded songs as an artist in his own right. He had the 1966 hit with 'Knock On Wood', a song that was originally written for Otis Redding. It was Otis Redding that then provided the inspiration for 'Big Bird'.

On a December day in 1967 Redding, along with members of his backing band and Stax musicians The Bar-Kays (who'd had a hit with 'Soul Finger') were flying

THE JAM

7

"I'd heard a lot of Motown and Stax when I was a kid, but the more well-known end of it. On Jam tours, we had a DJ called Ady Croasdell who ran a Sixties club. He turned me on to underground stuff and what people call Northern Soul. It just blew my mind."

Paul Weller

to Wisconsin where they were due to perform a concert. Bad weather caused their plane to crash. Otis, along with the pilot and all members of The Bar-Kays but one died. It was tragic. The world had lost one of its finest singers and performers. At the time Floyd was in the UK and whilst waiting at the airport he was flying back for Redding's funeral, he wrote 'Big Bird'.

'Big Bird' was released on Stax and recorded by Floyd and Copper along with Stax session musicians Booker T Jones, Donald 'Duck' Dunn and Al Jackson.

A live version of 'Big Bird' was included on the *Dig New Breed* album this was a recording from the Hammersmith Palais on 14 December 1981. It was later included on the *Fire And Skill* box set.

'Wonderful World' by Sam Cooke was recorded on 2 March, 1959 at Radio Recorders, Los Angeles and released the following year in April 1960. The song had been recorded during his last recording session with Keen Records, his label before joining RCA Victor. Cooke wrote the lyrics, the music was written by composers Lou Adler and Herb Alpert. Alongside their songwriting ventures and Alpert's successful career with the Tijuana Brass band Adler and Alpert had co-managed Jan and Dean.

Cooke, real name Samuel Cook was one of the pioneers of soul music. This led to him being known as The King of Soul and some even credit him as being the inventor of soul music. He had massive hits with songs like 'You Send Me' (1957), 'Cupid' (1962), 'Chain Gang' (1960), and 'Twistin' the Night Away' (1962). His version of 'Wonderful World' was used in a national Levi's 501 television commercial some twenty years after his death. Cooke

had been shot in 1964 at the Hacienda Motel, at 9137 South Figueroa Street, in Los Angeles, California. He was only 33 years old. Answering separate reports of a shooting and of a kidnapping at the motel, police found Cooke's body. The motel's manager, Bertha Franklin, said she had shot Cooke in self defence after he broke into her office and attacked her. Her account was immediately questioned and disputed by acquaintances.

Some of Cooke's family and supporters have rejected this version of events, believing that there was a conspiracy to murder Cooke and that the murder took place in some manner entirely different from the three official accounts.

Otis Redding and Herman's Hermits had success with 'Wonderful World' and Paul Weller laid down a version of the song at some point in 1980. This version has never been officially released but has found its way into the hands of Jam fans via other means. What it does show is that Paul respected the song enough to want to at least play around with it and record the track.

'My Girl' by The Temptations was the Motown group's first No 1 record. The song was actually written by The Miracles, which was Smokey Robinson and Ronald White, and Robinson said he wrote the song about his wife Claudette. The Temptations recorded the song in November 1964 in the 'snake pit' which was Studio A in Hitsville USA, the recording home of Motown. Musicians on the day included members of the Funk Brothers Benny Benjamin on drums, James Jamerson on bass and Robert White on guitar.

Otis Redding also recorded 'My Girl' in

7

THE JAM

1965 and his version was included on his album called Otis Blue: *Otis Redding Sings Soul*. Redding's version was never issued as a single in the US but it was in the UK on Atlantic UK and it reached No 11 in the charts. Both versions were embraced by the soul loving Mods in 1965.

The Paul Weller recording was laid down in the late Eighties. It's unconfirmed as yet regards who is actually playing the drums and bass on the song. There's also a prominent Hammond Organ that provides a really Sixties soul edge. This version has never been officially released but can be found on *YouTube*.

'My Mind's Eye' by the Small Faces was originally intended to be an album track by the band but was released as a single without their knowledge or consent whilst touring in the north of England. Their manager Don Arden had been eager for the group to release a song before Christmas and released an unfinished, rough demo copy in his possession. The single was a hit, reaching No 4 on the UK chart, but it was to signal the end of the group's relationship with both Arden and their label, Decca.

Even though Arden's decision paid off, the rewards didn't reach the band members because they failed to enjoy much of the financial success whilst under Arden's management. After 'My Minds Eye' was issued as a single it was then included on side one of the Small Faces second album *From The Beginning* which was released in June 1967.

The Small Faces were a Mod band from East London. The original members included Steve Marriott on guitar and vocals, Ronnie Lane on bass, Kenny

Jones on drums and Jimmy Winston on Hammond Organ. Winston was replaced by Ian McLagan just as the bands career was starting to take off. This was another decision made by Don Arden.

Arden achieved notoriety in Britain for his aggressive, sometimes illegal business tactics: which led to his being called 'Mr Big'. He was the father of Sharon Osbourne (and father-in-law of Ozzy Osbourne). In 1966, Arden and a squad of 'minders' turned up at impresario Robert Stigwood's office to 'teach him a lesson' for daring to discuss a change of management with Small Faces. This became one of the most notorious incidents in Sixties British pop business history. Arden reportedly threatened to throw Stigwood out of the window if he ever interfered with his business again.

The Small Faces loved the Mod way of life. They loved the clothes and would often get their royalties paid in the form of shopping trips in Carnaby Street. Arden's offices were located at 52-55 Carnaby Street and there's a commemorative plaque there now marking the spot which says 'Don Arden and Mod Band Small Faces (Steve Marriott, Ronnie Lane, Kenney Jones, Ian McLagan, Jimmy Winston) Worked Here 1965-1967'.

The Small Faces were heavily rooted in the Mod scene in the Sixties and have continued to be a source of reverence for every aspiring Mod since. This included a young Paul Weller. With songs like 'All Or Nothing' and 'Tin Soldier' it's easy to see why. A Jam or just a Paul Weller version of 'My Mind's Eye' from around 1981 can be found on *YouTube* and bootlegs, but it's not confirmed who is actually playing on the track.

'Give Me Just A Little More Time' by The Chairmen Of The Board was a song that was a UK hit for the group in 1970. It reached No 3 in both the UK singles chart and in the *Billboard* Hot 100. The Detroit outfit which consisted of General Johnson (birth name General Norman Johnson), Danny Woods, Harrison Kennedy and Eddie Custis, were signed to Invictus.

Invictus was founded by the Motown songwriting team Holland/Dozier/Holland in 1967. At the time of writing 'Give Me Just A Little More Time', with a co-writer Ron Dunbar (who later wrote the smash hit 'Band Of Gold' for Freda Payne), the trio were in a legal dispute with Motown. Holland/Dozier/Holland wrote 'Give Me Just A Little More Time' under the name Edythe Wayne.

The Chairmen Of The Board recorded their debut record in the HDH Studios in Detroit and drafted in Bob Babbitt and Richard 'Pistol' Allen from the Funk Brothers to play on it. One can only presume that this rattled Motown even more!

The Chairmen Of The Board went on to record several brilliant soul tracks that included 'You've Got Me Dangling On A String' and the amazing B-side 'Working On A Building Of Love'.

The Jam's version included some different lyrics and they performed it live on only a few occasions in late 1981. A version of The Jam performing the song was recorded at a Michael Sobell Sports Centre concert in December 1981. It has never been officially released.

'Uptight (Everything's Alright)' by Stevie Wonder was a hit for Motown in 1965. By the time the record was released Little Stevie Wonder had been with Motown for four years. Stevland Hardaway Judkins was born six weeks premature on 13 May 1950 which, along with the oxygen-rich atmosphere in the hospital incubator, resulted in retinopathy of prematurity, a condition in which the growth of the eyes is aborted and causes the retinas to detach, causing him to become blind.

As Wonder grew older he discovered his talents in playing the piano, but also the drums and harmonica. He also found that he could write songs and it was one of his own songs, 'Lonely Boy', that was played to Berry Gordy who signed up the eleven year old blind boy to his Motown label. Gordy then sent Wonder in the direction of one of Motown's producers, Clarence Paul and it was he who came up with the Little Stevie Wonder name. Wonder went on to have a long and successful career with Motown, with songs like 'Signed, Sealed, Delivered I'm Yours', 'Sir Duke', 'You Are the Sunshine of My Life', 'Superstition' and 'Fingertips'. He even wrote songs for other Motown artists, including 'Tears Of A Clown' for Smokey Robinson and The Miracles.

A cover of 'Uptight (Everything's Alright)' by The Jam was recorded in 1975 and nowadays can be listened to at a press of a button on *YouTube*. The Jam's version, which they included in their sets when they were just starting to venture into London, has that Pub Rock feel. It's urgent and prickly and clearly influenced by Dr. Feelgood.

'Reach Out I'll Be There' by The Four Tops was a No 1 record in both the USA and the UK in 1966. In fact it was Motown's second UK No.1 hit ('Baby Love' by The Supremes being the first).

7

THE JAM

7

By the time 'Reach Out I'll Be There' was released The Four Tops had been together for over a decade. The vocal quartet of Levi Stubbs, Lawrence Payton, Renaldo 'Obie' Benson and Abdul 'Duke' Fakir had been friends at High School and had formed the Four Aims, who signed to Chess Records.

Holland/Dozier/Holland, who wrote 'Reach Out I'll Be There', put Te Four Tops into Hitsville Studio A with the Funk Brothers and recorded the song.

The Four Tops would become one of Motown's most successful acts and, alongside the producers Holland and Dozier, they also worked with another Motown producer, Frank Wilson. Wilson gave Northern Soul the brilliant and extremely rare 'Do I Love You (Indeed You Do)'.

The Jam played this in 1980 and there's a recording of them playing the song during a soundcheck at the Music Machine on 12 December 1980. It's a punchy example of Jam muscle music.

'Stand By Me' by Ben E King was a No 1 hit in the US *Billboard* Hot R&B charts in 1961 but only a top thirty record in the UK. However, its popularity grew in 1986 following it being featured in the film *Stand By Me* that included a very young River Phoenix. It topped the UK charts over 25 years later in 1987.

Benjamin Earl King grew up in Harlem, New York. It was in Harlem that he got to know members of The Drifters, which he then joined, who were signed to Atlantic Records and had a hit with 'Save The Last Dance For Me'. King went solo in 1960 and staying with Atlantic on their ATCO label teamed up with Jerry Leiber and Mike Stoller to write 'Stand By Me'. Leiber and Stoller already had several hits with writing songs like 'Love Me' and 'Jailhouse Rock' for the other King - Elvis Presley. 'Stand By Me' was recorded in 1960 and released in 1961.

In 2012, it was estimated that the song's royalties had topped £17 million, making it the sixth-highest earning song of that time. In 2015, King's original version was inducted into the National Recording Registry by the Library of Congress for being 'culturally, historically, or aesthetically significant', just under five weeks before his death.

A version of 'Stand By Me' was included on *Direction Reaction Creation*. It's unconfirmed who is actually playing the bass, drums and organ with Paul. What is known is that it was recorded around late 1981 in Polydor's studios in Stratford Place, London.

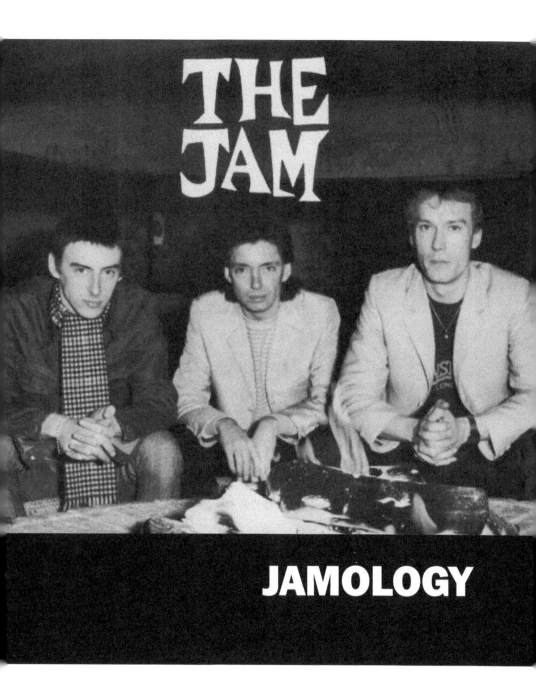

8

"*I was in the Speakeasy club in London years ago and The Who were there. We were young whippersnappers, thinking "God, they're 40 years old! What are they doing still around? Why don't they give up?"*

Bruce Foxton

JAM TOUR DATES  8

Here's a collection of Jam facts and information including television performances, tour dates, their final show, fans' memories, UK live recordings, books, web sites, ten key Jam locations, awards, Jam facts and a list of artists who've covered Jam tracks (and the tracks themselves). Prepare to be enlightened...

UK Recordings:

1. The Play House Theatre, Edinburgh, 07.05.77

2. Winter Gardens, Eastbourne, 09.06.77

3. Locarno Ballrooms, Portsmouth, 14.06.77

4. The Greyhound, Croydon, 26.06.77

5. 100 Club, London, 11.09.77

6. The Nashville Rooms, London, 10.09.77

7. The Odeon, Canterbury, 09.12.77

8. The Marquee, London, 24.02.78

9. The Marquee, London, 25.02.78

10. The Music Machine, London, 02.03.78

11. The Paris Theatre, London, 01.06.78

12. The Reading Festival, 25.08.78

13. Saint Andrews University, Fife, 07.11.78

14. The Apollo, Manchester, 13.11.78

15. The Apollo, Coventry, 15.11.78

16. Wembley Arena, The Great British Music Festival, 29.11.78

17. The Music Machine, London, 21.12.78

18. Reading University, Reading, 16.02.79

19. Liverpool University, Liverpool, 16.05.79

20. Strathclyde University, Glasgow, 18.05.79

21. The Guildhall, Portsmouth, 25.05.79

22. The Aylesbury Friars, Aylesbury, 17.11.79

23. The Wessex Hall, Poole, 18.11.79

24. The Apollo, Manchester, 20.11.79

25. The Gaumont Theatre, Southampton, 24.11.79

26. The Rainbow Theatre, London, 02.12.79

27. The Rainbow Theatre, London, 03.12.79

28. The Rainbow Theatre, London, 04.12.79

29. The City Hall, Newcastle, 07.12.79

30. The Conference Centre, Brighton, 15.12.79

31. The Guildhall, Portsmouth, 16.12.79

32. Bear Park, Loch Lomond, 21.06.80

33. The City Hall, Newcastle, 27.10.80

34. The City Hall, Newcastle, 28.10.80

35. The Play House, Edinburgh, 29.10.80

36. The Apollo, Glasgow, 30.10.80

37. The Wessex Hall, Poole, 09.11.80

38. The Rainbow Theatre, London, 16.11.80

THE JAM

8

39. The Royal Court Theatre, Liverpool, 27.04.81

40. The Guildhall, Portsmouth, 23.06.81

41. The Coliseum, St Austell, 25.06.81

42. The Magnum Centre, Irvin, 30.06.81

43. The Royal Hall, Bridlington Spa, 02.07.81

44. The Market Hall, Carlisle, 04.07.81

45. The Guildhall, Preston, 05.07.81

46. The Civic Hall, Guildford, 07.07.81

47. CND concert, Embankment, London, 28.10.81

48. The Michael Sobell Sports Centre, 12.12.81

49. The Michael Sobell Sports Centre, 13.12.81

50. The Hammersmith Palais, 14.12.81

51. The Hammersmith Palais, 15.12.81

52. BBC TV Theatre, London, 19.12.81

53. The Conference Centre, Brighton, 13.03.82

54. The Fair Deal, Brixton, 15.03.82

55. The Royal Bath and West Showground, Shepton Mallet, 17.03.82

56. Bingley Exhibition Hall, Birmingham, 21.03.82

57. De Montford Hall, Leicester, 22.03.82

58. The Apollo, Manchester, 25.03.82

59. The Apollo, Manchester, 26.03.82

60. The Deeside Leisure Centre, Wales, 27.03.82

61. The City Hall, Newcastle, 03.04.82

62. The Playhouse, Edinburgh, 05.04.82

63. The Playhouse, Edinburgh, 06.04.82

64. The Apollo, Glasgow, 07.04.82

65. The Showering Pavilion, Shepton Mallet, 21.09.82

66. The Conference Centre, Brighton, 22.09.82

67. The Granby Halls, Leicester, 23.09.82

68. The Royal Court, Liverpool, 24.09.82

69. The Royal Court, Liverpool, 25.09.82

70. The Edinburgh Ingliston Royal Hall, Edinburgh, 27.09.82

71. The Whitley Bay Ice Rink, Whitley Bay, 28.09.82

72. The New Bingley Hall, Stafford, 01.10.82

73. The Apollo, Glasgow, 25.11.82

74. The Poole Arts Centre, Poole, 27.11.82

75. The Coliseum, St Austell, 28.11.82

8

76. The Afon Lido, Port Talbot, 29.11.82

77. The Royal Hall, Bridlington Spa, 06.12.82

78. The Apollo, Manchester, 07.12.82

79. The Bingley Exhibition Hall, Birmingham, 08.12.82

80. The Civic Centre, Guildford, 09.12.82

81. Wembley Arena, London, 01.12.82

82. Wembley Arena, London, 02.12.82

83. Wembley Arena, London, 03.12.82

84. Wembley Arena, London, 04.12.82

85. Wembley Arena, London, 05.12.82

86. The Conference Centre, Brighton, 11.12.82

Overseas Recordings:

1. Malmo, Sweden, 23.09.77

2. The Paradiso Club, Holland, 30.09.77

3. Whiskey A Go-Go, USA, 08.10.77

4. The Rathskeller (The Rat), USA, 10.10.77

5. The Rathskeller (The Rat), USA, 13.10.77

6. CBGB's, USA, 15.10.77

7. CBGB's, USA, 16.10.77

8. Sportehall, France, 14.02.78

9. Four Acres, USA, 20.03,78

10. The Colonial, Canada, 21.03.78

11. CBGB's, USA, 31.03.78

12. Reims, France, 27.02.1979

13. Follies, Belgium, 06.03.1979

14. The Paradise Ballroom, USA, 12.04.79

15. The Palladium, USA, 14.04.79

16. University of California Royce Hall, USA, 21.04.79

17. Emerald City, USA, 27.02.80

18. The Palladium, USA, 29.02.80

19. Park West, USA, 06.03.80

THE JAM

20. Amusement Park, USA, 07.03.80

21. St Paul Civic Theatre, USA, 09.03.80

22. Fox Warefield, USA, 15.03.80

23. Civic Center Santa Monica, USA, 16.03.80

24. Armadillo Works, USA, 22.03.80

25. The Pink Pop Festival, Holland, 26.05.80

26. Sun Plaza Hall, Japan, 06.07.80

27. Nippon Seinenkan, Japan, 07.07.80

28. Nippon Seinenkan, Japan, 08.07.80

29. The Turku Rock Festival, Finland, 09.08.80

30. Gothenburg, Sweden, 22.11.80

31. Gota Lejon, Sweden, 25.11.80

32. Gota Lejon,, Sweden, 26.11.80

33. Rockpalast Dortmund, Germany, 30.11.80

34. Pavillon Baltard, France, 26.02.81

35. Olympian, Sweden, 01.03.81

36. Oddfellows, Denmark, 03.03.81

37. Market Hall, Germany, 06.03.81

38. Metropol, Germany, 08.03.81

39. L'Ancienne Belguique, Belgium, 10.03.81

40. The Paradiso Club, Holland, 14.03.81

41. Kinro Fukushi Kaikan, Japan, 13.05.81

42. Sun Plaza Hall, Japan, 15.05.81

43. Sun Plaza Hall, Japan, 16.05.81

44. The Ontario Concert Hall, Canada, 23.05.81

45. The Ritz, USA, 26.05.81

46. The Channel Club, USA, 29.05.81

47. Grona Lund, Sweden, 10.06.81

48. Johaneshovs Isstadion, Sweden, 16.04.82

49. The Olympian, Sweden, 18.04.82

50. The Faulkener Theatre, Denmark, 20.04.82

51. The Paradiso Club, Holland, 26.04.82

52. De Verenging, Holland, 26.04.82

53. Pantin Hippodrome, France, 29.04.82

54. Palais D'Hiver, France, 30.04.82

55. Richie Coliseum, USA, 14.05.82

56. The Palladium, USA, 15.05.82

57. The North Stage, USA, 16.05.82

58. The Palladium, USA, 18.05.82

59. The Trenton War Memorial, USA, 19.05.82

60. *The Orpheum Theatre, USA, 20.05.82*

61. *The Coliseum, Canada, 24.05.82*

62. *The Michigan Theatre, USA, 25.05.82*

63. *Perkins Palace, USA, 29.05.82*

64. *Perkins Palace, USA, 30.05.82*

65. *Perkins Palace, USA, 31.05.82*

66. *Fox Warfield Theatre, USA, 02.06.82*

67. *Kerrisdale Arena, Canada, 05.06.82*

68. *The Sun Plaza Hall, Japan, 14.06.82*

69. *The Mainichi Hall, Japan, 15.06.82*

70. *The Seinenkan Hall, Japan, 16.06.82*

71. *Kinro Kaikan, Japan, 17.06.82*

The Jam Tours:

The White Riot Tour: Included The Clash, Buzzcocks, The Slits and Subway Sect. The Jam pulled out of the tour after just three dates.

1. *The Playhouse, Edinburgh, 07.05.77*

2. *The Electric Circus, Manchester, 08.05.77*

3. *The Rainbow Theatre, London, 09.05.77*

4. *Newcastle University, Newcastle, 20.05.77 (Cancelled)*

5. *City Hall, St Albans, 21.05.77 (Cancelled)*

6. *The Civic Hall, Wolverhampton, 22.05.77 (Cancelled)*

7. *Top of the World, Stafford, 23.05.77 (Cancelled)*

8. *The Top Rank, Cardiff, 24.05.77 (Cancelled)*

9. *The Dome, Brighton, 25.05.77 (Cancelled)*

10. *The Colston Hall, Bristol 26.05.77 (Cancelled)*

11. *West Runton Pavilion, West Runton, 27.05.77 (Cancelled)*

12. *The Odeon, Canterbury, 28.05.77 (Cancelled)*

13. *The Chancellor Hall, Chelmsford, 29.05.77 (Cancelled)*

14. *The California Ballroom, Dunstable, 30.05.77 (Cancelled)*

THE JAM

8

The Jam – First British Tour:

Promoting their debut album *In The City* The Jam's first major UK tour saw the group playing 40 shows around the UK (after five were cancelled).

1. Barbarella's, Birmingham, 07.06.77

1. The Garibaldi Hall, Great Yarmouth, 08.06.77 (Cancelled)

2. The Twickenham Winning Post, London, 08.06.77

3. The Winter Gardens, Eastbourne, 09.06.77

4. The Corn Exchange, Cambridge, 10.06.77

5. The Polytechnic, Bristol, 11.06.77

6. Stamford Bridge, Chelsea, London, 12.06.77 (Cancelled)

7. The Top Rank, Reading, 13.06.77

8. The Locarno, Portsmouth, 14.06.77

9. The Village Bowl, Bournemouth, 15.06.77

10. Leeds Town Hall, Leeds, 16.06.77 (Cancelled)

11. The Seaburn Hall, Sunderland, 17.06.77

12. The Poplar Civic Hall, London, 18.06.77

13. UCI, London, 18.06.77

14. The Electric Circus, Manchester, 19.06.77

15. The Outlook Club, Doncaster, 20.06.77

16. The Top Rank, Cardiff, 21.06.77

17. Lafayette, Wolverhampton, 22.06.77

18. The Polytechnic, Huddersfield, 23.06.77

19. The Brunei Rooms, Swindon, 24.06.77

20. The Winter Gardens, Malvern, 25.06.77

21. The Greyhound, Croydon, 26.06.77

22. Battersea Town Hall, London, 27.06.77

23. The Drill Hall, Lincoln, 28.06.77 (Cancelled)

24. The Cat's Whiskers, York, 29.06.77

25. Rebecca's, Birmingham, 30.06.77

26. The Mayfair Ballroom, Newcastle, 01.07.77

27. Middleton Town Hall, Manchester, 02.07.77

28. The Top Rank, Brighton, 05.07.77

29. The Top Rank, Plymouth, 06.07.77

30. Mr Digby's, Birkenhead, 07.07.77

31. Town Hall, Middlesborough, 08.07.77

32. The California Ballroom, Dunstable, 09.07.77

8

33. *The Top Rank, Sheffield, 10.07.77*

34. *Tiffany's, Shrewsbury, 12.07.77*

35. *Shuffles, Glasgow, 13.07.77*

36. *The Maniqui Hall, Falkirk, 14.07.77*

37. *Clouds, Edinburgh, 15.07.77*

38. *Maxims, Barrow In Furness, 17.07.77*

39. *Eric's, Liverpool, 16.07.77*

40. *Maxims, Barrow In Furness, 17.07.77*

41. *The Pavillion, West Runton, 22.07.77*

42. *The Town Hall, High Wycombe, 23.07.77*

43. *Hammersmith Odeon, London, 24.07.77*

44. *Mont De Marson punk Rock Festival, 08.08.77 (Cancelled)*

45. *The 100 Club, London, 11.09.77*

First European Tour:

1. *Malmo, Sweden, 23.09.77*

2. *The Paradiso Club, 30.09.77*

THE JAM

8

The Jam then embarked on their first USA tour:

1. *The Whiskey-A-Go-Go, L.A, 08.10.77*

2. *The Whiskey-A-Go-Go, L.A, 09.10.77*

3. *The Rathskeller, Boston, 10.10.77*

4. *The Rathskeller, Boston, 13.10.77*

5. *CBGB's, New York, 15.10.77*

6. *CBGB's, New York, 16.10.77*

❝I remember four or five guys from England flew over to the States to see us with every penny they had managed to raise. Bruce and me used to let these guys sleep on the floor in our hotel rooms. They went to every gig we did in the States and they soon ran out of money. The Jam paid for them to get home. We got to know many of the fans on a personal level. We could go out and we were never bugged. The fans would just come up to us and chat. There was never a 'them and us' attitude, with The Jam and the fans. That was fantastic."

Rick Buckler

The Modern World Tour:

Promoting their second album *This Is The Modern World* this 24-date tour kicked off mid November 1977 finishing just before Christmas 1977.

1. *The Polytechnic, Huddersfield, 17.11.77*

2. *The Mayfair Ballroom, Newcastle, 18.11.77*

3. *Leeds University, Leeds, 19.11.77*

4. *The Empire Theatre, Liverpool, 20.11.77*

5. *The Top Rank, Cardiff, 22.11.77*

6. *Leicester University, Leicester, 24.11.77*

7. *Kings Hall, Derby, 25.11.77*

8. *The Friars, Aylesbury, 26.11.77*

9. *The Top Rank, Sheffield, 27.11.77*

10. *The Top Rank, Birmingham, 28.11.77*

11. *The Apollo, Manchester, 29.11.77*

12. *The Apollo, Glasgow, 30.11.77*

13. *The Sports Centre, Bracknell, 02.12.77*

14. *The Civic Hall, Wolverhampton, 03.12.77*

15. *The Locarno, Bristol, 04.12.77*

16. *The Village Bowl, Bournemouth, 05.12.77*

17. *The Top Rank, Brighton, 07.12.77*

18. *The Locarno, Coventry, 08.12.77*

19. *The Odeon, Canterbury, 09.12.77*

20. *The Greyhound, Croydon, 11.12.77*

21. *Lancaster University, Lancaster, 14.12.77*

22. *The Hanley Victoria Hall, Stoke, 15.12.77*

23. *The Corn Exchange, Cambridge, 16.12.77*

24. *The Hammersmith Odeon, London, 18.12.77*

Kicking off 1978 The Jam played two concerts in Europe: 13.02.78 Brussels, Belgium and 14.02.78 Paris Le Palace, Paris, France.

The London Blitz: Promoting the 'News Of The World' single.

1. *The Marquee Club, 24.02.78*

2. *The Marquee Club, 25.02.78*

3. *The 100 Club, 27.02.78*

4. *The Music Machine, 02.03.78*

Second tour of North America:

This second trip to

the US saw The Jam supporting American rock band Blue Öyster Cult in what their US promoter thought would get the group seen by a new 'rock' audience. The tour saw The Jam being booed off stage at some shows.

1. *The University of Bridgeport, Connecticut, 14.03.78*

2. *The Tower Theatre, Philadelphia, 18.03.78*

3. *The Agricultural Hall, Philadelphia, 19.03.78*

4. *The Four Acres Club, New York, 20.03.78*

5. *El Mocambo, Toronto, 21.03.78*

6. *El Mocambo, Toronto, 22.03.78*

7. *The Civic Center, Hammond, 24.03.78*

8. *The Richfield Coliseum, Cleveland, 25.03.78*

9. *The Coliseum, Fort Wayne, Indiana, 26.03.78*

10. *The Paradise Club, Boston, 29.03.78*

11. *CBGB's Club, New York, 30.03.78*

12. *CBGB's Club, New York, 31.03.78*

13. *The Four Acres Club, New York, 01.04.78*

14. *The Rupp Arena, Lexington, Kentucky, 02.04.78*

15. *St Louis, River Daze, Missouri, 03.04.78*

THE JAM

16. *Madison Bunky's, Wisconsin, 04.04.78*

17. *BJ's Concert Club, Detroit, 05.04.78*

18. *Bogarts, Cincinatti, 06.04.78*

19. *The Riviera Theater, Chicago, 07.04.78*

20. *The Celebrity Theater, Phoenix, 11.04.78*

21. *The Celebrity Theater, Phoenix, 12.04.78*

22. *The Santa Monica Starwood, L.A, 14.04.78*

23. *The Winterland Ballroom, San Francisco, 15.04.78*

24. *The Exhibition Hall, San Jose, 16.04.78*

The Jam were back in the UK to play at the Paris Theatre, London on 01.06.78 for the BBC show *Sight and Sound*. Some of the recordings from this show were later released on the *The Jam at the BBC* album.

British Tour 1978:

1. *The King George's Hall, Blackburn, 12.06.78*

2. *The Victoria Hall, Keighley, 13.06.78 (Cancelled)*

3. *The Pier, Colwyn Bay, 14.06.78 (Cancelled)*

4. *Barbarella's, Birmingham, 15.06.78*

5. *Barbarella's, Birmingham, 16.06.78*

6. *The Friars, Aylesbury, 17.06.78*

7. *The Lyceum, London, 18.06.78*

UK Seaside Tour:

1. *The Civic Hall, Guildford, 30.07.78*

2. *The Town Hall, Torquay, 31.07.78*

3. *Fiesta, Plymouth, 01.08.78*

4. *The Village Bowl, Bournemouth, 02.08.78*

5. *The Brunei Rooms, Swindon, 04.08.78*

6. *The Bilsen Festival, Belgium, 13.08.78*

8

7. The Reading Festival, Reading, 25.08.78

8. The Groningen Festival, Holland, 27.08.78

9. The Top Hat Club, Dublin, Ireland, 20.10.78

10. Galway Bay, Ireland, 21.10.78

The Apocalypse Tour 1978:

1. The Empire Theatre, Liverpool, 01.11.78

2. The De Montfort Hall, Leicester, 02.11.78

3. St George's Hall, Bradford, 03.11.78

4. The City Hall, Newcastle, 04.11.78

5. The Apollo, Glasgow, 05.11.78

6. The Capitol Theatre, Aberdeen, 06.11.78

7. St Andrews University, Fife, 07.11.78

8. The Polytechnic, Sheffield, 10.11.78

9. Leeds University, Leeds, 12.11.78

10. The Apollo, Manchester, 13.11.78

11. The Odeon, Birmingham, 14.11.78

12. The Coventry Theatre, Coventry, 15.11.78

13. The Corn Exchange, Cambridge, 17.11.78

14. The ABC Cinema, Great Yarmouth, 18.11.78

15. Cardiff University, Cardiff, 20.11.78

16. The Dome, Brighton, 21.11.78

17. The University of Kent, Canterbury (Cancelled)

18. The Guildhall, Portsmouth, 24.11.78

19. The Colston Hall, Bristol, 2611.78

20. Wembley Arena, London, 29.11.78

21. The University of Kent, Canterbury, 07.12.78

22. The Music Machine, London, 21.12.78

European Tour 1979:

Before The Jam embarked on their European tour they played one warm-up concert at Reading University on 16.02.79

1. Berlin, Germany, 20.02.79

2. The Star Club, Hamburg, Germany 21.02.79

3. The Star Club, Hamburg, Germany 22.02.79

4. Wiesbaden, Germany, 23.02.79

5. Paris, France, 26.02.79

6. Rennes, France, 27.02.79

7. The Royale, Lyon, France, 28.02.79

8

8. Marseille, France, 04.03.79

9. Follies, Brussels, Belgium, 06.03.79

The Jam's Third Tour of the USA and Canada 1979:

1. The Rex Theatre, Toronto, 10.04.79

2. The Orpheum Theatre, Boston, 12.04.79

3. The Tower Theatre, Philadelphia, 13.04.79

4. The New York Palladium, New York, 14.04.79

5. The Agora Ballroom, Cleveland, 16.04.79

6. The Punch and Judy Theatre, Detroit, 17.04.79

7. The Oakland Auditorium Theatre, San Fancisco, 20.04.79

8. The University of California Royce Hall, L.A, 21.04.79

9. The Commodore, Vancouver, 24.04.79

The Jam Pact Tour 1979:

1. The Sheffield University, Sheffield, 04.05.79

2. The Sheffield University, Sheffield, 04.05.79

3. The City Hall, Newcastle, 06.05.79

4. The Salford University, Salford, 08.05.79

5. The Rainbow Theatre, London, 10.05.79

6. The Rainbow Theatre, London, 11.05.79

7. The Auditorium, Loughborough, 12.05.79

8. The Exeter University, Exeter, 14.05.79

9. The Liverpool University, Liverpool, 15.05.79

10. The Liverpool University, Liverpool, 16.05.79

11. The Strathclyde University, Glasgow, 18.05.79

12. The Strathclyde University, Glasgow, 19.05.79

13. The Colston Hall, Bristol, 21.05.79

14. The Odeon, Birmingham, 22.05.79

15. The Guildhall, Portsmouth, 24.05.79

16. The Saddleswoth Arts Festival, Saddlesworth, 09.06.79

The Setting Sons Tour 1979:

Before The Jam set off on their Setting Sons tour, earlier in November they played two secret shows under two different names. The Jam/John's Boys played at The Marquee, London 02.11.79 and The Jam/The Eton Rifles at the Nashville, London 03.11.79

1. *The Aylesbury Friars, Aylesbury, 17.11.79*

2. *The Poole Arts Centre, Poole, 18.11.79*

3. *The Apollo, Manchester, 20.11.79*

4. *The Civic Hall, Wolverhampton, 21.11.79*

5. *The Gaumont, Southampton, 23.11.79*

6. *The Gaumont, Southampton, 24.11.79*

7. *Bingley Hall, Birmingham, 25.11.79*

8. *Trentham Gardens, Stoke, 26.11.79*

9. *The Royal Hall, Bridlington Spa, 27.11.79*

10. *The Deeside Leisure Centre, Deeside, 29.11.79*

11. *The Lancaster University, Lancaster, 30.11.79*

12. *The Sophia Gardens, Cardiff, 01.12.79 (Cancelled)*

13. *The Rainbow Theatre, London, 02.12.79*

14. *The Rainbow Theatre, London, 03.12.79*

15. *The Rainbow Theatre, London, 04.12.79*

16. *The City Hall, Newcastle, 06.12.79*

17. *The City Hall, Newcastle, 07.12.79*

18. *The Apollo, Glasgow, 08.12.79*

19. *The Caird Hall, Dundee, 09.12.79*

20. *The Odeon, Edinburgh, 10.12.79*

21. *The Queens Hall, Leeds, 11.12.79*

22. *The King George's Hall, Blackburn, 12.12.79*

23. *The Sophia Gardens, Cardiff, 13.12.79 (Cancelled)*

24. *The Brighton Conference Centre, Brighton, 15.12.79*

25. *The Guildhall, Portsmouth, 16.12.79*

26. *The De Montfort Hall, Leicester, 18.12.79*

27. *The Pavilion, Bath, 20.12.79*

28. *The Pavilion, Bath, 21.12.79*

The Jam's Fourth USA Tour:

Before heading off on their fourth tour of the USA The Jam prepared themselves by playing four UK dates:

1. *The Corn Exchange, Cambridge, 11.02.80*

2. *The University of Kent, Canterbury, 12.02.80*

THE JAM

3. The Winter Gardens, Malvern, 13.02.80

4. The YMCA, Woking, 15.02.80

1. The Emerald City, New Jersey, 27.02.80

2. Stage West, Connecticut, 28.02.80

3. The New York Palladium, New York, 29.02.80

4. The Triangle Theatre, New York, 01.03.80

5. JB Scotts, New York, 03.03.80

6. The Motor City Roller Rink, Detroit, 05.03.80

7. Park West, Chicago, 06.03.80

8. The Old Chicago Amusement Park, Chicago, 07.03.80

9. The Showbox, Seattle, 13.03.80

10. The Fox Warfield Theatre, San Francisco, 15.03.80

11. The Santa Monica Civic Center, L.A, 16.03.80

12. The Palace, Houston, 21.03.80

13. The Armadilo HQ, Austin, 22.03.80

14. The Capitol, New Jersey, 28.03.80 (Cancelled)

Following the fourteen dates in the USA The Jam returned home and throughout the spring and early summer played a handful of concerts that included:

1. The Rainbow Theatre, London, 07.04.80

2. The Rainbow Theatre, London, 08.04.80 (Mick Talbot of the Merton Parkas joined The Jam on stage).

3. The Civic Centre, Guildford, 18.04.80

4. The Pink Pop Festival, Holland, 26.05.80

5. The Civic Hall, Wolverhampton, 02.06.80

6. The King George's Hall, Blackburn, 03.06.80

7. The Hanley Victoria Hall, Stoke, 04.06.80

8. The Loch Lomond Festival, Scotland, 21.06.80

First Tour of Japan:

1. The Mainichi Hall, Osaka, 03.07.80

2. The Kaikan Hall, Osaka, 04.07.80

3. The Sun Plaza Hall, Tokyo, 06.07.80

4. The Nippon Seinenkan, Tokyo, 07.07.80

5. The Nippon Seinenkan, Tokyo, 08.07.80

6. Cancelled concert in Tokyo, 10.07.80

8

On their way back to the UK The Jam stopped off in America to play one concert at Flippers, Los Angeles. They then played a few more gigs before launching into the Sound Affects Tour.

1. The Civic Hall, Guildford, 22.07.80

2. The Friars, Aylesbury, 02.08.80

3. The Poole Arts Centre, Poole, 03.08.80

4. The Turku Rock Festival, Finland, 09.08.80

5. The Technical College, Bromley, 18.10.80

The Sound Affects UK Tour:

1. The Top Rank, Sheffield, 26.10.80

2. The City Hall, Newcastle, 27.10.80

3. The City Hall, Newcastle, 28.10.80

4. The Playhouse, Edinburgh, 29.10.80

5. The Apollo, Glasgow, 30.10.80

6. The Apollo, Manchester, 31.10.80

7. The Apollo, Manchester, 01.11.80

8. The Deeside Leisure Centre, Deeside, 02.11.80

9. The Queens Exhibition Hall, Leeds, 03.11.80

10. The Brighton Conference Centre, Brighton, 05.11.80

11. The Brighton Conference Centre, Brighton, 06.11.80

12. The Sports Centre, Bracknell, 07.11.80

13. The Sports Centre, Bracknell, 08.11.80

14. The Poole Arts Centre, Poole, 09.11.80

15. The Sophia Gardens, Cardiff, 10.11.80

16. The Bingley Hall, Birmingham, 11.11.80

17. The De Montfort Hall, Leicester, 12.11.80

18. The De Montfort Hall, Leicester, 13.11.80

19. The Rainbow Theatre, London, 15.11.80

20. The Rainbow Theatre, London, 16.11.80

21. The Hammersmith Odeon, London, 18.11.80

22. The Hammersmith Odeon, London, 19.11.80

The Sound Affects European Tour:

1. Gothenburg, Sweden, 22.11.80

2. Stockholm, Sweden, 24.11.80

3. Gota Lejon, Sweden, 25.11.80

4. Gota Lejon, Sweden, 26.11.80

5. Lund, Sweden, 27.11.80

6. The Karregat, Holland, 29.11.80

8

7. The Rockpalast TV Show, 30.11.80

8. The Utrecht Westfalenhalle Concert House, Holland, 01.12.80

9. Oosterpoort, Holland, 02.12.80

10. Hofterlo, Belgium, 03.12.80

11. The Fort Regent, Jersey, 04.12.80

The Jam then finalised the Sound Affects tour by adding some extra UK dates:

1. The Coliseum, St Austell, 08.12.80

2. The Colston Hall, Bristol, 09.12.80

3. The Winter Gardens, Malvern, 10.12.80

4. The Civic Hall, Guildford, 11.12.80

5. The Music Machine, London, 12.12.80

6. The Coliseum, St Austell, 14.12.80

Going into 1981 The Jam continued to promote the Sound Affects album by playing some more concerts: these would warm them up for the second leg of Sound Affects European Tour. The Jam went under the name The Jam Road Crew and played at The Cricketers Pub, Woking, 14.02.81

1. The YMCA, Woking, 16.02.81

2. The Sheerwater Youth Club, Woking, 17.02.81

3. The Norwich University, Norwich, 21.02.81

4. The Nottingham University, Nottingham, 22.02.81

5. The Crawley Leisure Centre, Crawley, 23.02.81

6. The Pavilion Baltard, France, 26.02.81

7. The Olympen, Sweden, 01.03.81

8. The Oddfellows, Denmark, 03.03.81

9. The Market Hall, Germany, 06.03.81

10. The Metropole, Germany, 08.03.81

11. Ancienne Belguique, Belgium, 10.03.81

12. The Tivoli Hall, Belgium, 12.03.81 (Cancelled)

13. The Paradiso Club, Holland, 13.03.81

14. The Paradiso Club, Holland, 14.03.81

15. The Palais St Sauver, France, 15.03.81

16. Studio 44, France, 16.03.81

The Jam returned to the UK to play at the Royal Court Theatre, Liverpool for a benefit concert in support of the March Against Unemployment cause.

and then it was back home again to perform at a 'Funeral Pyre' promotion concert at the Rainbow Theatre, London on 17 June 1981.

Second Tour of Japan:

1. *Kinro Fukushi Kaikan, Tokyo, 13.05.81*

2. *The Mido Kaikan Hall, Osaka, 14.05.81*

3. *The Sun Plaza Hall, Tokyo, 15.05.81*

4. *The Sun Plaza Hall, Tokyo, 16.05.81*

Fifth North American Tour:

1. *Le Club, Montreal, 20.05.81*

2. *The Concert Hall, Toronto, 21.05.81*

3. *The Concert Hall, Toronto, 22.05.81*

4. *The Concert Hall, Toronto, 23.05.81*

5. *The Ottawa Technical High School, Ottawa, 24.05.81*

6. *The Ritz, New York, 26.05.81*

7. *The Channel Club, Boston, 29.05.81*

Arriving back in the UK there was only a short opportunity for The Jam to catch their breath before heading out to Sweden to play two concerts: Grona Lund, Stockholm 10.06.81, and onto Borlanger

The Bucket And Spade Tour

1. *The Festival Pavilion, Skegness, 20.06.81*

2. *The Granby Hall, Leicester, 22.06.81*

3. *The Guildhall, Portsmouth, 23.06.81*

4. *The Coliseum, St Austell, 25.06.81*

5. *The Bingley Hall, Stafford, 27.06.81*

6. *The Magnum Leisure Centre, Irvine, 30.06.81*

7. *The Royal Hall, Bridlington Spa, 02.07.81*

8. *The Market Hall, Carlisle, 04.07.81*

9. *The Guildhall, Preston, 05.07.81*

10. *The Civic Hall, Guildford, 07.07.81*

11. *The Civic Hall, Guildford, 08.07.81*

It was October before The Jam performed again and this was at a CND benefit concert held at the Rainbow Theatre on 23.10.81. The following day The Jam played at another CND organised event on the Embankment, London. Going into December more CND benefit concerts were supported and these included: The Michael Sobell Sports Centre on 12.12.81

THE JAM

and 13.12.81 and at Hammersmith Palais on 14.12.81 and 15.12.81

The Jam signed off 1981 by performing a set for the *BBC's In Concert* series at Golders Green Hippodrome, London on 19.12.81

1982 had started off quieter on the performing front, with only gigs at Central London Polytechnic on 24.02.81 and an appearance at the JOBS Not YOPS event in Guildford on 06.03.81.

The Trans-Global Express UK Tour:

1. *The Guildhall, Portsmouth, 12.03.82*

2. *The Conference Centre, Brighton, 13.03.82*

3. *The Conference Centre, Brighton, 14.03.82*

4. *The Fair Deal, London, 15.03.82*

5. *The Alexandra Pavilion, London, 16.03.82*

6. *Royal Bath and West Showground, Shepton Mallet, 17.03.82*

7. *The Afan Lido, Port Talbot, 18.03.82*

8. *The Bingley Hall, Birmingham, 20.03.82*

9. *The Bingley Hall, Birmingham, 21.03.82*

10. *The De Montfort Hall, Leicester, 22.03.82*

11. *The De Montfort Hall, Leicester, 23.03.82*

12. *The Apollo, Manchester, 25.03.82*

13. *The Apollo, Manchester, 26.03.82*

14. *The Deeside Leisure Centre, Deeside, 27.03.82*

15. *The Opera House, Blackpool, 28.03.82*

16. *The Top Rank, Sheffield, 29.03.82*

17. *The Top Rank, Sheffield, 30.03.82*

18. *The Top Rank, Sheffield, 31.03.82*

19. *The Queens Exhibition Hall, Leeds, 01.04.82*

20. *The City Hall, Newcastle, 03.04.82*

21. *The City Hall, Newcastle, 04.04.82*

22. *The Playhouse, Edinburgh, 05.04.82*

23. *The Playhouse, Edinburgh, 06.04.82*

24. *The Apollo, Glasgow, 07.04.82*

25. *The Apollo, Glasgow, 08.04.82*

The Trans-Global Express European Tour:

1. *Johaneshovs Isstadion, Sweden, 16.04.82*

2. *The Olympen, Sweden, 18.04.82*

3. *The Faulkner Theatre, Denmark, 20.04.82*

4. *The Vesiby-Risskov Hall, Denmark, 21.04.82*

5. *The Paradiso Club, Holland, 24.04.82*

6. *The Paradiso Club, Holland, 25.04.82*

7.

Harvey Goldsmith Entertainments And M.C.P Present

THE JAM

Wembley Arena

DECEMBER 1st - 5th 1982

GUEST

THE JAM

De Vereniging, Holland, 26.04.82

8. Ancienne Belgique, Belgium, 27.04.82

9. The Pantin Hippodrome, France, 29.04.82

10. The Palais D'Hiver, France, 30.04.82

Sixth North American Tour:

1. The Richie Coliseum, Washington, 14.05.82

1. The Palladium, New York, 15.05.82

2. Northstage, New York, 16.05.82

3. The Palladium, New York, 18.05.82

4. The Trenton War Memorial, New Jersey, 19.05.82

5. The Orpheum Theatre, Boston, 20.05.82

6. The Verdum Auditorium, Montreal, 22.05.82

7. The Coliseum, Toronto, 24.05.82

8. The Michigan Theatre, Michigan, 25.05.82

9. The Aragon Ballroom, Chicago, 26.05.82

10. Perkins Palace, Los Angeles, 29.05.82

11. Perkins Palace, Los Angeles, 30.05.82

12. Perkins Palace, Los Angeles, 31.05.82

13. The Fox Warfield Theatre, San Francisco, 02.06.82

14. The Kerrisdale Arena, Vancouver, 05.06.82

Third and Final Japanese Tour:

1. The Kaikan Hall, Tokyo, 11.06.82

2. The Sun Plaza Hall, Tokyo, 14.06.82

3. The Mainichi Hall, Osaka, 15.06.82

4. The Seinenkan Hall, Tokyo, 16.06.82

5. Kinro Kaikan, Nagoya, 17.06.82

The Jam were back in the UK in late June were due to play two concerts at the Queens Park Rangers Football ground, Loftus Road (26.06.82 and 10.07.82). Both were cancelled.

A Solid Bond In Your Heart Tour (Some gigs cancelled):

1. The Leacliff Pavilion, Southend, 20.09.82

2. The Showering Pavilion, Shepton Mallet, 21.09.82

3. The Conference Centre, Brighton, 22.09.82

4. The Granby Hall, Leicester, 23.09.82

8

5. *The Royal Court, Liverpool, 24.09.82*

6. *The Royal Court, Liverpool, 25.09.82*

7. *The Edinburgh Inglestone Royal Exhibition Hall, Inglestone, 27.09.82*

8. *The Whitley Bay Ice Rink, Whitley Bay, 28.09.82*

9. *The Whitley Bay Ice Rink, Whitley Bay, 29.09.82*

10. *The Queens Exhibition Hall, Leeds, 30.09.82*

11. *The Bingley Hall, Stafford, 01.10.82*

12. *The Gloucester Hall, Jersey, 09.10.82*

13. *The Beau Sejour Leisure Centre, Guernsey, 11.10.82*

A Solid Bond In Your Heart European Tour:

14. *Paris, France, 13.10.82*

14. *Strasbourg, Belgium, 14.10.82*

15. *Genk, Belgium, 15.10.82*

16. *Poperinge, Belgium, 16.10.82*

17. *Amsterdam, Holland, 17.10.82*

18. *Amsterdam, Holland, 18.10.82*

Beat Surrender Tour:

1. *The Apollo, Glasgow, 25.11.82*

2. *The Poole Arts Centre, Poole, 27.11.82*

3. *The Coliseum, St Austell, 28.11.82*

4. *The Afan Lido, Port Talbot, 29.11.82*

5. *Wembley Arena, London, 01.12.82*

6. *Wembley Arena, London, 02.12.82*

7. *Wembley Arena, London, 03.12.82*

8. *Wembley Arena, London, 04.12.82*

9. *Wembley Arena, London, 05.12.82*

10. *The Pavilion, Bridlington Spa, 06.12.82*

11. *The Apollo, Manchester, 07.12.82*

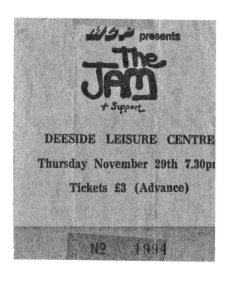

WSP presents

the JAM + Support

DEESIDE LEISURE CENTRE

Thursday November 29th 7.30pr

Tickets £3 (Advance)

Nº 1994

THE JAM

12. *The Bingley Hall, Birmingham, 08.12.82*

13. *The Civic Hall, Guildford, 10.11.82*

14. *The Conference Centre, Brighton, 11.12.82*

11 December 1982 - The Brighton Centre.

Simon Wells saw The Jam play their final ever concert:

Can it really be over 30 years since The Jam, Britain's favourite ever Mod sensation, last trod the boards? Well, those yellowing press cuttings I carefully filed away in an oversize scrapbook under my bed tell me this is so. It all just seems a hell of a long time ago. And as it's December again outside my window, I thought it more than pertinent to share a few reflections on the day The Jam called it a day.

With the forgiving benefit of retrospect, Paul Weller's decision in 1982 to walk out on the band when they were at the top of the pop tree seems an astute and thoughtful decision. One only needs to look at Weller's lyrics to realise that they were drawn from the urgency and immediacy of youth, and with two of the band nearing their thirties, there was no way that they could sincerely deliver that sort of material without hypocrisy: something that had become a minor obsession with Weller.

Their last album, The Gift, was an uneasy mix of soul, gospel and punk-funk, sowing seeds that would only begin to fully germinate once Weller had moved on from the creative confines of The Jam. Still, with the most loyal fan-base since The Beatles, pulling the plug on the nation's favourite threesome was going to be an explosive, if risky, finale. The question on everyone's lips was, "Well, what happens next?" Ever the professional, Weller had announced the split well before the final tour, ensuring that the band would be greeted by a three-week standing ovation.

Even after five sell-out nights at Wembley Arena and a barnstorming UK tour, demand for tickets was still throbbing. The Jam were at No 1 in both album and singles charts, and so a Saturday night at Brighton's Conference Centre (reportedly Weller's favourite venue at the time) was slotted in to satisfy the final demand. To many, it seemed fitting that the band chose Brighton for their last hurrah. Brighton will always be a Mod town, forever smothered with a fur-rimmed parka since the ersatz Mods adopted it for many a well-documented 'haveitawaydays' in the Sixties. Quadrophenia the movie unwittingly re-baptised the town with the hand of Mod in the late Seventies, sending further confused Moddies into Tamla Toytown in search of pills and soap.

As a Jam devotee, the few days prior to the concert were full of great expectations. Indeed when you hear of 'last' concerts, you conjure up images and expectations that a band can't simply hope to achieve. Nonetheless as I hadn't attended The Beatles' last soiree at Candlestick Park in 1966, nor Cream's farewell fandango at the Albert Hall, I was sure as hell going to be at The Jam's (my generation's Beatles) last bash.

I think it was Mike Read on Radio One who announced that the band was to play the final gig the Wednesday before the show, and that the tickets were going on sale the following morning.

A few of us from deepest Sussex made the pilgrimage down to Brighton to secure those prized bits of paper, paper that would be later passed around public houses like tablets from the Mount. By the time we got down to the box office at 9.00am, there was an enormous queue and our collective hearts sank. Imagine the embarrassment down later at the pub if we hadn't scored the tickets! Eventually though, we did get to the counter and happily acquired four tickets at £5.00 each.

The anticipation a few days before the gig was unbearable. The band's new live opus, Dig the New Breed, was played and played till a hole went through track three on side two. Over beer and bullshit, we planned to individually storm the stage to say our own fond farewell to the boys - naturally all recorded on a mate's pocket Instamatic. The dreams of children no less.

One thing I do clearly recall about the day (a Saturday) was that it was miserably wet and overcast: not unusual for the South Coast in December. The Centre, Brighton's conference venue, had actually put on their hoarding that fronts the building 'The Jam's Last Concert' (as if we didn't know!). We managed to miss the soundcheck (something that had become a ritualised matinee of Jam gigs) but were informed that it had been a miserable affair, Weller and Foxton barely communicating with each other. Later that afternoon, Weller (without

Bruce and Rick) had been seconded to Brighton Pier by the BBC's *Nationwide* to explain his reasons for leaving the group.

In characteristic mode atop a windy prom he spat: "I feel we've achieved enough y'know. I think we've done all we can do as the three of us, and I think it's a good time to finish it. I don't want to drag it on, and go on for like the next twenty years doing it, and become nothing: mean nothing: end up like all the rest of the groups. I want this to count for something."

As we approached the gig. There were hordes of people outside literally begging for tickets and handing over extortionate sums to the parasitic touts that flocked around the venue like flies on rotten meat. I clearly recall too, a large posse of skinheads milling around. (Note: this was the time of the pathetic skinhead vs Mods vs anybody confrontations that had brought Brighton to a standstill the previous summer). In our innocence, the group I'd gone down with had decided to make our way to the front of the stage as soon as we got into the hall. Once inside though, it was clear that several hundred people had had the same idea. It was packed solid at the front, well before the first support came on.

Given the layout of the venue - the ground floor area was standing and the three facing tiers were seated - many people had tried to gatecrash the arena floor and, obviously aware that this might happen, extra security staff were placed on the doors to prevent this. It was no surprise then, Jam fans being what they were, that those with seating tickets simply leapt the 12 to 5 foot drop from

THE JAM

8

the gallery and hastily buried themselves in the crowd. Once the lights went down it was like a sea of Mod lemmings. One enterprising Mod even used his parka to lever his mates down onto the floor!

The first support group – I don't remember their name – came on looking and sounding very amateur, but full of enthusiasm.

The next group on were Apocalypse, a band from Weller's Jamming label-stable. I personally didn't think much of them, and neither did a lot of the crowd - but it was brave move to put them on that night. The biggest cheer they got was when the lead guitarist played the first few bars of 'Start!' After they'd left the stage I wandered to the back of the hall to ask the sound desk guy if the concert was being recorded (answer: "no"). What I did notice, however, was John Weller setting up a video camera on the mixing board. The footage would later surface some years later on the bootleg market.

Then something very strange appeared.

As the lights dimmed, a disembodied voice bellowed out the arrival of the 'Eton Rifles Dance Troupe'. Then to a soundtrack of some of the worst Seventies musical travesties, shambled on a gang of the weirdest looking bunch of plonkers you could imagine, prancing around decked out in glitter, flares and even Bay City Rollers gear. (One I believe was Gary Crowley and possibly Paul's sister Nicky). Understandably they were met with a huge barrage of abuse and a sizeable number of coins! Just why they were there though (other than a wind-up) remains a mystery to me. It did nothing but antagonise most of the crowd, who were now getting very impatient.

There was one moment when I turned around (I was about ten to 12 rows from the front) to see the whole of the hall completely full, with more and more people streaming in. We later found out that in an act of goodwill the doors had been left open

to those without tickets. There also seemed to be a huge contingency of skinheads present who were pushing their way through the crowd, hurling abuse at everyone and making it all very uncomfortable. Looking back, and having attended hundreds of gigs since, this was the most frightening moment I've ever experienced. However, I'll never forget that the last two records the warm up DJ span that night were the Small Faces' 'Whatcha Gonna Do About It' and (poignantly) The Kinks' 'Waterloo Sunset', which played as the lights dimmed.

With the atmosphere in the hall on fire, some bloke (Swedish? Dutch? I don't know) came on to introduce the band: "For the last time, the only band to leave a solid bond in your heart - The Jam!"

The group came on to the loudest roar imaginable, Weller resplendent in a red polka dot button down and tonic strides and Bruce and Rick in their familiar stage garb. Kicking off with 'Start!' The Jam were obviously out to finish on the highest possible note. Paul initially was so highly charged he managed to break three strings in as many songs. I hadn't seen the band play at Wembley, but I was struck by the uneasy mass of people on stage: brass, sax, keyboard, two backing singers - it all seemed far too congested.

The last gig I'd seen The Jam do on the Solid Bond tour a month or so previous, was the best I'd ever witnessed them perform - and that was as a three piece. This night though, Paul and Bruce kept up their wall of silence with each other, although there was one touching moment when, during 'It's Too Bad', Bruce's mike temporally conked out, leaving him to join Paul on his mike for the last part of the song.

I seem to recall Paul getting more and more pissed off − first with the lights, and then even more so as guitar string after guitar string kept snapping. During 'Down in the Tube Station at Midnight' he actually walked off stage mid-song to retrieve another guitar. Towards the end of the gig during 'Town Called Malice', some prick threw a glass bottle on stage, narrowly missing Bruce, but exploding all over Rick's drum kit. Understandably the group walked off. A few minutes later they sombrely returned. Bruce Foxton addressed the crowd - sounding well upset: "I wanna remember this gig for the good things, not the fucking bottles!"

Paul by this point seemed detached from everything, saying little or nothing between numbers. A couple of songs later (a lamentable rendition of 'In the City', an unforgivable version of 'Going Underground') the band performed their very last number, an overlong and fragmented rendition of 'The Gift'. They then left the stage and the house lights went up − although most present had to double back as Paul, Bruce and Rick came back on for a final goodbye. I distinctly remember Paul hanging back by the drum kit as Bruce gave a "thank you very much" speech, and then darting off the stage very, very quickly. And that, as they say, was that.

It seemed that the band had thrown everything in on this tour. Brighton, though, was just one gig too many, especially after their previous appearance a few days before at Guildford, close to their hometown of Woking. That, for all intents and purposes, was to be the full-circle gig.

8

THE JAM

8

Those present recall an emotional night where the band played their hearts and souls out to fans, friends and family. As a band they'd mentally worked towards Guildford as being the final hurdle, making a further gig an emotionally redundant affair. According to Foxton and Buckler in their lamentable biography, Our Story, Brighton was slotted in to satisfy 'monetary reasons'.

There was an almighty scramble at the merchandise stall on the way out, but more concerning for myself and my friends was the mass of skinheads who had assembled outside the front doors, and so we beat a hasty retreat out of the side entrance. None of us were that impressed with the night's activities, although it was always going to be something to say you'd seen The Jam's final concert.

> ## "Well, that's that then. What do we do now?"
>
> ### Bruce Foxton

As the crowd made their weary way back up the hill to Brighton station, the ticket stubs from the concert had been ceremoniously dumped on the street outside the rear of the venue. The majority of fans just walked over them.

Bruce Foxton

When we did the last concert I was going through the set list thinking, 'This is the last time I'm going to play these numbers.' We always knew nothing lasts forever. We always talked about that at some point The Jam was going to come to an end. It just came a little too soon.

All change for Foxton, Weller and Buckler. Pic Anton Corbijn

JAM SPLIT

THE JAM are to break up right after their pre-Christmas concerts — and that is now official.

[newspaper article body text]

PAUL WELLER'S PERSONAL GOODBYE TO HIS FANS

Rick Buckler

It was a great gig, so we were all fired up from having just played better than ever, but creeping in was the realisation of just what was ending. At each venue, fans would ask us why we were splitting up, and at that stage neither Rick nor I knew the answer because it was entirely Paul's decision: he wanted a clear end to The Jam, and although we tried to talk him round, we had to respect his wishes. After the show we went our separate ways, as happened often at gigs that our friends and families attended – but this time we stayed apart. It didn't really hit me until the next morning. I woke up in the Grand Hotel on the seafront with a very thick head, thinking.

THE FINAL CONCERT: BRIGHTON 11 DECEMBER 1982

8

Set list:

Start!

It's Too Bad

Beat Surrender

Away From the Numbers

Ghosts

In The Crowd

Boy About Town

Get Yourself Together

All Mod Cons

To Be Someone (Didn't We Have a

Nice Time)

Smithers-Jones

Tales From the Riverbank

Precious

Move On Up

Circus

Down in the Tube Station at

Midnight

David Watts

Mr. Clean

Going Underground

In the City

Town Called Malice

The Butterfly Collector

Pretty Green

The Gift

8 FROM THE FANS

The connection between The Jam and their fans has become legendary. Few comparisons can be made and few can feel as passionate about a band that moved them so much when they were young. This was evidenced by the interest and pull that the *About The Young Idea* exhibition had some thirty plus years after The Jam had split. There have also been numerous compilation and live albums released and books published on The Jam. The Jam's music lives on, as does the love for the band from their loyal fans. Blessed are The Jam Army!

Fè Mensah

The Jam were a strong part of my musical upbringing as a growing child. Whenever a new song by them was on the radio or on *Top of the Pops* my elder sisters especially were likely to turn up the volume or sing it aloud word for word. My elder brother also purchased their Greatest Hits. Also around the age of five I thought the song 'Eton Rifles' was in fact called 'Eton Riots' - oops!'

Phil Potter

I first got into The Jam at a very early age. While most of the kids I grew up with were singing along with John Travolta to 'Greased Lighting' I was singing the lines of 'Mr Clean'. It was mid 1978 when I first really heard a Jam album in full at my cousin's house, that album being *This Is The Modern World* which had been released late the year before but it was from then on that I developed a serious love for this band. Move forward 18 months to around December 1979, and by now I was collecting everything I could with pocket money and birthdays; it was always The Jam that I wanted as a present.

So by the time their fourth album *Setting Sons* was released, I wanted, needed, had to, see them live. The Setting Sons tour was announced in all the music press papers, *NME*, *Sounds*, *Melody Maker* etc. I was 11 or 12 at this time and a few older blokes from my secondary school had managed to get tickets. I asked my Mum and Dad if I could go, but even before asking I knew the answer would be no, my mum said there was no way she was letting me go all the way to Finsbury Park at night on my own (well, with another load of boys a year or so older). I begged for days, but nothing was going to change their minds.

Back then a few bands would soundcheck during the mid afternoon and it was a major event for fans to go along and try their luck at getting in and The Jam were known for being a band that welcomed fans into the hall/theatre/arena to hear them run through a small set list. So this was a chance for me to try my luck, and if I couldn't go to the gig at night then an afternoon soundcheck would be second best. The London dates were three nights at the Rainbow Theatre in North London's Finsbury Park.

I came from Paddington West London so it was a short trip on the Piccadilly Line. This meant of course bunking off school.

On the morning it was up for school like normal, into my uniform and out the door and then I waited until my mum had gone to work (dad went much earlier). I then went back inside the house, off with the uniform and into my Jam stage shoes, Fred Perry, Levis and jacket and off to North London. I went with a few mates from school, who for most of the time talked about the gig ahead of that night. I could only sit on the train, thinking that perhaps even at the eleventh hour my mum would change her mind. We arrived at Finsbury Park tube station and walked the short distance to the venue. My heart was beating ten to a dozen, excitement was an understatement.

As we got nearer I could see a rather large crowd already outside the main doors. Most were a bit older - mods, rude boys and girls – and we got in line and spoke to a few that were in front and asked if the band had arrived. Kenny Wheeler, the band's head of security, said that no one would be allowed in until the band's roadies had set up all the equipment and this could be a while. It was around 2.00pm by now and I was thinking about what to tell my mum to explain why I was so late home from school because I'd never be back by 4.00pm, the time I roughly got home normally.

We stood outside for what seemed like ages and I was starting to think how bad is my luck. I go to the only soundcheck and no one gets in. Then someone in the queue shouted out that he could see John Weller talking to a few of the security men inside, and with that they came towards the main doors and said that we would be allowed in providing we keep quiet during the songs, and after that the band would sign anything and chat for few minutes.

Wow! It was finally going to happen - I was to see The Jam live, albeit a soundcheck. We finally got inside and took our places on the floor where later it would be packed to the rafters. There must have been around 100 to 150 people let in. The Jam and John Weller were always good for this. The lights were up bright and then they dimmed then up again and down, and so on.

I was too busy looking up to notice everyone had moved towards the stage and a cheer went up as Paul, Rick and Bruce walked on and they ran through about seven songs. I can only really remember 'When You're Young' and 'Private Hell', but it was definitely a good 50 minutes of The Jam on stage. After that they came to the edge of the stage. It was packed down at the front by now and a lot of older fans had made their way to speak to the band. I managed to sort of shake Bruce's hand but that was about it - only being 11 it was always going to be hard to get in front of blokes of about 18.

Still, I had finally seen the band I loved. We were asked to leave the venue and made our way back to the tube station. I turned around to see above the main doors "The Jam – Sold Out - 2nd, 3rd and 4th December" and once again my heart sank. I so badly wanted to be back on that train coming to the venue a few hours later that night.

In all I went to a few soundchecks and did manage to meet the band properly. We owe a lot to the late John Weller (RIP) for these special afternoons. He always had time for us fans. Oh and yes, I did finally manage to see The Jam Live properly in the end.

THE JAM

8

Shane Juson

We travelled up from Leominster, a small town in Herefordshire, on a cold mid-March Sunday morning to see the best band in the fucking world at Birmingham Bingley Hall.

I was with my friends Terry, April and Karen, and Karen's dad Dick was driving. Terry and myself were 15 years old and April and Karen both 14. We got into the short queue as soon as we got there at around 3pm and left Dick to his own devices.

Resplendent in my beige suit, button down shirt, US Army parka and black bowling shoes, I was absolutely freezing stood outside. I thought I'd be nice and warm at least stood in the queue for the next four hours!

At around 3.30pm the doors opened up to the venue and everyone started rushing in. I hadn't got a clue what was happening, as this was only the third gig I'd ever been to.

Obviously I ran in too, to be amazed to see The Jam on stage! What the hell was happening? Everyone around me seemed to know what was going on and rushed to the barrier. I followed suit and ran to gain my own spot at the barrier in front of Paul Weller.

Paul was wearing his black jumbo cord Crombie, a college scarf, the famous Rupert The Bear trousers and black bowling shoes, Bruce had a black Crombie and Rick a denim jacket on behind the drum kit.

The Jam kicked off with 'Precious' and I just felt like a guilty schoolboy watching them without showing a ticket! I still didn't have a clue what was happening.

> *"It seemed to go by in an absolute flash but I was so much in awe of being able to witness the band in such a fantastic atmosphere."*

Our own small, intimate gig by the biggest band of the time and one to make a huge impression on me for the rest of my life.

They played around four songs in total and then, all too soon, it was over. The security started ushering us out of the hall as soon as they got the nod and I noticed Paul starting to come to the right hand side of the stage, down the steps, through the barriers and onto the floor of the venue.

Now was my moment I thought! I ran back towards Paul, skirting past the burly security - I was only about five foot two at the time - and said "hello" and shook Paul's hand in good old-fashioned schoolboy style. I don't know who was more shocked out of the two of us to be honest, Paul being taken aback as a short-arse kid ran toward him or me at meeting Paul Weller, my idol! I was in such shock that I didn't even ask for an autograph, I thought I'd never get the chance again.

The gig followed that night and was an amazing experience, (the show was filmed for Trans-Global Express). I was again in my spot in front of Paul, still in my parka and suit, front row on the barrier and sweating my bollocks off.

I also managed to get onto the video for a few seconds between 'Ghosts' and 'Precious!' The clip has appeared on a couple of Paul Weller DVDs and also on *About The*

Young Idea film. Unbelievable!

I have probably told everyone I've ever met my story of that soundcheck. One of the best days of my life. I was like a star myself the next day at school as the lad who had met Paul Weller!

In the *About The Young Idea*, Paul said "I don't know if it ever made a difference to anybody when we let the kids into the soundchecks?" Did it ever! Keep the faith.

Rob Ross

These are the recollections - mostly from emotion - of having been a fan of The Jam, as a teenager in the suburbs of Staten Island, New York. And that would be the most oft-repeated word from me, when talking about The Jam: emotion. From the moment they connected with me, it was like osmosis: Paul Weller's lyrics, the power of the melodies and the all-encompassing image/vibe I took from The Jam was one of complete emotion, which became a part of me. In short, it became the foundation of my soul.

Staten Island in the Seventies and Eighties wasn't exactly a thrilling place to grow up. It was (and still is) a very closed off physical location - an island in between New York and New Jersey, connected by four bridges and the only means of getting into Manhattan - the city - was via the Staten Island Ferry. Someone very astutely called it a cultural purgatory wedged between New York and New Jersey and although my views have changed dramatically since (I still live here), it would be apt for the time. It was/still is very conservative: in many ways very old guard and people here had their own Staten Islandness, which I could never describe accurately.

Musically, most Staten Islanders of that period were either oldies fans, since you could always hear doo-wop blasting from car radios, or disco people who would make their weekly trek over the Verrazano Bridge to the discos of Brooklyn, thanks to the *Saturday Night Fever* phenomenon. The rest who were into rock music were predominantly stoners - the AC/DC/Black Sabbath/Led Zeppelin crowd. If there were any people into punk at that earliest of moments, I wouldn't have known about them. I was 12 when punk occurred, especially being from New York and having an older cousin who was as astute a music fan as one could hope for: he was (and still is) the older brother I never had (I'm an only child). I worshipped him and his tastes and took endless cues from him since he was my hero. So when he instantly took to this new, exciting thing called punk, I got swept up in it with him.

Naturally, even though I was on the cusp of adolescence, I already had some very firm favourites that I'd grown up with, coming from parents with an incredible and extensive record collection. And as that 12 year old, my preferences were The Beatles, The Who, The Yardbirds, The Kinks, The Hollies, Paul McCartney, Todd Rundgren, Harry Nilsson, Pink Floyd and, yes, Led Zeppelin.

There were some prog things I liked as well, but I was a fan of the three-minute song: I didn't love ten-minute epics. When I heard the things my cousin was listening to, the one band that I immediately took notice of was The Jam, especially with their obvious Who/Beatles influences - and I should note: at that time, I'd been getting more into The Who over The Beatles! Being a teenager into this music - and finding a group of people I could connect with who were like-minded, not just musically, but on other levels - was near impossible. I was a very clumsy and awkward teen. At times I had this blinding

THE JAM

anger that I could never understand or describe; I had no ability in speaking to girls or carrying on a meaningful conversation with anyone.

But listening to The Jam and absorbing Paul's lyrics gave me an outlet. By 14, I'd finally bought a guitar because I desperately wanted to write songs and play like Pete Townshend. I was obsessed with playing. I'd come home from school and play until I went to sleep. I was a quick study. The more I listened to the The Jam, the more I read about The Jam and saw their photos, I began to come out of this self-absorbed social coma I was in. Yes, I wasn't a great speaker but I learned how to be a bit deeper with the things I said because of what I was learning and picking up on and from The Jam's influences or something that Paul may have said. I was reading books and poetry: listening to artists I'd never picked up on before: the Mod influence was already there, thanks to my long-standing love and knowledge of The Who, but The Jam was mine. I would try and spread the gospel to all of my friends: when the band would come to town and with the passage of time, we would go see every gig (the 1981 gig at The Ritz is still my favorite memory of them live and at their peak of performing power).

And time was passing. One minute I was 13, buying *All Mod Cons*: the next I was 17 and waiting for the guy behind the counter of Bleecker Bob's record store to open the box of new singles and hand me the latest from The Jam called 'Town Called Malice'. Most importantly, by the time I was 17, 18, I was writing song lyrics.

There were hundreds upon hundreds, the majority of which were absolute garbage, but there were several that I deemed worthy. And 90% were all born out of the influence Paul Weller had on me. There were songs of frustration, questioning why things were the way they were around me: not standard teen love songs but asking about the connectivity between two people - I credit all of it to wanting to write with a sense of consequence and confidence like Paul. I'd finally gotten a Rickenbacker and decided sooner or later, I'd form or join a band.

When I heard word that The Jam were splitting up - and I'll never forget it - it was a Monday night in November 1982 on the old WPIX radio station after they played 'Circus' and I was on the phone with a friend of mine who said "yeah, sad news out of England: those guys are breaking up at the end of the year." I was devastated. It was, at that moment, the worst possible news I could have heard. And even though I mourned and kept wondering why, a few months later, I finally graduated high school. And at 18, now with The Jam gone, I was going to have to form a band and carry on my version of The Jam's tradition and influence. And I did. But it was because of The Jam I managed to keep my wits about me and my head on straight as a teenager: they were always the musical light at the end of the tunnel in a narrow place like Staten Island. And there were, indeed, others who were like me and who heard the same things I heard and felt the same things I felt - especially about The Jam. So were it not for Paul, Bruce and Rick, I might not have survived the teen years. I certainly wouldn't be the person I'd like to think I became.

Craig Barden

I first heard The Jam quite late, aged 17, once I'd gotten over my initial obsession with The Beatles. Being born in 1997 didn't stop me from accessing great music, I'd always been aware that The Jam had existed, and the impact they'd had on the British people, yet I never actually got round to giving their music a proper listen.

I joined a three-piece Britpop/ Indie inspired band, The Gallerys, and my audition song was 'In The City' by The Jam. Having never heard the song properly before, I went on *YouTube* to listen to the track to learn it and I was after a few seconds was speechless. The *Top of the Pops* video showed The Jam, three working class lads with no formal musical education jumping up and down, aggressively hitting their instruments yet managing to demonstrate so much skill, shouting the opening lyrics "In the City there's a thousand things I want to say to you". I was blown away.

The band was clearly an energetic trio, capable of portraying their frustrations in life through their aggressive and hard hitting music. Though fairly punk-like in ferocity, there are massive amounts of musical skill and careful consideration in The Jam's impressive catalogue. Ranging from the skilful guitar in 'News of The World' to the rhythmic drums of 'Down in The Tube Station at Midnight', it's clear The Jam were well and truly skilled musicians.

For me, however, Bruce Foxton's bass lines blew me away the most. Not only are his bass lines creative, innovative and fit for purpose in The Jam's catalogue, they add flavour to the tunes. You only need to listen to 'Funeral Pyre' for thirty seconds to be exposed to Foxton's brilliance. The catchy bass riff at the beginning of the track establishes the sinister feel of the tune, as Foxton provides a whipping bass line to hold together the verses and hold the track together.

It's clear that in 2017 The Jam are more relevant than ever. There are political, social, and cultural tensions in the world, and what better way to voice one's frustrations with the issues of the world than by listening to the carefully controlled anger of The Jam, a three piece essential not only for British musical culture, but for the history of popular music. The Jam were one of a kind.

Richard Houghton

The late Seventies and early Eighties were a great time to be buying singles. Punk had led to the reintroduction of picture sleeves and the use of coloured vinyl after years of singles coming out in plain paper sleeves or advertising the record label rather than the artist whose single was inside. To add insult to injury, some 45s didn't even come with a record middle, so you'd fork out 55p for a single and then have to shell out again. And the music! You had artists like Elvis Costello, Madness and The Clash all putting out singles that weren't necessarily going to feature on an album, which was a welcome throwback to the Sixties, when a seven inch was something to be treasured in its own right, and which made them all the more desirable. And then there was The Jam. I would read about a new Jam single in the *NME* and two weeks later it would be in the shops. None of this waiting for months

THE JAM

for something to appear that you seemed to get with the more established acts. It was just single after single after single, and each one was an event. Paul Weller seemed to be a man on fire, bubbling with creative energy, and the videos and the appearances on *Top of the Pops*, together with the interviews he gave, seemed to suggest someone who really gave a toss, which appealed to me.

I got to see The Jam once, at Loughborough University students union on 12 May 1979, on The Jam Pact Tour. I remember the set was lit only in white and green, and they finished with 'A' Bomb In Wardour Street' and a stage explosion at the end of the song which had the lighting gantry wobbling and looking like it was about to collapse. I think the roadies must have overdone the pyro that night because it was the size of explosion you might see in a venue five times that size. I walked out of the venue, with the dry ice filling the place, knowing that I'd seen a band at the absolute height of their powers. I don't think Weller spoke a single word to the audience. All his passion and energy was devoted to delivering that set. Fabulous!

Mark Bunyan

Myself and my mate Gary Simmons went to the Rainbow gig in December 1979. We were 13 years old and I remember the older fans watching over us and the pure excitement of seeing The Jam live. Also on the way home we sung every song that was played that night. We got kicked off the bus for being too noisy!

Mick Hughes

I arrived at Hammersmith for The Jam soundcheck a bit late due to getting the paper train at 3.50am after the gig the night before. I looked around and it seemed a bit quiet, but I hooked up with a few other Jam fans outside the Odeon.

I was gutted as I heard 'Billy Hunt' being played and realised it was quiet as everyone was already in for the soundcheck. Not wanting to miss any more, four of us went round the side of the Odeon searching for a way in. In those days security was a lot easier then today. Anyway, we found a door that opened and we told each other to be quiet.

We crept in and saw some stairs, so went up trying not to be noticed. As we went up all we found was some bloke sitting warming his hands over a stove. Realising this was not the way, we crept down again. The other three went out but I wasn't giving up that easy as I was normally lucky and didn't miss a soundcheck.

I could hear them playing and it seemed very close. A door with a glass top to my surprise said 'Top Stage'. I looked in and could see Paul Weller and Bruce Foxton. Half way through a song I tried the door and couldn't believe it when it did open. A roadie saw me but ignored me. I waited until the end of the song then went in and walked up to Paul Weller and said "hello".

Paul said, "You better go and sit with the others down there before security get you." John Weller was laughing at the fans sitting for the soundcheck that had already given me a cheer. Paul patted me on the back as I jumped into the pit and sat with the others. After the soundcheck had finished Rick, Paul and Bruce spoke to me, saying they couldn't believe it when I appeared from nowhere!

8

"I walked out of the venue, with the dry ice filling the place, knowing that I'd seen a band at the absolute height of their powers."

Richard Houghton

8 THE JAM ON TV

The Jam appeared on the weekly UK TV show *Top of the Pops* on at least 30 different occasions. In May 1977, 'In The City' made the Top 40 and The Jam became the first 'punk' band to appear on the show, though their Rickenbacker guitars and sharp suits owed just as much to the Sixties. At its peak in the late Seventies, *Top of the Pops* reported viewing figures of 19 million.

Top of the Pops was traditionally shown every Thursday evening on BBC1, except for a short period on Fridays in mid 1973. Each weekly programme consisted of performances from some of that week's best-selling artists, with a rundown of that week's singles chart. With its high viewing figures the show became a significant part of British popular culture. Everybody wanted to appear on *Top of the Pops*!

In 1980 more of a party atmosphere was introduced to the show, with performances often accompanied by balloons and cheerleaders, and more audible audience noise. The programme had been broadcast live in its early editions, but then being recorded on the day before transmission for many years. However, from May 1981, the show was sometimes broadcast live for a few editions each year, and this practice continued on an occasional basis (often in the week of a bank holiday, when the release of the new chart was delayed, and for some special editions) for the rest of the decade.

The programme moved in September 1985 to a new regular half-hour timeslot of 7pm on Thursdays, where it would remain until June 1996. After falling viewing figures for many years, the show was final axed by the BBC in 2006 after 42 years on air.

19 May 1977 – 'In The City'
21 July 1977 – 'All Around The World'
4 August 1977 – 'All Around The World'
18 August 1977 – 'All Around The World'
3 November 1977 – 'The Modern World'
9 March 1978 – 'News Of The World'
24 August 1978 – 'David Watts'
7 September 1978 – 'David Watts'
21 September 1978 – 'David Watts'
19 October 1978 – 'Down in the Tube Station at Midnight'
15 March 1979 – 'Strange Town'
5 April 1979 – 'Strange Town'
23 August 1979 – 'When You're Young'
1 November 1979 – 'The Eton Rifles'
15 November 1979 – 'The Eton Rifles'
20 March 1980 – 'Going Underground'
27 March 1980 – 'Going Underground'
3 April 1980 – 'Going Underground'
21 August 1980 – 'Start!'
4 September 1989 – 'Start!'
1 January 1981 – 'Going Underground'
4 June 1981 – 'Funeral Pyre'
22 October 1981 – 'Absolute Beginners'
11 February 1982 – 'Town Called Malice'
18 February 1982 – 'Precious / Town Called Malice'
25 February 1982 – 'Town Called Malice'
1 July 1982 – 'Just Who Is The 5 O'Clock Hero'
16 September 1982 – 'The Bitterest Pill (I Ever Had To Swallow)'
2 September 1982 – 'Beat Surrender'
9 December 1982 - 'Beat Surrender'

Bruce Foxton:

I would rush home from work or wherever I was in order to watch *Top of the Pops*. It was the only way really to see the bands that you liked at that time. So for me it was very exciting to be appearing on *Top of the Pops*. In terms of the technical side it was a let down because you were miming, and you could hear your foot tapping louder than your track they were playing back to you to mime to. We were all moving around on the *Top of the Pops* stage and you could hear us clunking around louder than the music.

THE TUBE

The Tube, which was first aired on 5 November 1982 and ran until 1987, was fronted by Jools Holland, the former keyboard player from Squeeze, and Paula Yates, and was named after the plexiglass tunnel which led down into Studio Five at Tyne Tees TV, Newcastle upon Tyne, the place where all the stars from the Eighties subsequently appeared.

Holland, who had quit Squeeze to pursue a solo career, had branched out into TV as well. His hit-and-miss, laid-back style worked a treat and, backed by his vast musical knowledge, Holland held the show together. He later achieved notoriety by injudiciously using the phrase "groovy fuckers" in a live early evening TV trailer for the show, causing the show to be taken off air for three weeks as a result.

And then there was Paula Yates: young, naughty, cheeky and very sexy. Yates, who had posed naked for *Penthouse magazine* in 1978, had become a music journalist, writing a column called 'Natural Blonde' in the British weekly music paper *Record Mirror*. She became a fan of The Boomtown Rats and their lead singer, Bob Geldof, with whom she became involved and who fathered her first three daughters.

Yates later met Michael Hutchence when his group INXS appeared on the show. Recalling that first meeting, Yates said that she had essentially interviewed Hutchence's crotch and he had invited her back to his hotel room. Geldof and Yates divorced in 1996 after she and Hutchence became an item, it all becoming rather messy, with the whole episode played out in the British tabloid press.

On 22 November 1997, Hutchence was found dead in his hotel room in Sydney, Australia. His death was reported by the New South Wales Coroner to be the result of suicide. On 17 September 2000, Yates died of a heroin overdose.

The list of acts who appeared live on *The Tube* reads like a Who's Who of Eighties music: Tina Turner, The Cure, U2, INXS, R.E.M, Bon Jovi, The Smiths, Iggy Pop, Dire Straits, The Pretenders, The Cramps, Tears For Fears, Culture Club, The Jam and Wham! all appeared between 1982 and 1987. *The Tube* provided a turning point for many new acts who appeared, bringing their music to the masses. U2, Paul Young, Frankie Goes To Hollywood and The Proclaimers, to name a few, all saw giant leaps in their careers after being on the show.

What made *The Tube* great was the edgy style of the presenters and live performances from three or four artists each week. Throw in some shambolic interviews and bits of comedy and you had great TV.

8 THE YOUNG IDEA DOCUMENTARY

8

In May 2015 Paul Weller arrived at some rehearsal studios in Woking. Wearing a pink Chelsea Football Club badge on his jacket. He was greeted by Bob Smeaton and his team and, once the seating had been arranged and the cameras prepared, Paul's interview began for the new documentary that was being made on The Jam called *The Jam: About The Young Idea*.

The documentary was linked to the exhibition on The Jam that had officially opened on 26 June 2015 at Somerset House, London, England. There had been an opening party the previous night for friends and family of the team behind the exhibition that included Nicky Weller, her partner Russell Reader, and Jam fan and memorabilia collector Den Davis. The preview night was also attended by various TV and radio presenters, journalists and long time Jam fans such as Martin Freeman, Al Murray, Sex Pistol Paul Cook, Gem Archer (from Oasis and Noel Gallagher's High Flying Birds) and others.

Radio presenter Gary Crowley had also been instrumental in getting the exhibition off the ground, along with the documentary.

The exhibition included an array of Jam-related items. There were clothes that had been worn by Paul, Rick and Bruce, thousands of photographs and newspaper cuttings, and instruments that had belonged to the band including some of Paul and Bruce's Rickenbacker's and Rick's "Great White" drum kit.

For the first time the Wellers shared photographs and memorabilia from their own archives and these included some of Paul's old Sheerwater school books that contained examples of his early attempts at poetry and sketches - some of which showed images of himself playing in The Jam.

As The Jam fan walked from room to room in the amazing setting of Somerset House, they would be treated to countless Jam songs and film footage of the band playing. Every step took The Jam fan on a journey through The Jam's story. It was an enjoyable experience and for many, certainly an emotive one too. The exhibition had over 57,000 people through the doors at Somerset House in a little over two months, including many die-hard Jam fans from around the world.

The second phase of The About The Young Idea exhibition was hosted in the summer of 2016 by the Cunard Building in Liverpool.

The exhibition in Liverpool was bigger and better and the tears of joy flowed again, such was the meaning of the band to so many people.

The Liverpool exhibition ended with a concert held in honour of The Jam. On the night From The Jam, featuring Bruce Foxton on bass, headlined. In some ways the concert brought to a head what had been a jam-packed two years. Not since The Jam had split had there been so much interest or activity on the band.

In 2015 Rick Buckler had published his autobiography *That's Entertainment: My Life in The Jam* and *The Jam: About The Young Idea* documentary had also been released.

The Jam: About The Young Idea documentary had been in safe hands from the start. Rumour has it that it was Paul who suggested that Bob Smeaton direct it. Paul was familiar with some of Bob's previous works, namely the brilliant *The Beatles Anthology*.

THE JAM

By the time Bob began working on *About The Young Idea* he was already a double Grammy Award winner and a three times Emmy nominated director of music and arts documentaries. Alongside The Beatles he'd directed films on The Who, Elton John, Jimi Hendrix and Pink Floyd and many more. Bob Smeaton came with a seal of approval, and Paul Weller approved.

The day that Bob spent with Paul in Woking included taking Paul around Jam-related locations around the town. Paul was filmed walking down Stanley Road for instance. Bob had done exactly the same with Rick and Bruce. They were taken to their various homes and other places of interest to The Jam fan and what had contributed to The Jam's story. Woking for The Jam fan has the same meaning as Liverpool for The Beatles fan. The importance just cannot be underestimated.

The documentary premiered on Monday 24 August 2015 at the Ham Yard Hotel in Ham Yard, London. This in itself seemed appropriate because the recently built hotel stood just feet from the entrance of where the legendary Sixties Mod hangout The Scene Club was. On the night of the premiere, only Bruce Foxton out of the three members of The Jam made an appearance. *About The Young Idea* then aired on Sky Arts on 5 September 2015 and would get repeated many times thereafter, reaching Jam fans globally.

"Put your hands together for the best band in the fucking world." This is how *The Jam: About The Young Idea* begins, with

John Weller announcing the band live on stage, something he did countless times.

The documentary rolls on teasing with snippets of what is to come. One of the contributors, Keiko Egawa, sits in her home telling the interviewer about how, when she first heard The Jam, something hit her soul and how it felt like an almost spiritual thing. Later in the documentary, she talks about her relationship with the band.

Nicky Weller recalled spending much of her adolescence running The Jam fan club from the family home, opening letters addressed only 'The Jam, Woking' and 'Paul Weller, Woking'. She was only 14 when their career took off and Nicky would sort through sacks of post that started to turn up on the doorstep at the family home in Stanley Road.

Nicky said, "You sort of forget how big The Jam were really, and how quickly they became so popular. It wasn't an overnight success either. They worked hard to get there, but it was quite amazing the extent of it. We were always playing music around our home in Stanley Road. We had a record player that could stack up to six records at any one time. Mum was always playing records by Chuck Berry, Elvis or the various artists on the Tamla Motown label. She was always singing along with them. It was Mum who was really into her records and different sorts of music and I think that's what helped to inspire Paul to discover various genres of music."

Next 'Going Underground' plays in the background as Steve Cradock talks about how The Jam changed his life and if it hadn't have been for The Jam he'd probably still be a window cleaner.

There are further snippets of Jam songs, 'The Bitterest Pill', ''A' Bomb In Wardour Street' and 'In The City'. Actor, Jam fan and friend of Paul Weller, Martin Freeman makes an appearance saying "I know every beat, every lick - it's (The Jam) a huge part of who I am." And this is the kind of statement that reaches out and touches Jam fans from all around the world. The Jam were a shared experience in so many ways and throughout the documentary the viewer is reminded of this.

Next Paul Weller makes his first appearance. He stands holding an enlarged black and white photograph of himself as a teenager. Throughout the documentary, holding up a photograph of their younger self would be repeated by each contributor. Each contributor would also follow the same pattern of introducing themselves: "Paul Weller, born Woking, Surrey, 1958." This was a nice touch because it placed each contributor on a level playing field. One thing that The Jam were recognised and applauded for was being to relate to their fans and not be like so many of their peers in the lofty rock and roll world of 'them and us'. This just wasn't in the natures of Paul, Bruce and Rick.

'That's Entertainment' plays as Paul is filmed, wearing a blue jacket, jeans and blue suede shoes, walking through various locations in Woking. This includes strolling down Stanley Road. The viewer can almost imagine a younger Paul, guitar in hand, Steve Brookes and his family by his side, as he heads to play another gig at Woking Working Men's Club.

Paul talks about his first live performance as a fourteen-year old boy in the Working Men's Club and it is here that Steve Brookes gets introduced. At the time of making the documentary, Paul and Steve had been friends for over forty years. Their friendship shines through as they sit beside each other clutching acoustic guitars and talk about first meeting and discovering music and how important The Beatles were to them. There's even mention of how they wanted to be "bigger than The Beatles".

Paul and Steve's conversation flows and they even launch into a duet of the Everly Brothers song 'Bye Bye Love' before talking about learning three-chord songs from groups that they loved from the Fifties and Sixties. An example is 'Slow Down' by Larry Williams, which they treat the viewer to with a more original version, unlike the version that appeared on *In The City*.

At no point in the documentary are all three members of The Jam filmed together in the same room, despite attempts by the film makers to organise this. Therefore Paul, Bruce and Rick's interviews were all filmed on separate occasions (Paul's interview in the Woking rehearsal studio was filmed in the same room the day before Rick's).

Rick Buckler is introduced next. Rick stands outside the Sheerwater Youth Club holding a picture of his younger self and says, "Rick Buckler, born Woking, Surrey, 1955." 'Absolute Beginners' plays.

Rick goes on to talk about the time he played with Paul and Steve at the Sheerwater Youth Club and he is filmed walking into the very room in which the performance took place. Rick looks astonished as he glances around a room in which he hasn't set foot in for over three decades. Rick then talks about first meeting Paul and Steve and how he had

been impressed because they could "actually play guitar properly".

Paul and Steve return for the next scene and this is where John Weller gets introduced. Paul talks about how his dad "just loved it" and how he became The Jam's manager. This is followed by some older footage of John being interviewed where he talks about how he knew he couldn't provide Paul with an education or with money, but what he could give him was "inspiration".

Paul continues by talking about how his dad encouraged him and how he was a bit of a hustler and how this helped The Jam to get gigs and start to make a name for themselves.

The camera cuts to Rick at this point, who adds that John Weller was very important in the early days in the way he got the band gigs.

Next up is Bruce Foxton "born Woking, Surrey, 1955". 'All Around The World' plays as Bruce starts to talk about how he met with Paul, Steve and Rick. An old photograph of

The Jam flashes up. Each member is dressed in their stage outfit of the day - black shirts with white kipper ties, black flares and white plimsolls. It would be another two years before the band members would be seen again sporting the monochrome look. The photograph is backed up with a rough recording of The Jam playing 'Walking The Dog'.

Some footage of Dr. Feelgood then bursts onto the screen, as only the Feelgoods could and Paul talks about the influence that they had on him. Paul says "the only band that made any sense was Dr. Feelgood" adding that they "were brash and aggressive". Steve Brookes chips in by describing the Feelgoods as playing "hard-edged R&B". Hearing Paul and Steve's thoughts on Dr. Feelgood helps to understand how the early Jam songs started to get influences and take shape and how this is probably best demonstrated on the *In The City* album. 'Blueberry Rock', an early songwriting attempt from Paul and Steve, gets played. The song was recorded in 1973. It's rock and roll, it's innocent, and it helped to set Paul on his songwriting career.

Following the timeline of The Jam's story Rick talks about Steve Brookes' departure and explains how Paul took over the lead role and effectively became the band's leader.

Paul returns and starts to talk about discovering The Who and liking their sound of "edge, aggressiveness and violence". He reminisces about The Who as they perform 'My Generation' on stage at The Marquee in London and he shares with the viewer that that 'My Generation' is his favourite Who song. This leads Paul onto talking about discovering Mod and the impact that had on him: "This was me from here on." Paul goes on to say how the Mod image fitted with The Jam's direction and how Rick and Bruce accepted this too.

'We Got By In Time' plays as Paul next talks about punk and how he felt he was "waiting for it". Some footage of The Sex Pistols takes centre stage as Paul talks about how he felt a "connection" between what he and The Jam were doing. He stresses the importance of how punk was about being part of something with the "same age kids" and how it was a "good scene".

Paul's description on the explosion of punk and its impact leads on to Bruce talking about The Jam getting interest from A&R men, because they were now playing regularly at many of the London hot spots, like The Red Cow and the Nashville. There is footage in the documentary of The Red Cow and Paul talks about getting a residency there and how on week one there were just a handful of people but a couple weeks on there were kids lined up down the street trying to get in.

At this point another contributor is introduced. Adrian Thrills talks about first seeing The Jam when he was sixteen years old. He describes The Jam's sound as having a "strong Sixties influence" and their songs being played with better musicianship than most of the other punk bands around at the time. Adrian talks about the punk fanzine that he published called *48 Thrills* (the title was lifted from the lyrics of The Clash song '48 Hours') and how this possibly includes the first interview with The Jam.

A&R man Chris Parry is next up. He talks about how he'd been on the hunt for punk bands as he was looking to sign one up. Chris describes how he saw The Jam and how he found Paul to be "outstanding as a frontman". Chris says he could see that The Jam were a group that "was going to deliver"and offered to sign them up to Polydor. Paul cuts in saying how The Jam got signed for "six grand and how John didn't even have a bank account at the time.

The next contributor to make an appearance is Vic Coppersmith-Heaven. Vic talks about being "blown away" after seeing The Jam and how he wanted to capture that "high energetic set" on tape in the studio.

At this point both Paul Weller and Chris Parry talk about the making of *In The City* and there is footage of The Jam's debut *Top of the Pops* appearance, where they performed their debut single 'In The City'.

Rick talks about how "fabulous" it was to play on *Top of the Pops* and Bruce adds to this by saying "it was great getting on *Top of the Pops*". Paul agrees but adds that it was also a bit of a let down too.

Music journalist and editor of the fanzine *Flexipop* Barry Cain makes an appearance. Barry was always very supportive of The Jam and helped to establish them with

THE JAM

his supportive and positive reviews. Barry talks about his "love affair" with The Jam, describing the sound of The Jam as "it was The Who kissed by Motown, with a dash of Clash".

Barry goes on to explain that because of The Jam's songs, look and ability to play their instruments they were able to appeal to a wider audience. At the time The Jam were building a punk-based fan base, but they were also being dismissed too. In 1977 The Jam had one foot in the punk scene and another in a scene that they were creating for themselves - and this became what has since been termed as the Mod revival. Not that this was deliberate or even conscious thing on Paul, Rick and Bruce's part - but it happened and it's believed and accepted by many that the second wave of Mod owes a great deal to The Jam. It may have not even happened if it wasn't for them.

Paul returns to the screen saying how he feels about being in The Jam in 1977. "They were my favourite times," adding, "There was still a sense of innocence about it all." Paul is referring to a time when things were simpler. The Jam were still travelling to shows in old vans with just a couple of road crew. The hotels were cheap and the wages just got them by. But they were a part of something, there was a buzz and an energy that only youths can create and, what was more, Paul was realising his dream of being in a band and making records. In many ways 1977 was the start for The Jam.

Amateur photographer and Jam fan Derek D'Souza makes an appearance and talks about the beginnings of his connection with The Jam. He talks about how they stood out from all the other groups around at that time and "how The Jam felt like one of us". Derek picks up on the point of The Jam relating to

their fans and the fans relating to them.

Adrian Thrills returns to explain how 1976 was like "year zero" with the "newness of punk". He then talks about going to interview Paul at his home in Stanley Road. Adrian describes walking into Paul's bedroom and being taken aback by all the Sixties and Beatles-related memorabilia that Paul had. Adrian points out that this was at the "height of punk" and seeing what Paul had not only demonstrated his "real love of that era" but also surprised him - it also made sense what was influencing Paul's songwriting.

Paul is then seen talking about seeing Joe Strummer at a Jam gig, when they played upstairs at Ronnie Scott's in Frith Street, Soho. Paul noted that Strummer was wearing a t-shirt that said 'Chuck Berry Is Dead'. Paul pulled him up on it saying "you don't really mean that, do you?" and saying how he was a fan of Chuck Berry. This of course was at the time when punk was all about trying to shock, so it's quite possible that Strummer was only joking.

The documentary moves towards the release of the *In The City* album. Bruce talks about it being "pretty much our live set". Vic Coppersmith-Heaven joins the conversation and describes what it was like being in the studio during the making of the album. Paul also joins in, saying "I remember feeling disappointed with it", explaining that he didn't think it had captured the band's sound at that time. A sentiment perhaps not shared by Rick or Bruce or the fans for that matter.

Keiko Egawa talks next about how New wave hit Japan in 1977. She remembers how she loved The Jam's songs, but not being able to speak English she couldn't understand any of the lyrics. But the music was enough to hook her in.

Some of the 'Art School' video gets shown

THE JAM

8

next before Martin Freeman explains how he got into The Jam after hearing his older brother playing 'In The City' and how he felt The Jam were not just a "punk band" but a "really good pop band" too.

Founder of Acid Jazz Records, DJ and friend of the band, Eddie Pillar next introduces himself and talks about seeing The Jam when he was fifteen. He talks about The Jam being different and not like the "poncey middle class punks, who took heroin and walked down the King's Road". Eddie goes on to say that he believes 'All Around The World' to have been the first Mod record for his generation - the 'post punk' generation.

Adrian Thrills, Rick and Bruce next talk about how The Jam released two albums in 1977. Rick describes how the band "leapt in" without really understanding the demand that quickly making a second album would put on the band and Bruce explains how there was a lot of pressure on himself, Rick and Paul and this was how he stepped up to help out by writing some songs. At this point 'Don't Tell Them You're Sane' starts to play.

Barry Cain contributes to the conversation by talking about how he got a credit on the *Modern World* album. He said he told Paul how going to a Jam concert was like going through three moods: "Red heat expanding into white heat, expanding into teenage blue". Paul borrowed "teenage blue" and included it into his lyrics for 'Life From A Window'.

The 'News Of The World' video gets used next in the documentary as Bruce continues to talk about how he was starting to contribute songs. And Paul talks about feeling like the *This Is The Modern World* got "written off" by some and how

at that time he didn't really care because he was too busy falling in love with a girl called Gill Price. He continues by saying that some demos were being recorded for the third album but Chris Parry had to point out that the songs weren't really "cutting it" and this helped galvanize him into writing songs. "I had to get my head out of my girlfriend's blouse and get back into writing," says Paul. This part of the documentary ends with 'English Rose' being played.

Paul Weller and Vic Coppersmith-Heaven next talk about being in the studio and trying to do something with 'Down in the Tube Station at Midnight'. The story is told about how Paul tossed the lyrics he'd scribbled out onto a piece of paper into the wastepaper bin and how Vic retrieved them and encouraged Paul and Rick and Bruce to persevere with it. Thankfully The Jam did persevere and 'Down in the Tube Station at Midnight' has since gone down as one of The Jam fans' most appreciated songs. Barry Cain also celebrates the originality of the song and stresses the point of how there was nothing else around at that time that could be compared to the song.

Martin Freeman steps up next and goes on to talk about how *All Mod Cons* was the album where The Jam "set their sound". Eddie Pillar supports this by saying that "somehow they get it right". He is referring to the timing of *All Mod Cons* and the impact it had on the revivalist Mod scene. There's footage of Mods from that period in their parkas and riding scooters.

The subject of "what is Mod? How can it be defined?" then gets discussed by Martin Freeman and Eddie Pillar, which is in itself informative and makes sense, especially

Eddie's comment that Mod is a "classic, timeless thing".

'Strange Town' is the next Jam song to get played as the next contributor, TV writer Paul Abbott, talks about discovering The Jam in 1977 and how he was struck by the "melodic nature" of Paul Weller's songwriting skills.

The topic of Paul's lyrics is picked up by Paul himself who explains that he was writing about his own generation, adding "I didn't have to put myself in their shoes - I was already in their shoes." The point of Paul being labelled a spokesman for his generation is also mentioned, which Paul informs the viewer that he felt uncomfortable about.

The brilliant 'When You're Young' video gets shown next. Paul, Rick and Bruce are smiling, happy and clapping along with the street kids that helped make the video. The video is followed by Paul talking about being young and remembering his twenty first birthday. And he talks about The Jam's music being about youth, a belief which Paul held onto throughout The Jam's life, which further adds weight to Paul's interview on that cold and windy day in Brighton in 1982, where he talked about wanting The Jam to have "meant something", "count for something" and "not gone on for the next twenty years, like the rest of the groups."

There's some footage of The Jam performing live on stage whilst in the States. Paul introduces 'Strange Town' with a reference to zip codes, the American equivalent of a British postcode. This is a demonstration of Paul's humour, which has often been misunderstood. Next Martin Freeman talks about how The Jam "were very British" and how they never really made an impact on America.

The next contributor, Marie McHugh, is now introduced. She talks about her experiences of being a London girl and a Jam fan and spending hours listening to *Setting Sons*. She talks about how she and her friends 'obsessed' about the band and how they loved Paul and thought he was 'wise beyond his years'.

'Thick As Thieves' explodes into the documentary, which is quickly followed by Paul explaining how he originally intended *Setting Sons* to be about three friends. But he describes how that was never realised because he lost his way with it and decided to "just make a record".

Paul then goes on to talk about 'Eton Rifles' and how he felt this song "elevated" his lyrics. He also told the story of the Right To Work march and how it passed by Eton College and some of the students mocked the marchers. Paul explains how he saw this as an 'opportunity to write about class'. Paul also has a dig at David Cameron for his comment about liking the song.

Jam fan and possessor of the largest memorabilia collection in the world on The Jam, Den Davis, features next. Den is seen walking into the Apollo, Manchester, the venue where he first saw his beloved band. He goes on to talk about the audience that night and the energy and the impact it had on him.

The documentary provides several accounts of the impact that The Jam had on its fans, and still do. Keiko returns to talk about how she moved to England, just so that she could be closer to The Jam and get to concerts more easily. She talks about seeing The Jam at the Rainbow Theatre, London and her constant renewing of her visa, which

THE JAM

allowed her stay in the UK. She lights up the screen as she chuckles about having now lived in the UK for over thirty years, and it all started because of her passion for The Jam.

Ian 'Snowy' Snowball (co-author of this book) is next up, holding up a photograph of his twelve-year old self. He stands just feet away from the youth club where he used to attend and first heard 'Going Underground' and 'Start!' on the youth clubs juke box. He goes on to talk about how The Jam was responsible for firing up his interest in politics and how The Jam provided an education that has helped shape him as a man. He adds that he wouldn't have got such an education listening to Duran Duran.

'Going Underground' is played and Rick talks about The Jam getting their first No 1 record and how they cut short their tour of the States so they could return home and perform their No 1 record on *Top of the Pops*.

Paul's comments about 'Going Underground' getting to No 1 are about it scaring him and how he was left thinking "where do you go after getting a No 1 record?" He adds, "At least it was song that was saying something." Here Paul is talking about the threat at the time of a nuclear war.

Rick continues with talking about the connection that The Jam had with CND and the Cold War and he credits Paul with helping to raise awareness about the issues with a younger generation.

The documentary moves on, helped by a snippet of 'Pretty Green', and Marie McHugh talks about the sound that The Jam as a three-piece was able to create. Den Davis pitches in by making the point that each member of The Jam was as important as the other. He says no one thought of The Jam as being just Paul Weller and that the fans held each Jam member in equal regard.

The *Sound Affects* album gets discussed, firstly with Martin Freeman and then by Rick, who says he felt the album "was very close to how we saw ourselves". Paul continues with the thread of describing the process of making the album.

The 'That's Entertainment' video gets shown next, which serves as an introduction to writer and documentary maker, and friend to Paul, Mark 'Bax' Baxter. He talks about how The Jam were the first band to really do anything for him and how Paul Weller was a "massive influence" on him and also the "inspiration" behind much of what Bax went onto achieve.

It was the point of what The Jam inspired in people that Bob Smeaton wanted as a theme running through the documentary. The people chosen to contribute to the documentary had all done something that they, in some way, however small or subconsciously, ascribed to the influence that The Jam had had upon them.

The theme of being inspired by The Jam continues with Derek D'Souza telling his story of how he fancied himself as a bit of an amateur photographer and sent some photographs from a Jam concert to The Jam fan club and got a response. Derek describes how he not only got a response but also got a letter from Paul, which Paul reads out in the documentary. Derek also talks about his invite to photograph The Jam, which he did in Chiswick Park for the 'Absolute Beginners' record. Of the opportunity and the session Derek concludes "it changed my life".

The topic of soundchecks and how The Jam welcomed fans into the venues to observe them is next talked about, firstly by Den Davis and then by Bruce and Rick, who both agree that they "appreciated the support" of the fans. They also talk about the unique relationship that The Jam had with their fans.

'Absolute Beginners' is the next Jam song to get played and with it comes the next contributor, a young Mod and Modernist blog writer named David Pottinger. David talks about discovering the band after his dad had pre-loaded 'Absolute Beginners' onto his iPod. This was it for David and he describes how he then went and sought out other Jam songs and became hooked, saying "it changed everything for me".

The documentary then moves towards one of the most moving sections where David is filmed interviewing Paul Weller. The Modfather and the Mod apprentice sit opposite one another. David asks the questions and Paul replies. David wants to know how the name The Jam came about and what was the thinking behind using the Shelley poem on the *Sound Affects* album sleeve.

Mark Baxter continues with the discussion about poetry and explains that if it hadn't have been for that Shelley poem being included on the album sleeve he wouldn't have gone out and bought a book on poetry. Mark describes how the influence compelled him to want to "find out more". Ian Snowball adds to this, crediting The Jam with giving permission to young boys like himself, who went to an all boys comprehensive school in a working class area, to explore a subject like poetry.

Steve Cradock is next up, talking about hearing 'Town Called Malice' on *Top of the Pops* and being "hooked". Paul then talks about the songs meaning and how it reflected a 'desolate time'. Martin Freeman talks about the brilliance of the song and its usage of "the most commercial beat of the twentieth century", the Motown reference, and Rick says that the song was probably "our most commercial song", adding "the one that got through to a lot of people". And three

decades after its release, 'Town Called Malice' is probably still the 'go to' Jam record for any radio DJ to play, anywhere in the world.

The documentary is now deep into 1982, the final year of The Jam, and the subject of *The Gift* enters the story. McHugh talks about how she felt The Jam's final studio album "reached new heights, but lost some fans that had been there from the start".

Regarding *The Gift*, Paul talks about how he was going back to listen to soul music again and how, because of this, it influenced his songwriting on the album. 'Precious' also gets a mention and how it seemed to cause a "division amongst Jam fans" because some thought it was jazz funk.

Eddie Pillar picks up on the point of the "division amongst fans" saying that he was aware that some fans struggled with the transition from where The Jam had been but were clearly going - or at least where Paul's songwriting was going, a point also made by Martin Freeman who says that *"The Gift* gives clues to where Paul was going regards the whole soul thing".

There is some footage of The Jam performing 'Ghosts' from the Trans-Global Express Tour and Paul starts to talk about the last months of The Jam and how he'd been in the band for ten years and how it had been "full on" and he was ready for something else.

The next part of the documentary is devoted to exploring the final months and Paul's decision to leave The Jam. Bruce says "I sensed Paul needed a break, but didn't know the end of the band was nigh" and Rick adds, "I didn't know it was the end of the line."

Paul talks about being still only 24 years old and wanting to see what else he could do and what else he could make. Rick describes the meeting that included John Weller, where

THE JAM

Paul announced his intention to leave the band and Bruce describes how, on hearing the news, his "mouth dropped" and they all knew there was no way of "talking Paul around".

'The Bitterest Pill' plays as Keiko Egawa, Derek D'Souza, Marie McHugh and Eddie Pillar all comment on the impact that hearing about The Jam splitting up had on them. Keiko says she cried for three days.

The documentary includes a snippet of the interview that Paul gave to the UK TV News programme *Nationwide*, where he talked about leaving The Jam. There are photographs from The Jam's final concert in Brighton and Rick and Bruce share their feelings about the concert and what their thoughts were about and what they meant to do next.

The documentary tactfully pulls away from the end days. There is some footage of The Kinks and of Paul saying "I want to play with other musicians and see what happens". The Jam are no more.

Fast forward to 2015 and the documentary focuses on the legacy that includes From The Jam and Bruce saying of the band that "it's a testament to those great songs" and "people still want to hear them". And no one can deny that From The Jam are crowd pullers and seem to go from strength to strength.

The front cover to Rick's autobiography *That's Entertainment: My Life In The Jam* fills the screen and Rick talks about teaming up with "Snowy and putting the book together".

Steve Cradock talks about being in Paul Weller's band for twenty one years and being included on most of his studio albums since Paul left The Style Council and Paul talks about "pushing it as far as it can go", adding "I don't know where it will end up" and "I think it's my job to do that".

As the documentary draws to a close there is footage of the *About The Young Idea* exhibition at Somerset House and a brief appearance of Nicky Weller talking about it. "The Jam did speak for a generation," she says, and never a truer word has been spoken.

And then there is Paul Weller. The man who started The Jam. When considering the reforming of The Jam he answers "absolutely, categorically, no". Rick goes on record, saying, "I don't think it would be the wisest thing to do" and Bruce confirms, "It's probably best just left there." And Paul's final words are, "We stepped out at the right time."

And there ends a fantastic documentary about an amazing band - The Jam.

> ## *"The Jam changed my life."*
>
> **Derek D'Souza**

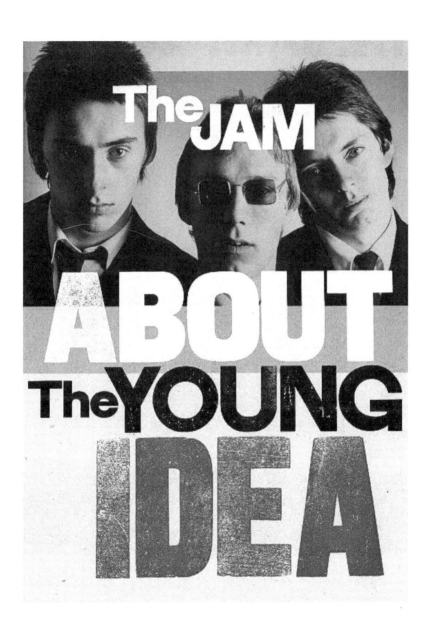

8 THE JAM: 10 KEY LOCATIONS

BOND STREET TUBE STATION

On 12 September 1978 photographer Martyn Goddard and the three members of The Jam entered Bond Street tube station to shoot the 'Down in the Tube Station at Midnight' single cover. They chose Bond Street station on the Central line (between Marble Arch and Oxford Circus) as it was the nearest station to their record company offices. They waited until late evening before attempting the quick shoot as they didn't have permission from the London Underground. The band pitched themselves at the end of the platform and waited until a speeding train emerged out of the tunnel before Goddard took a series of shots.

In 2015 Rick Buckler returned to be photographed there again and that photo was used in promotional posters when he toured a series of Q&A events he was doing to support his autobiography *That's Entertainment: My Life In The Jam*.

SOHO MARKET

In an attempt to gain some publicity in the music press The Jam set up and played for almost an hour on the pavement in Soho Market during 1976. Rick Buckler said: "The Jam went to Soho Market with the sole purpose to be arrested. Which would lead to some coverage in the papers. No one was writing anything interesting about The Jam. The *NME*, *Melody Maker*, and *Sounds*, they saw us as just another band from the punk rock scene.

We set up and started playing. Hoping it would annoy someone so much that they would complain and we would be nicked. The police did turn up, but they just watched the show. They didn't even ask us to turn the music down! We had to play our set twice, as we ran out of numbers to play. So, we got fed up, packed up and went back to Woking." Apart from drawing a large crowd, three members of The Clash, Joe Strummer, Mick Jones and Paul Simonon who were living in a nearby squat, also stood and watched the performance.

QUEEN'S PARK – WHEN YOU'RE YOUNG VIDEO

The footage in the park was filmed in Queen's Park, in North West London, England. The footage showing the high road is Kilburn High Road and the footage of the escalator was filmed in Kilburn Square which is almost directly opposite Woolworths (which is no longer there).

The escalator has long since been removed (it was out of order most of the time!) and the filming took place in summer 1979. The Jam perform the song on the now historic bandstand which was built in 1887 (with all the Ironwork supplied by Walter Fariane & Co. of Glasgow). The video features lots of children joining in singing and dancing with The Jam.

THE JAM

POLYDOR RECORDS HQ - STRATFORD PLACE, LONDON W1

Polydor offices were then in Stratford Place, W1. It was here that The Jam signed their recording contract with Polydor and would subsequently have many meetings. The Jam also recorded their debut album *In The City* here in Polydor's in-house recording studio.

WOKING LIBERAL CLUB

Formerly the Working Men's Club, the venue was one of the first places The Jam's founding members Paul Weller, Steve Brookes and Rick Buckler rehearsed at and where the band first played on 31 December 1974. They would rehearse on Sunday afternoons when the place was shut. Paul Weller used to live just around the corner on Stanley Road. The club is now demolished.

BATTERSEA POWER STATION

The video for 'News of the World', was filmed on the roof of Battersea Power Station in London. Battersea Power Station was built in the 1930s and ceased generating electricity in 1983, but over the past 50 years it has become one of the best known landmarks in London and is a Grade II listed building.

The station's celebrity owes much to numerous popular culture references. Alfred Hitchcock used it in early scenes of his 1936 film *Sabotage*, the cover art of Pink Floyd's 1977 album *Animals* features the building and it appeared in the 1965 Beatles' film *Help!*

STANLEY ROAD

Paul Weller grew up in a small house with an outside toilet on Stanley Road with his parents and sister Nicky Weller. It was from this house that the young members of The Jam would rehearse and later his mother Ann and Nicky

8

would run The Jam Fan club. The house isn't standing any more after being demolished.

CHISWICK PARK

The Jam did the photo shoot for the 'Absolute Beginners' sleeve on 31 August 1981 with photographer Derek D'Souza who had the three members standing next to stone steps, walls and gates. Weller was sporting his Steve Marriot haircut and wearing round sunglasses. The Beatles had also used the same location in 1966 when they shot the promotional videos for 'Paperback Writer' and its B-Side 'Rain'.

WEMBLEY ARENA

The Jam played five sold out nights at Wembley Arena in December 1982 during their farewell Beat Surrender tour. They then played just five more live shows ending in Brighton on 11 December.

Originally the Empire Pool, the venue was built for the 1934 British Empire Games by Arthur Elvin, and originally housed a swimming pool, as reflected by its former name. The Empire Pool hosted the annual *New Musical Express* Poll Winners' concert during the mid Sixties. Audiences of 10,000 viewed acts like The Beatles, T. Rex, David Bowie, The Monkees, Dusty Springfield, The Rolling Stones and Pink Floyd.

HORSELL COMMON

The video for The Jam's 1981 single 'Funeral Pyre' was shot here. It shows the group playing very close to a large bonfire.

Horsell Common is an ancient village near Woking. It includes a Muslim burial ground and a number of Bronze Age barrows and protected heathland and is surrounded by thousands of trees.

The Jam spent all day and into the night filming at this location where they were joined by friends and fans who also took part in the filming. A huge fire was built which was lit once it went dark which you can see behind the group as they play in the video.

One of the most recognisable features of the common is the sand pits. The pits were used by H.G. Wells as the site of the first Martian landing in his novel *The War of the Worlds*.

8

JAM FACTS

'In the City' is the only Jam single to chart higher as a reissue than as an original release in the UK, reaching No 36 in 2002

'All Around the World' was featured in *A Year in Yellow*, a documentary about British cyclist Bradley Wiggins' attempts to win the 2012 Tour de France. Wiggins, who is a self-confessed fan of The Jam, can be heard listening to it in his hotel room in the days leading up to the tour.

The single version of 'The Modern World' had slightly changed lyrics, replacing the words "I don't give two fucks about your review" with "I don't give a damn about your review".

Some copies of 'Down in the Tube Station at Midnight' single were pressed with 'Down in the Tube Station' as the B side, with 'So Sad About Us' and 'The Night' appearing on the A Side.

'That's Entertainment' is the group's lone entry, at No 306, on *Rolling Stone's* 500 Greatest Songs of All Time list released in 2004.

'Town Called Malice' was featured prominently in the 1985 comedy film National Lampoon's *European Vacation*.

When U2's Bono was unavailable to perform 'Do They Know It's Christmas' on *Top of the Pops* in 1984 as part of Band Aid, Paul Weller mimed the U2 man's famous line "Tonight thank God it's them, instead of you."

In Australia, the songs 'Going Underground', 'The Eton Rifles', 'That's Entertainment' and 'Start!' made up an Australia-only EP entitled *4 Side Affects*.

The Gift spent 25 weeks on the UK album charts, rising to No 1. In the US, the album spent 16 weeks on the *Billboard* 200 album charts

The Polydor US LP release of *Setting Sons* in 1979 reversed the sides and inserted the single 'Strange Town' as the second song on side two between 'Girl on the Phone' and 'Thick As Thieves'.

In February 1982 The Jam became the first band since The Beatles to play two numbers on the same edition of *Top of the Pops* when they performed 'A Town Called Malice', and 'Precious'.

All Mod Cons is listed as one of the *1001 Albums You Must Hear Before You Die*.

LIVE!

8

THE JAM
Fair Deal

*"See me walking around —
I'm the boy about town that
you've heard of"*

The JAM are The Gift, the fair deal from heaven, because, even if they do nothing else, they FIT. At the beginning of their career they had the mark of a group, especially of a Polydor "new wave" group, that would quickly be forgotten. The mod image looked so blasé, and the then pro-Tory politics rankled without actually disturbing. But in fact, mod turned out to be the perfect start — its social ambiguity gave them a diffident, lower-middle-class less

distance from the sweat and stupor of things like punk and heavy metal. Weller used mod as a perspective rather than an engrossing style, as a fan rather than a champion. True, The Jam could play The Who's 'Much Too Much' with more confidence and dynamism than The Who themselves ever mustered. But Weller was no mere revivalist. Before he could even be sure of his musical bearings, the mantle of working-class hero had been placed on his shoulders, and The Jam were all of a sudden filling the gap between punk's irresponsible glee and rock's sedated sleepwalk. To this day Weller has never sold out mod, never pensioned it off; his relevation to the status of hero enabled him simply to

ignore the rapid rise and fall of its official revival.

The Jam's solid entrenchment in the Sixties is a crucial part of their success and it works because they adapt r'n'b for an audience that knows little about the original music. Weller's open perspective allows him to draw into his songs whatever trademarks seem appropriate for individual themes without slavishly reproducing them. As he can phrase it to this day — with reference to both the funk of 'Precious' and the Motown bass lift of 'Town Called Muller' — *"Take a pinch of white and a pinch of black/Mix it together and makes movin' flavms . . ."*

'Pinch' is the key word, for by "pinching" the '60s and its endless memories, The Jam have somehow attracted vast legions of the disaffected, the non-aligned, and the nobodies, who flock to Weller because no one style confines him and because he has not been "corrupted" by his fame. When he inherited Townshend's guitar techniques, he also took on the man's acute sense of responsibility.

A Jam gig is thus a fairly joyless spectacle. The Lonsdale sweatshirts are

eloquent symbols of its rigour and sobriety; what we are really witnessing is a gymnasium of exhortation. Weller never preaches, but he never sings either. Where the Stones made up for not being black by being camp, The Who and The Jam strip r'n'b of its sexual and sexuality. By using it as a basis for social anthems, they kill off the humour and narcissism of its five performance.

With a banner proclaiming the legend "Trans-Global Unity Express" pinned above them, there was a fine irony in the almost total absence of non-white faces in the audience. But The Jam's a definitively white, unsensual sound, and not simply because Buckler's drums are a battery blam bam pickup job. No, the real reason is Weller's voice. The words he sings are never integrated into the overall sound; they exist outside the engine-room of rhythm because they are not born of musical instincts in the first place. Every emotion, every potential inflexion, is thrown out with the same aggressive urgency — so that a great song like 'Happy Together' carries exactly the same degree of imploring and

hopefulness as an ephemeral fling like 'Precious'.

The problem is that too many Jam fans are constantly looking to Weller to 'speak' to them, to somehow explain them. A Jam audience really works for its heroes, chanting for encores like possessed football supporters and loving themselves in their benevolence; a suggested mass identity. It's irrelevant to them that 'A Town Called Malice' is just a case of Madness meet the Four Tops down in the tube station at midnight, because Weller's the authority, the figurehead against which we are all of us marshal and judged wanting.

On 'The Gift' Weller's confusion under the burden of this responsibility is almost pathetic. He can conclude 'Precious' with the confession that *"I feel trapped in somew/in this imagery"*, and then immediately plunge into 'Just Who Is The 5 O'Clock Hero?' with 'Hello darlin' — I'm home again/Covered in shit and aches and pains" — and both sung in precisely the same cockney monotone! What one feels most powerfully of a Jam gig is Weller straining to keep up with the expectations and assumptions which have been forced on him. His every movement is a genuflection of rhetorical presence — his torso muscling into his guitar, his neck thrusting out at the mike as if it would throw the whole of Paul Weller at the heart of his audience.

Bruce Foxton is of course the perfect complement to this bursting charisma: everything about him, from his early '70s sex-skin brushtop to his hideous sky blue suit, is plain naff.

At the Fair Deal The Jam made it clear just how extensively they are prepared to compress their manifold

sources in the service of social conscience. As if 'Heat Wave' weren't enough, amazingly flatulent versions of 'Fever' and 'Hit The Road Jack' forced the point home. A handful of really exciting numbers — like 'Funeral Pyre' and 'Private Hell' — stood out from a predominantly safe and "assured" set, but they were flawed for between 'Weller even felt obliged to advise us that the two new "important" songs — presumably the ones we should be studying and learning — were 'The Gift' and 'Trans-Global Express'.

Paul Weller no longer swallows anything; he simply fits the bill, meets the demand for a certain sanity with the contrived authority of his voice and his equalised emphases. As Richard Cook said, or at least implied, the sheep that are buying 'The Gift' are the very people who should be listening to The Fall.

As they stand at present, The Jam are a strident summation of traditional pop forms and archaic rock attitudes, the pivotal point of white youth as it is. Weller himself sits so easily between the messiah, Joe Strummer, and the craftsman, Elvis Costello; it's unreal — yet he touches mother of their heights.

What is more bewildering still is how he manages year after year to ignore the extreme conservatism of his fans, instead actually paying to the condescending lengths of thanking them in full page ads for their undying "trust and loyalty".

"I believe in life" — and I believe in love . . .

But the world which I live in — keeps trying to prove me wrong . . .

— and what you give is what you get!

Barney Hoskyns

THE
GIFT OF
UNSOUND
VISION

White man's burden. Paul Weller pic: Peter Anderson

NME AWARDS

8

NME Awards 1978

Best Male Singer: David Bowie
Best Female Singer: Debbie Harry
Best Album: The Jam - 'All Mod Cons'
Best Single: The Clash - '(White Man) In Hammersmith Palais'
Best Songwriter: Elvis Costello
Best Dressed Sleeve: The Rolling Stones - 'Some Girls'
Best Group: The Clash
Best New Group: Public Image Ltd
Best Guitarist: Mick Jones
Best Bassist: Jean Jacques Burnel
Best Keyboardist: Dave Greenfield
Best Drummer: Keith Moon
Best DJ: John Peel
Best Radio Show: John Peel Show
Best TV Show: 'Revolver'
Most Wonderful Human Being: Sid Vicious
Pin-Up Of The Year: Debbie Harry
Film: 'Close Encounters of the Third Kind'
Creep Of The Year: John Travolta

NME Awards 1979

Male Singer: Sting
Songwriter: Paul Weller
Best Group: The Jam
Guitarist: Paul Weller
Bassist: Bruce Foxton
Keyboards: Dave Greenfield
Drums: Rick Buckler
Female Singer: Kate Bush
Best New Act: The Specials
Most Wonderful Human Being: John Peel
Image Of The Year: Gary Numan
Creep Of The Year: Gary Numan
Single: The Specials - 'Gangsters'
Album: The Jam - 'Setting Sons'
TV Programme: 'Fawlty Towers'
Best Dressed Sleeve: Public Image Ltd - 'Metal Box'
Disc Jockey: John Peel
Radio Show: John Peel Show
Face Of The Decade: Johnny Rotten
Farce Of The Decade: Mod Revival
Film Of The Year: 'Quadrophenia'

THE JAM

NME Awards 1980

Best Group: The Jam
Best New Act: UB40
Best Male Singer: Paul Weller
Best Guitarist: Paul Weller
Best Drummer: Rick Buckler
Best Songwriter: Paul Weller
Best Bassist: Bruce Foxton
Best Keyboardist: Dave Greenfield
Best Other Instrumentalist: Saxa
Best Single: The Jam - 'Going Underground'
Best Album: The Jam - 'Sound Affects'
Best Dressed Sleeve: The Jam - 'Sound Affects'
Best Disc Jockey: John Peel
Best Dressed Person: Adam Ant
Haircut Of The Year: Eugene Reynolds
Most Wonderful Human Being: Paul Weller
Creep Of The Year: Margaret Thatcher
Event Of The Year: Death Of John Lennon
TV Programme: 'Not the Nine O'Clock News'
Movie Of The Year: 'The Elephant Man'

NME Awards 1981

Best Group: The Jam
Best New Act: Altered Images
Most Missed Person: John Lennon
Best Songwriter: Paul Weller
Best Female Singer: Siouxsie Sioux
Best Male Singer: David Bowie
Best Single: The Specials - 'Ghost Town'
Best LP: Echo & The Bunnymen - 'Heaven Up Here'
Best Dressed Sleeve: Echo & The Bunnymen - 'Heaven Up Here'
Best Guitarist: Paul Weller
Best Bassist: Bruce Foxton
Best Drummer: Rick Buckler
Best Keyboardist: Dave Greenfield
Best TV Programme: 'Coronation Street'
Best Radio Show: John Peel
Best Film: 'Gregory's Girl'
Most Wonderful Human Being: Paul Weller
Best Dressed Person: Michael Foot

NME Awards 1982

Best Group: The Jam
Best Male Singer: Paul Weller
Best Female Singer: Siouxsie Sioux
Creep Of The Year: Margaret Thatcher

Most Wonderful Human Being: Paul Weller
Best Songwriter: Paul Weller
Best Single: The Jam - 'Town Called Malice'
Best Longplayer: The Jam - 'The Gift'
Best Live Act: The Jam
Best Dancefloor Favourite: Wham! - 'Young Guns (Go for It)'
Best Dressed Sleeve: Siouxsie and the Banshees - 'A Kiss in the Dreamhouse'
Event Of The Year: The Jam Split
Best Dressed Male: Paul Weller
Best Dressed Female: Siouxsie Sioux
Best Haircut: Paul Weller
Best Electronics: Vince Clarke
Best Guitarist: Paul Weller
Best Bassist: Bruce Foxton
Best Drummer: Rick Buckler
Best Miscellaneous Instrument: The Emerald Express, Violin
Best Radio Show: John Peel
Best Music Video: Madness - 'House of Fun'
Best TV Show: 'The Young Ones'
Best Film: 'E.T. the Extra-Terrestrial'

NME Awards 1983

Best Group: New Order
Best New Act: The Smiths
Best Dressed Female: Siouxsie Sioux
Female Singer: Siouxsie Sioux
Songwriter: Elvis Costello
Male Singer: David Bowie
Best Dressed Male: David Bowie
Best Long Player: Elvis Costello - 'Punch the Clock'
Best Single: New Order - 'Blue Monday'
Best Film: 'Merry Christmas, Mr. Lawrence'
Best Promo Video: Michael Jackson - 'Thriller'

Most Wonderful Human Being: Paul Weller
Creep Of The Year: Margaret Thatcher
TV Show: 'The Tube'
Best Dressed Sleeve: New Order - 'Power, Corruption & Lies'
Best Radio Programme: John Peel
Best Guitarist: The Edge
Best Drummer: Budgie
Best Miscellaneous Musician: The TKO Horns
Best Bassist: Peter Hook

8

WEBSITES

THE OFFICIAL JAM WEBSITE

http://www.thejamofficial.com/

The official Jam site with everything you'd expect. Biography, plenty of photos in the gallery section, full discography, The Jam store, (full of trendy Jam t-shirts), latest news and you can receive all the latest news on Jam happenings when you sign up to The Jam newsletter.

UDISCOVERMUSIC

http://www.udiscovermusic.com/artists/the-jam

Universal Records have several pages all dedicated to The Jam. As part of their uDiscover site, they have a dedicated Jam page with a selection of videos and an official biography all of which link to other Jam related pages linking to all releases on iTunes, Spotify and Amazon.

THE JAM FAN

http://www.thejamfan.net/welcome.htm

The only Jam website run by a member of the band, (Rick Buckler), features a gig list from 1974 and ending in 1982, an 'On This Day' Jam happenings section and a forum for Jam fans to discuss all things Jam related.

THE JAM INFORMATION PAGES

http://thejam.org.uk

Full of information on The Jam run by Kevin Lock. Listing all the singles, albums and compilations, lyrics, gigs from 1973 until 1982. A section with quotes and reviews on the group from all the British music press and a very interesting section listing and linking to every Jam appearance on *Top of the Pops*.

PAUL WELLER

http://paulweller.com/akr/

The official Paul Weller site. Contains a very comprehensive discography covering The Jam, The Kinks and all of Paul's solo work. As well as news and tour dates the site has a lovely media gallery with photographs covering Paul's entire career.

RICK BUCKLER

http://www.rickbuckler.net

Rick's very own web site with all his latest news. The site features a page for drummers everywhere that lists all of Rick's drum kits from his time with The Jam to the current times.

THE JAM

8

BRUCE FOXTON
https://www.brucefoxton.com/about

The official page of Bruce Foxton with news, tour dates and a news blog.

FROM THE JAM
https://www.fromthejamofficial.com

The official site of Bruce Foxton and Russell Hastings with all the latest news and tour dates for From The Jam including a news blog, shop, links and gallery.

STRANGE TOWN
http://www.strangetown.net

Strangetown.net offers links to everything about The Jam including books, posters and memorabilia

On Metronome Records (Import)

A police car and a screaming siren
Pneumatic drill and ripped up concrete
A baby wailing and stray dog howling
The screech of brakes and lamp light blinking

That's entertainment, that's entertainment

A smash of glass and the rumble of boots
An electric train and a ripped up phone booth
Paint splattered walls and the cry of a tomcat
Lights going out and a kick in the balls

I tell you, that's entertainment, that's entertainment

Days of speed and slow time Mondays
Pissing down with rain on a boring Wednesday
Watching the news and not eating your tea
A freezing cold flat and damp on the walls

I tell you, that's entertainment, that's entertainment

Wake up at 6am on a cool warm morning
Opening the windows and breathing in petrol
An amateur band rehearsing in a nearby yard
Watching the telly and thinking about your holidays

That's entertainment, that's entertainment

Wake up from bad dreams and smoking cigarettes
Cuddling a warm girl and smelling stale perfume
A hot summer's day and sticky black tarmac
Feeding ducks in the park and wishing you were far away

That's entertainment, that's entertainment

Two lovers kissing amongst the scream of midnight
Two lovers missing the tranquillity of solitude
Getting a cab and travelling on buses
Reading the graffiti about slashed seat affairs

I tell you, that's entertainment, that's entertainment

Words and music by Paul Weller
Reproduced by permission of And Son Music Ltd.

8 THEY COVERED THE JAM

THAT'S ENTERTAINMENT
Morrissey
Sing Your Life / That's Entertainment
HMV 1991

THAT'S ENTERTAINMENT
Billy Bragg
Workers Playtime (CD Reissue)
Cooking Vinyl 2006

THAT'S ENTERTAINMENT
Reef
Fire and Skill: The Songs of the Jam

START!
Beastie Boys feat. Miho Hatori
Fire and Skill: The Songs of the Jam
Ignition 1999

PRETTY GREEN
Mark Ronson feat. Santigold
Version Columbia 2007

278 THIS DAY IN MUSIC'S GUIDE TO **THE JAM**

8

TOWN CALLED MALICE
McFly
Radio 1 Established 1967
Universal 2007

TOWN CALLED MALICE
Gene
Fire and Skill: The Songs of the Jam
Ignition 1999

TO BE SOMEONE
Noel Gallagher
Fire and Skill: The Songs of the Jam
Ignition 1999

DOWN IN THE TUBE STATION AT MIDNIGHT
Carter the Unstoppable Sex Machine
Do Re Me, So Far So Good (Single)
Chrysalis 1992

GOING UNDERGROUND
Lostprophets
4:AM Forever / Going Underground
Columbia 2007

GOING UNDERGROUND
Buffalo Tom
Fire and Skill: The Songs of the Jam
Ignition 1999

GOING UNDERGROUND
Down by Law
When You're Young: Songs Originally Recorded by the Jam
Young Mood 1998

ENGLISH ROSE
Everything But The Girl
Fire and Skill: The Songs of the Jam
Ignition 1999

ENGLISH ROSE
Journey South
Journey South Syco 2006

THE BUTTERFLY COLLECTOR
Noel Gallagher feat. Paul Weller
The Dreams We Have as Children - Live at the Royal Albert Hall
Big Brother 2009

THE JAM

8

THE BUTTERFLY COLLECTOR
Garbage
Queer (Single)
Mushroom 1995

CARNATION
Liam Gallagher and Steve Cradock
Fire and Skill: The Songs of the Jam
Ignition 1999

GHOSTS
Suran Song in Stag
Cowboys and Indians
Crue 2000

THE MODERN WORLD
Ben Harper
Fire and Skill: The Songs of the Jam
Ignition 1999

MODERN WORLD
Less Than Jake
Goodbye Blue & White
Less Than Jake 1999

ART SCHOOL
Silver Sun
Fire and Skill: The Songs of the Jam
Ignition 1999

ART SCHOOL
Melvins
Everybody Loves Sausages
Ipecac 2013

THE GIFT
Heavy Stereo
Fire and Skill: The Songs of the Jam
Ignition 1999

STANDARDS
Crummy Stuff
The Way We Listen To..
Ammonia 2002

THE JAM LITERARY EVENT

8

On 4 June 2015 *Thick As Thieves* authors Stuart Deabill and Ian Snowball organised and hosted the first Jam literary event at the Cockpit Theatre in London. Appearances included Nicky Weller, Derek D'Souza, Dennis Munday, Bill Smith and Stu and Ian.

An intimate audience of 150 hardcore Jam fans respectfully listened to what turned out to be an amazing day and Jam fest. Shane Juson was one of the attendees on the day.

Shane Juson review: I didn't know what to expect when I first booked to go to this event but the names on the list were too much of a pull.

We travelled down from rural Herefordshire to the big city early in the morning so we weren't late. We got to the venue about an hour early so went for a coffee. On the way back to the venue, through the market, I heard a familiar voice telling me to get a move on. It was Derek D'Souza!

We got in and there were so many familiar faces around in the bar all eagerly waiting to get in. I had a chat with a few people while my wife sat down and read her magazine. She's usually the social one!

The event kicked off with some fantastic stories and great insights into people's association with the band. All

the guests were captivating the whole crowd.

One of the best for me was Stuart Deabill who had educated me in the art of swearing. The only words beginning with F or C that I could probably put down in writing are either football or Chelsea!

Such a great sense of humour though. Another highlight was when Nicky Weller was talking too and interacting with Steve Carver and Steve recalling some of his memories too. We all wished we were in his shoes!

I even got a mention off Nicky when she said I was one of the most regular visitors to the exhibition and probably the most emotional! I accept that allegation! Throughout Nicky's interview there was a guitar case in front of her. We all wondered what was inside...Then it was revealed.

One of the Weller Holy Grails. The boys' Rickenbacker from *All Mod Cons!* After the event was over there was even an opportunity to have a photo taken with The Boys which I think most of the audience took up as I've seen the pic on Facebook so much, my own included.

All in all a fantastic day that was over too quickly as I could listen to people talking about The Jam forever.

THE BOOKS

THE MODFATHER: MY LIFE WITH PAUL WELLER
David Lines
William Heinemann/Arrow Books
2006

'Introducing the Adrian Mole of Mod' said Q Magazine when the book was published. *The Modfather - My Life With Paul Weller* is the author's personal story of growing up with Paul Weller and The Jam. Lines writes about his love affair with the group after first hearing 'This Is The Modern World'. In the opening paragraph on page one, Lines says that as soon as he discovered The Jam "they changed his life forever". His story is about how much his life revolved around The Jam and this is something that other Jam fans can relate to. Adrian's book is autobiographical and filled with humour and references the period when The Jam poured into the lives of numerous young people. It's an easy to read, well-written book and - most importantly - enjoyable.

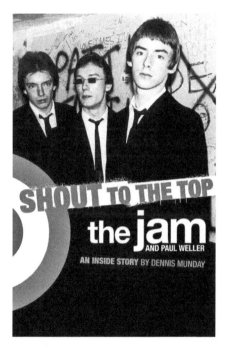

SHOUT TO THE TOP: THE JAM AND PAUL WELLER: AN INSIDE STORY
Dennis Munday
Omnibus Press
2006

8

Dennis's book was written from a unique perspective. In 1978 he started working directly with The Jam. *Shout To The Top* is an honest account (Dennis is an honest bloke) of being involved with Paul, Rick and Bruce and many others that helped the band become a successful group. There are numerous recollections of interactions between the band members and John Weller, the fans, the record label and others from the music industry. The insights in the book are second to none.

What really comes through in *Shout To The Top* is Den's passion for The Jam. This he admits in his book as he describes what it was like for him having one foot in the Polydor camp and the other in The Jam camp. Den provides several stories of how this wasn't always an easy thing to live with and how, in the end, as The Kinks were in their *Our Favourite Shop* phase, he felt he needed to make his exit.

For The Jam fans there are tales galore as Den describes the joys and challenges of being in the studio with The Jam, in meetings, on the road and also some of the events at various video shoots (a couple of which he ended up being in).

Dennis also provides some insightful explanations on how the music industry works and the various situations that the group had to endure and the 'games' that record labels play. And on several occasions he relates these to The Jam, which in itself helps to explain a few things.

Shout To The Top is without a doubt one of the 'go to' books that a Jam fan will reach for to remind them about some fact, but its also a book that Jam fans can feel they can relate to. After all Den was another Jam fan and he'd been a Mod in the Sixties - so he knows what he's talking about!

Throughout Den's book there are several references to how *Direction Reaction Creation* came into existence and his part in the researching, compiling and production of the product and this is something that Jam fans are very grateful for.

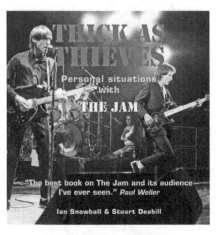

THICK AS THIEVES (PERSONAL SITUATIONS WITH THE JAM)
Ian Snowball & Stuart Deabill
Marshall Cavendish
2012

"The best book on The Jam and its audience I've seen" wrote Paul Weller about *Thick As Thieves*, which came as a pleasing response to the authors, whose "intention was always to gather a diverse collection of people from all ages, locations and backgrounds" and this book achieved this.

Thick As Thieves was originally to be titled *Saturday's Kids* by the authors, but during the writing of the book, another book was published using the title. That particular book wasn't about The Jam, but about Mods in general, but it made no sense to publish another book with the same name so quickly, so *Thick As Thieves* was decided upon - it was the nearest title that the authors could find that related to the fans.

A book such as this one hadn't been attempted. The authors used a format that they used for a previous book they'd had published called *From Ronnie's To Ravers (Personal Situations In London's Club Land)*. The format depended on contributions from people who knew the subject matter. In this case it was about a fifty-year history of clubbing in London. So there were people who'd gone to the jazz dens of the Fifties, the Mod clubs of the early and mid Sixties and the psychedelic clubs of the late Sixties the punk, funk and soul clubs of the Seventies and Eighties and then into the acid house and rave clubs as the Eighties slipped into the Nineties.

It was important for the authors that their book not be just text heavy, they knew fans had photographs, as well as their stories of their own 'personal situations' and over the course of the next few months hundreds of photographs were handed over to be used in the book which helped to tell the story of The Jam in a chronological way.

Whilst the photographs stacked up the authors interviewed Jam fans for the book. Those interviewed included: Pat Nevin, Dennis Munday, Pete Wilson, Bill Smith, Steve Brookes, Brett 'Buddy' Ascott, Eddie Pillar, Garry Bushell, Ady Croasdale, Tracey Young and Jennie McKeown and a whole army of Jam fans. An especially nice section included a feature on John Weller and Derek

D'Souza and his experience of the Absolute Beginner's photo shoot.

Its felt by many Jam fans that *Thick As Thieves* helped to kickstart a new, invigorated wave of interest in The Jam. After its publication in 2012, there was a flurry of Jam activity that included more books, literary events, exhibitions, CDs and album releases (some deluxe versions of The Jam's studio albums), climaxing in the documentary *The Jam: About The Young Idea*.

Paul Weller was initially hesitant to get involved with the book. It was suspected that previous books on the band that had focused on his career had perhaps soured his support. However, the authors had a close friend called Mark Baxter and he was able to assure Paul that the authors had the band's best interests at heart and really just wanted to produce a book that celebrated The Jam and its fans. And then early one Sunday morning Paul sent a text to Mark containing his foreword. The authors were naturally delighted and grateful.

Paul Weller (April 2012): "I'm always amazed at how young our audience was! I thought I was young, but looking back, a lot of our fans were just 12 or 13. Have a look at the front row of kids in *The Tube* TV performance we did. You'll see they were proper kids!"

"The Jam army were committed, dedicated and ferocious. There was a tremendous sense of occasion at our gigs. There was also an air of violence and tension. But then so was our music, so we reflected off each other, as all great art does - though none of us would have called it that at the time. I am glad I was on stage and not in the audience, as most

8

nights were fucking scary!"

"But young passions run high and passion it most definitely was. It was also very tribal, whether style tribes or football ones. Every night would kick off and the sea would part in the middle and blood and beer would fly. Scary but always exciting."

"Towards the end though, I'd had enough. I saw what the Thatcher gang were doing to the country and the working class and I thought, why do we have to fight each other when we could be fighting those fuckers? But it was divide and rule in motion and I had to move on."

"God bless The Jam army, almost every day of my life I have a person in their forties or fifties come up to me and say how much our music meant to them and telling me of their Jam gig experiences. They've never forgotten that gig or that song. That says an awful lot about how passionate those gigs and songs and kids were. That passion never withered or died."

It was around the time that Paul loaned his support that Rick Buckler also stepped up to be interviewed and offer his support and then Bruce quickly followed, which meant that, for the first time in a long time (over thirty years), all three members of The Jam were included in a book about their band.

The first print run of Thick As Thieves quickly sold out and a second and then third followed before the year was finished. The following year the first Apple iBook on The Jam was published - it was an updated version of Thick As Thieves, this time including an interview with Nicky Weller too.

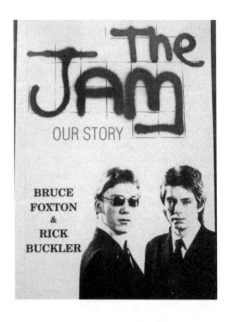

THE JAM: OUR STORY
Bruce Foxton and Rick Buckler
Castle Communications
1993

This book was actually written by Alex Ogg who did a series of short interviews with Rick and Bruce to capture their memories. Ogg then filled in the gaps and it's really Ogg's story of The Jam with a little help from Rick and Bruce. But at the time it was an opportunity for Rick and Bruce to tell some of their stories and share some of their recollections about how things happened.

The Jam: Our Story walks the reader through the history of the band. It describes how Paul, Bruce and Rick met and talks about the parts that the other significant people in The Jam story played.

The book provides accounts of what was going on with The Jam at the time of making albums and going on tour. It also describes the tensions and differences within The Jam band camp and what it was like for Rick and Bruce when they found out that Paul wanted to end the band. This part of the band's story isn't dealt with in too much depth like future books (as Rick's autobiography *That's Entertainment* would do) but it provides the reader with a sense and overview, and that is good enough.

The book came out just as the first scent of Brit Pop was being sniffed out. Over the next couple of years bands like Oasis, Blur and Ocean Colour Scene would all cite The Jam as one of their major influences and after *The Jam: Our Story* was published there seemed to be a flurry of excitement about The Jam and more books about the band found themselves being written. Not that that was a negative thing in any way, after all if you like jam, keep on eating it.

The book includes some photographs of The Jam from the video shoot at Battersea Power Station, with the road crew, Polydor press shots and live shots which all help to bring the book to life.

KEEPING THE FLAME
Steve Brookes
Sterling Wholesale
1996

This book came out just three years after *The Jam: Our Story*. Maybe Steve felt the need to provide Jam fans with a different point of view. Maybe he just wanted to write a book about the time when he was a founding member of The Jam.

Steve Brookes's personality shines through in *Keeping The Flame*: it has wit, humour, a simplicity and an innocence about it.

Contained in the book is a handwritten note from Paul where he has jotted down his response to what his old friend had written: "The best thing I've ever read on The Jam. The most accurate, honest and endearing.

THE JAM

8

It's also a great picture of a young group determined to escape and make it big time."

Steve begins his introduction with the words "So why did I leave?" He then explains that answering this question was one of the reasons why he decided to write his book. Steve then goes on to tell how he ended up living in Woking and indeed with the Wellers, going to Sheerwater and meeting Roger Pilling and Paul Weller on his first day and how he and Paul became the best of friends.

Throughout Steve's book he is respectful regards his relationship with Paul and his association with the Wellers. *Keeping The Flame* is probably the best book that provides insight into what the Wellers were like and what it would have been like for Paul Weller as he grew up with parents like John and Ann and a sister in Nicky.

Steve describes the efforts that he and Paul put into learning their guitars, poring over the Beatles songbook, how they went about recruiting other band members, playing their earliest gigs in the Woking Working Men's Club and Michaels, and then how band members made their exits, including himself.

Steve included in his book some set lists from The Jam's earliest days. The list contains a mixture of the standards they were playing like 'Roll Over Beethoven', 'Long Tall Sally' and 'Great Balls Of Fire' and some of their own songs like 'Takin' My Love' and 'Some Kinda Lovin'. It shows what music The Jam were listening to and playing live to punters in smoky working men's clubs and pubs. The list, like Steve's book, also captures a very special and charming part of The Jam's career.

When Stuart Deabill and Ian Snowball were putting *Thick As Thieves* together they contacted Steve and asked if he'd be willing to give an interview for the book. Being the generous man that he is he agreed and invited them down to his home. They sat and drank tea and fired questions at him about his memories of being in The Jam. And in amongst this he momentarily disappeared into another room only to return a few seconds later carrying an acoustic guitar. Steve plonked himself back onto his chair, got comfortable with the acoustic and launched into playing 'Some Kinda Lovin'. It was a special moment for the *Thick As Thieves* authors and one which would stick with them forever - they also captured it on the Dictaphone they were using, but haven't and wouldn't ever share it with anyone else.

An enjoyable aspect to Steve's book is that he writes about keeping an eye on The Jam's career and what he knew it would mean for Paul, Bruce and Rick and that he doesn't hold any grudges or to his credit share any disappointments that he may have. *Keeping The Flame* is, without doubt, a book that should be on every Jam fan's bookshelf.

GROWING UP WITH THE JAM

Nicky Weller, Gary Crowley, Russell Reader, Den Davis
Nicetime Inc Productions
2015

With a foreword from all three members of the band, heart-warming personal recollections and unseen photos. This book was compiled by the team who brought us the *About The Young Idea* exhibition. Their idea was to approach household names from the world of music, film and media who they knew had a love for The Jam. The list was lengthy and included Ray Davies, Pete Townshend, Mick Jones, Sharleen Spiteri, Andy Partridge, Nick Haywood, Jonny Marr, Billy Bragg, Noel Gallagher, Jools Holland, Kelly Jones, Martin Freeman, Max Beesley and many more. Each contribution provides an explanation why they loved The Jam's songs and what the songs had meant to them.

The book was published by Nicetime Inc Productions following a successful crowdfunding campaign and it was first made available during the exhibition at Somerset House in the summer of 2015.

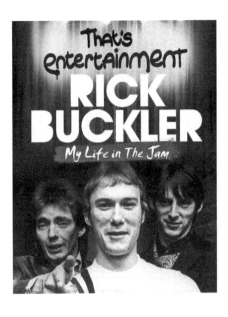

THAT'S ENTERTAINMENT
Rick Buckler and Ian Snowball
Omnibus
2015

In the spring of 2014 Ian Snowball approached Rick with the idea of putting together his autobiography. He had heard rumours that Rick had been making a start, but progress was slow and as is often the case when writing a book, the idea is much easier than the actuality of putting a book together. In the first instance writing a book takes time and time in the modern world is a precious luxury.

Ian spoke to Rick on the phone and Rick invited him down to his local pub to discuss the matter further. One Saturday morning they met up and over breakfast (Rick's local does a fine breakfast, so it was easy to see why he uses it) it was apparent they both

8

had something they wanted to say about the idea and something that would need to be established and agreed upon before any further steps were taken.

Ian said, "It was important to me that Rick understood that I wouldn't want to write about anything negative as it related to The Jam, Paul or Bruce. This is just not my style and besides - why would I want to have a dig at Paul, who only a few months earlier had provided such a positive and supportive foreword for *Thick As Thieves*? But thankfully, in a matter of a few minutes Rick had pretty much said the same, and we both realized that we were on the same page. So with our wishes and needs established and an agreement in place, we spent the remainder of the meeting sipping our teas, shovelling in mouthfuls of egg and beans and putting our heads together regards a framework and structure in which Rick's story could be told. We also established that my role would be to act as a sort of ghostwriter and tease the story out of Rick. I left that meeting with a belly full and buzzing with ideas. Not only was I excited about writing another Jam book and pleased that Rick was giving me the opportunity to try my hand at ghostwriting (I'd never tried it before and so was grateful to Rick that he trusted me enough), but I was also fully aware that if we could pull this off, this would be the first autobiography from a member of The Jam. A few weeks later Rick and I met up again in his local. Again we spent the first hour chatting over breakfast before spending the next couple of hours drawing out the story, which I would capture on my dictaphone. This was to be our first session and what I had suggested we do was start at the end. What this meant was talking to Rick about the final days leading up to The Jam splitting it. It seemed to make perfect

sense to begin the book in this way, as if to get this bit out of the way. Rick agreed and he provided me with his account of that period in The Jam's story and what it had meant to him."

That's Entertainment: My Life In The Jam was a bestseller and Omnibus's biggest seller of the year it was published. That is indeed entertainment!

A BEAT CONCERTO
Paulo Hewitt
Boxtree Ltd 1983 (2nd Edition 1996 with Foreword By Noel Gallagher)

This book was really the first book that the fans truly embraced. Published the year after The Jam split up it was purchased by seemingly every Jam fan, young and old. With contributions from Paul, Rick and Bruce *A Beat Concerto* was insightful. Adding to this

8

family members and friends (like Steve Carver and Steve Brookes) were also interviewed and they add another dynamic to the story of The Jam. Paolo was the person best placed to write such a book at such a time. He knew The Jam and the people connected to band on a very personal level and he was a fan himself.

The book provides a chronological account of The Jam's story and the lives of the three band members. Contained in the book are photos of a very young Paul and members of his family and throughout the book there are additional photographs that take the reader on a step by step down Jam lane.

Paolo also included reviews of Jam songs and releases from the likes of Dave McCullough, Paul Du Noyer and Barry Cain and these help to paint a picture of the band from the point of view of other respected music journalists. The book ends with a discography and an early photograph of Paul handing his Rickenbacker to a member of the road crew as he leaves the stage. *A Beat Concerto* certainly set the bar for any Jam books that followed.

THE JAM UNSEEN
Twink
Cyan Books
2007

This was a must-have book for any Jam fan. 21-year old freelance photographer Twink was commissioned by The Jam to be their official photographer, capturing them not only on stage, but also during their life out of the public eye. He went on to tour with the band and spend time with them in studios and other photoshoots. It was Twink's photographs that were used on the front sleeve of *The Gift*.

These images capture The Jam's electrifying live performances as well as their quieter moments - backstage, travelling and relaxing. "When we needed a photographer to come on the road with us - someone who could access all areas and take candid fly-on-the-wall shots - we had no doubt that he was our man," write Bruce Foxton and Rick Buckler in the foreword to this book.

The Jam Unseen included 200 of Twink's photographs of the band and, when published, a photographic exhibition was held in London.

POP ART POEMS (THE MUSIC OF THE JAM)
Shaun Hand
Self published
2016

The author, clearly a Jam fan, provides a detailed account of each Jam song. These accounts take into consideration the songs' structures, meanings and context. The book is very well researched and borrows bits and pieces from other books on The Jam which helps to paint a full picture. Full credit should be given to the author for it's clear the book took time, blood, sweat and tears to put together. It's another must have for Jam fans.

8

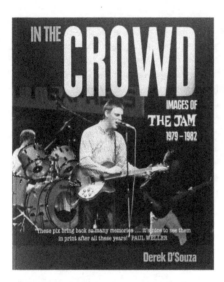

IN THE CROWD: IMAGES OF THE JAM

Derek D'Souza
Marshall Cavendish International
2013

Derek's book was picked up by the same publishing house that published *Thick As Thieves* and came out the following year. The Jam army never shy away from a good book on The Jam and a book that contains rare and never-before-seen photographs is a pure delight.

Most of the images in the book were taken at gigs and sound checks between 1979 and 1982 and capture how most Jam fans who managed to see the band perform live remember them best, seen from the crowd level up there on stage.

Derek would partner up with writer Simon Wells to create another Jam book, *In Echoed Steps, The Jam and a Vision of Albion*.

PAUL WELLER - THE CHANGING MAN

Paolo Hewitt
Corgi
2008

Paolo Hewitt has known Paul Weller since they were both teenagers in the depths of Woking, through his ascent to fame with The Jam, the halcyon years of The Style Council and for all of his critically acclaimed solo career. Hewitt has even been the inspiration for some of Weller's songs - and he has extraordinary in-depth knowledge of the inspiration behind the rest.

Once, when Hewitt interviewed Weller for a music magazine, he complained,

"I don't know why people ask me all these questions. All the answers are in my songs." Largely unnoticed, Weller has used thirty years of lyrics to explore his personal history and beliefs. Taking as his starting point these lyrics, alongside a lifetime's friendship, Paolo Hewitt shows us the real Paul Weller, the man inside the music.

AIM HIGH: PAUL WELLER IN PHOTOGRAPHS

Tom Sheehan
Omnibus Press
2016

Tom Sheehan is one of the premier UK rock photographers and one of the great post-punk photographers with a catalogue of image that define so many of his subjects. Sheehan is one of the photographers that made sense of those times and freeze-framed the very perceptions of many of these musicians. His work with Paul Weller and The Jam is iconic and it took

someone who as a real character like Tom to get the best out of the band. With many never-before-seen images, this is a unique body of work that shows the brilliant talent of Tom via a fantastic visual journey from The Jam, through The Style Council and the solo years. The book is arranged in three chapters covering Paul's career in chronological order. Every photograph has been carefully scanned and re-touched to produce the images in their glorious best and every element of this deluxe book is produced to the highest specification.

The book features a foreword by Paul Weller himself and an essay written by the critically acclaimed music journalist Simon Goddard.

THE JAM: THE START TO 77

Rick Buckler, Ian Snowball, Richard Schalle
2017

2017 is the 40th anniversary of The Jam's first two albums *In The City* and *This Is The Modern World*. In this graphic novel The Jam's drummer Rick Buckler tells the story of

8

PAUL WELLER

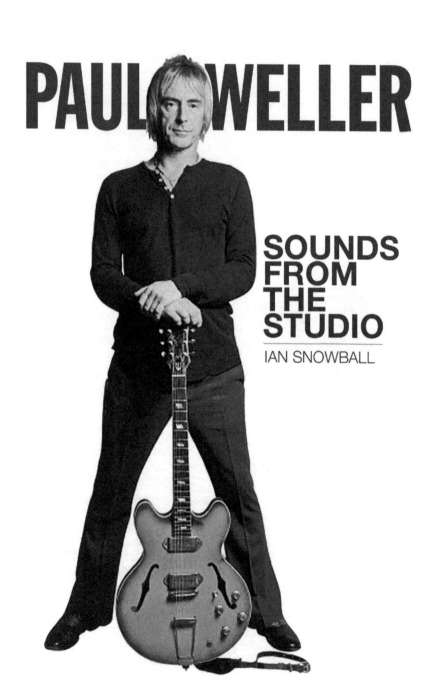

SOUNDS FROM THE STUDIO

IAN SNOWBALL

the bands evolution from the early days up until the end of 1977.

PAUL WELLER: SOUNDS FROM THE STUDIO

Ian Snowball
This Day in Music
2017

2017 was the 40th anniversary of the start of Paul Weller's recording career. His first album, *In The City*, which he recorded with The Jam, was released in 1977. He then went on to record a further 22 albums with The Jam, The Style Council and his solo career. *Sounds from the Studio* starts in 2015 with the release of his most recent album *Saturn's Pattern* then works backwards to the groundbreaking debut from The Jam - *In the City*.

The book includes interviews with artists who have worked with Paul including Noel Gallagher, Steve Cradock, Sir Peter Blake, Mick Talbot, and both Rick Buckler and Bruce Foxton from The Jam as well as many of the studio hands, sleeve designers, as well as interviews with members from Paul's family.

Other books also written about The Jam or have the band heavily referenced include:

The Jam: The Modern World By Numbers (Plexus Publishing, 1995)

About The Young Idea: The Story Of The Jam 1977 - 1982 by Mike Nicholls (Proteus Books, 1984)

The Jam by Miles (Music Sales Card, 1982)

The Jam Retrospective: A Visual History 7- 12 Rare Albums by Agent Provocateur (Retro Publishing, 1997)

The Jam Modern Icons by Richard Lowe (Virgin Books, 1997)

Maximum Jam & Paul Weller – Audio Book Only - By Ben Graham (Chrome Dreams, 2003)

Long Hot Summer by Ian Snowball (Heavy Soul Books, 2010)

The Jam Chord Songbook by Peter Evans (Music Sales Ltd, 1999)

The Sound Of The Jam – Guitar Tab (Music Sales Ltd, 2002)

The Jam Greatest Hits in Guitar Tab – David Holmes (Music Sales Ltd, 1997)

The Jam – START! Again Book – Anthology 1 – 8 Of The Jam Fanzine START! By Neil Allen (Self published, 2016)

The Complete Guide To The Jam & Paul Weller by John Reed (Omnibus Press, 1999)

INDEX

7

7

7

THE JAM

INDEX

THE JAM

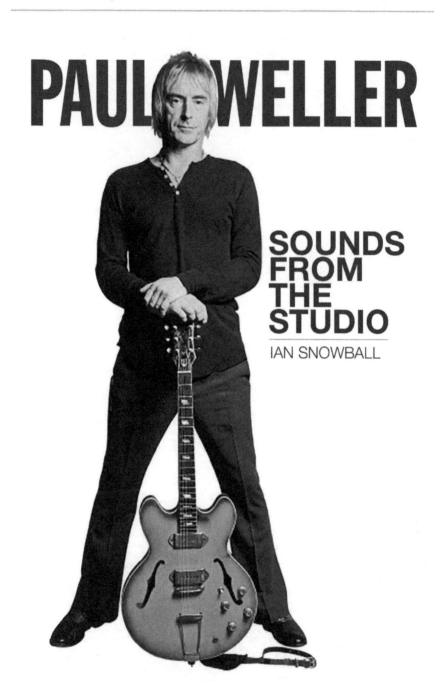

PAUL WELLER

SOUNDS FROM THE STUDIO

IAN SNOWBALL

For more info, visit www.thisdayinmusic.com

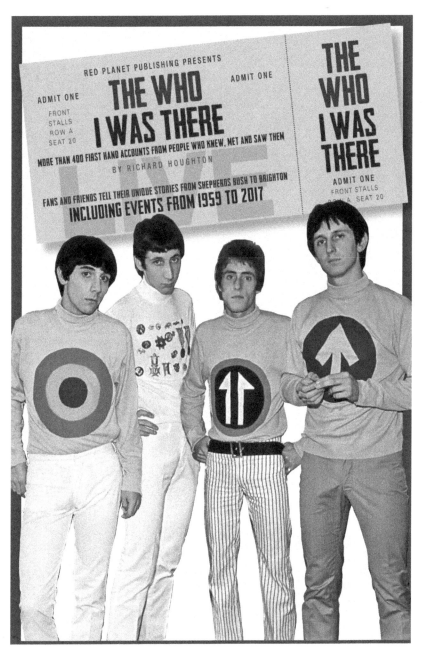

For more info, visit www.thisdayinmusic.com

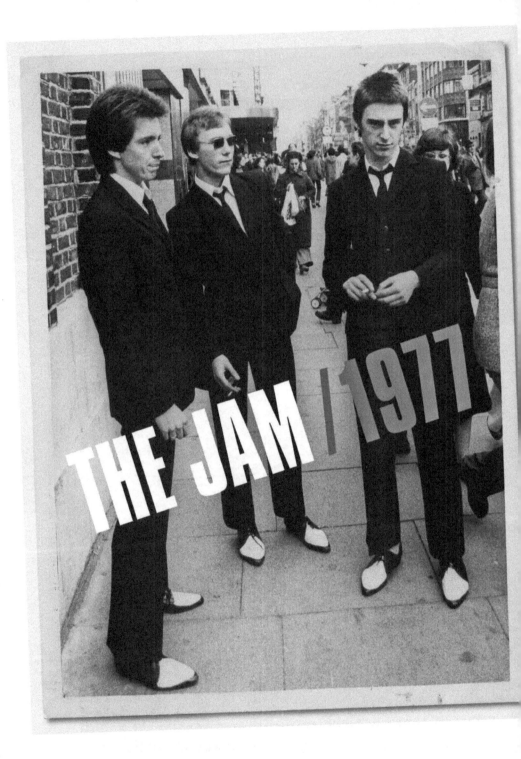

THE JAM / 1977

Polydor

THE JAM / 1977

40th Anniversary
five-disc boxset
Original albums
remastered
144-page book
& postcards
Unreleased demos
& live recordings

UMC

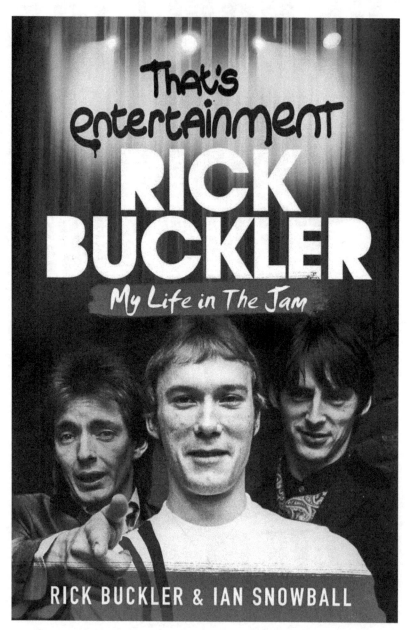

That's entertainment

RICK BUCKLER

My Life in The Jam

RICK BUCKLER & IAN SNOWBALL

For more info, visit www.strangetown.net

For more info, visit
www.strangetown.net

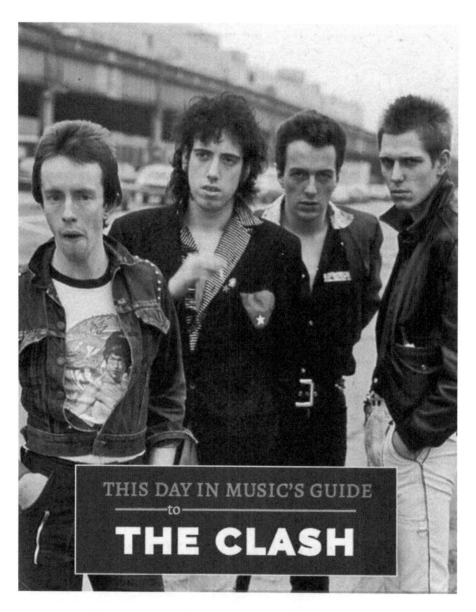

THIS DAY IN MUSIC'S GUIDE
— to —
THE CLASH

For more info, visit www.thisdayinmusic.com

For more info, visit www.thisdayinmusic.com

BOB DYLAN
THE DAY I WAS THERE

For more info, visit www.thisdayinmusic.com

JIMI HENDRIX
THE DAY I WAS THERE

For more info, visit www.thisdayinmusic.com